C000216651

Imperium Press was founded in 2018 to supply students and laymen with works in the history of rightist thought. If these works are available at all in modern editions, they are rarely ever available in editions that place them where they belong: outside the liberal weltanschauung. Imperium Press' mission is to provide right thinkers with authoritative editions of the works that make up their own canon. These editions include introductions and commentary which place these canonical works squarely within the context of tradition, reaction, and counter-Enlightenment thought—the only context in which they can be properly understood.

AMERICAN EXTREMIST

THE PSYCHOLOGY
OF
POLITICAL EXTREMISM

JOSH NEAL

PERTH
IMPERIUM PRESS
2020

Published by Imperium Press

www.imperiumpress.org

First Edition

A catalogue record for this
book is available from the
National Library of Australia

ISBN 978-0-6488593-6-9 Paperback
ISBN 978-0-6488593-7-6 EPUB
ISBN 978-0-6488593-8-3 Kindle

CONTENTS

ACKNOWLEDGEMENTS

This work would not have been possible without the contribution and support of a great many people, the vast majority of whom I do not know and will sadly never have the pleasure of meeting. First and foremost among them are the guests and audience of the various programs I have hosted over these last few years. The former greatly expanded my knowledge and awareness of the world and its workings while the latter made the success of these programs possible. Second, I owe a great deal to Joel Davis for introducing me to the work of Chris Bond and ultimately to the fine people at *Imperium Press*. Without them, this book may never have seen the light of day. My brief tenure with the *Radix* team was also pivotal to the production of this work, and so I thank them as well (Jefferson, Tyler, Nils, Mark, and Richard). I feel no shame in admitting that the initial phase of this work was fraught with great difficulty and terrifying confusion, and that I might not have persevered without the careful eyes of a handful of generous people and so my thanks goes out to you as well (Caroline, Miss White). However, the most pivotal, and also paradoxical, contributions—perhaps this work's raison d'être—came from the very people who were responsible for revealing my identity to the public, and thus precipitating a very difficult but necessary period in my life. I am unreservedly, and eternally, grateful to that group of dedicated miscreants (and their collaborators), for without them I would not have strove to achieve as deep an understanding of this subject as I now possess. Truly, it is a debt I will never be able to repay. Of course, I am also indebted to you, the reader. It is my hope that in reading this, you find my work as illuminating as I did writing it.

AMERICAN
EXTREMIST

From There to Here

Upon what force do we call to conceive a soul?
Not woman, but circumstance.
Not man, but haughty arrogance.
Many have asked, as have many answered, but truth be told –
That the measure of a man can be found through
   so-called happenstance.

November 18th, 2016

With the help of my closest friend of over fifteen years, I started my career as a broadcaster and commentator the week after the 2016 presidential election. At that time, I could not have imagined where this decision would take me or how it would impact my life. I certainly did not anticipate that just three years later, my foray into the world of politics would lead to the publication of over a dozen hit pieces which would render me persona non grata. But to tell that story (and ultimately the story of this book's publication) necessitates a trip down memory lane.

Only a few months prior to embarking upon this new venture, I was knee deep in doctoral applications and seeking to climb the final hurdle on my way to becoming a licensed clinical psychologist. Deeply ambivalent about this goal, I was desperately seeking other alternatives; I was not enthusiastic about the prospect of spending another four years in school at the expense of other ambitions. To make matters worse, many of the programs I was considering had faculties staffed by, shall we say, academics of a certain persuasion. Many of my would-be mentors were pursuing areas of research that hardly excited me. As for the ones that did, I couldn't shake the nagging feeling that there would be significant compatibility issues. I wanted to practice my craft, but the cost seemed too high. Cautiously, I began searching for potential off-ramps to liberate me from the highway of stagnation and conformity I saw unfolding before me. I did not want to spend half a decade in classrooms, especially if that meant walking on eggshells around my fellow classmates, and more significantly, my instructors and mentors. Further complicating the matter was the distressing fact that I still did not know where I stood, intellectually. I had spent the preceding decade floating in and out of various artistic and philosophical subcultures—richer for the experience, yes—but with no surer footing beneath me to show for it. Certainly, I had developed a keen sense of what I stood against. But what I stood *for*? That was a bit trickier.

In the half decade or so prior to 2016 I had been working as an adjunct and a research assistant, picking up classes at various schools in the New York area and jumping from laboratory to laboratory vainly pursuing the singular golden opportunity which would snap the pieces of my life together. These experiences were profoundly startling. Conversations with fellow adjuncts, professors, and even department chairs, while often congenial, over time took on a distinctly sinister quality. Even innocuous comments about psychology or current events would trigger intense disgust and revulsion from my peers and superiors. Being a naturally curious and open-minded person with a great many sympathies for left-wing politics, the degree of hostility to anything outside of their narrow field of permissible opinions was beyond staggering. This trend would only intensify in the months leading up to and immediately following Donald Trump's victory. As that fateful day drew nearer and nearer, it became impossible to do anything other than smile and nod during interactions with my colleagues. And while I did not find this to be a problem for my career as a researcher, the idea of applying for a position to yet another laboratory where I would inevitably find myself going through the motions proved to be rather disheartening to say the least.

Circumstances *inside* the classroom were hardly any better.

My experiences as an adjunct involved at least as much un-teaching as it did actual productive instruction. It was shocking to see just how poorly educated, or rather, *how well miseducated* many of my students were. Moreover, they had grown accustomed to viewing education—not just the discipline of psychology—as superfluous, deliberately uninteresting and irrelevant, if not something completely antagonistic. It was a task I felt unfit for, but I gave my best effort to meet the challenges presented to me. Largely I was a success, and my students appreciated these efforts even if some still found the course material unnecessary to their larger ambitions. Not that the climate permitted simple discussions of these topics *prior* to my tenure as an adjunct, but with time it became increasingly difficult to discuss issues related to sexuality, intelligence, ethnic and racial differences in human development, family structure, and the principles of social psychology, without confronting the political veil shrouding each subject. As the country inevitably lurched toward November 8th, 2016, the question of Donald J. Trump also became difficult to avoid. Generally, these were multiethnic classrooms, diverse in every sense of the word, thus necessitating an approach to each lecture that demanded a grace and finesse befitting a world-class neurosurgeon. In many ways, I learned the skills of diplomacy, persuasion, and rhetoric which would prove invaluable as a commentator by virtue of having to confront some hundred or more students, often four to six days a week, in virtually every borough of New York City.

But it wasn't just the challenges of navigating an ideologically paralyzed workplace or the Trump campaign that led me into the milieu in which I have now found myself; pivotal moments both culturally and personally took their toll, forcing me to undergo a difficult period of intellectual maturation. The dissolution of important relationships, the deterioration of formerly good health, and the dashing of certain naïve aspirations were all as critical in changing my attitude as the larger national and international events that occurred alongside them. Events such as the removal of Muammar Gaddafi; the Trayvon Martin and Michael Brown shootings (and the subsequent assassination of five Dallas law officers by Micah Xavier Johnson); the escalating migrant crisis throughout Europe; the rash of domestic terror attacks in California, Florida, and New York during the second term of then President Obama's administration; and yes, the Brexit and Trump votes collectively forced a reevaluation of my worldview. Over a period of four or five years, my worldview—that of a coolly dispassionate, agnostic, scientific and libertarian-minded individual—was throttled beyond repair. I was moved, more accurately *pushed*, into a position where I felt the only way to understand what was going on was to go where I was not supposed to go.

The challenges posed by the political and cultural climate of the time doubled as golden opportunities. I had the chance to refine my worldview every day, sometimes for free—with friends and family—and sometimes for a living, whenever I spoke with my students and colleagues. Trump's campaign was a kind of divining rod that (at the time) seemed to point with brilliant clarity towards what was true and real. My future broadcast partner and I were among the only people in our social circles to see this and it gave us a sense of tremendous confidence. For the first time, things were starting to make sense. The world was becoming more comprehensible. Not only were the great mysteries of life proving more sensible, but we were beginning to feel as though we could make accurate predictions about cultural and political events. Feeling like a pair of 21st century Nostradami, my friend and I decided to join the podcast circuit. We finally had the answers and now it was time to step out of the minor league and into the big time. The wind was firmly beneath my wings, and so I entered the arena of political commentary assured that I had something to say, that it was the truth, and that people needed to hear it. But within a few months, the cracks in the Trump façade began to emerge and that sense of invulnerability gave way to a nagging, creeping, doubt.[1] Certainly, there were prior

1 Reflecting on that period—a full five and a half years later—has proven to be quite revealing. I couldn't have believed it at the time, but since then, Donald J. Trump has proven himself to be the man many of his detractors claimed he was all those years ago. Weak-willed, self-aggrandizing, narcissistic, and a con man through and through. The real tragedy is to see how many people continue to fall prey to the spectacle. What I thought was the beginning of a new American epoch in fact proved to be more temporally limited than that. 2016 was an event, a revelation, an apocalypse. The cosmic hand of God reached through the clouds to slap a little sense into as many receptive people as he could, and I, fortunately (and I hope, not hubristically), happened to be one of them. Today, peo-

incidents which had delivered moments of pause; the selection of Mike Pence as running mate was one such instance. Looking back at that time now, there were quite a few of these moments. However, the euphoria produced by Trump's campaign and subsequent victory overrode any capacity for a rational analysis of these events. Once a colder political sobriety began to settle in, it became clear to the both of us that our journey was only just beginning. Cognizant of this we continued along the path, demoralized and confused but also primed for something new.

January 4ᵗʰ, 2018

Roughly thirteen months after the election, another pivotal moment occurred which set me on the path I am on now, and without which I could never have written this book. Shortly after Trump announced his candidacy, I had begun to abandon most of the programs which comprised the bulk of my media consumption habits for nearly a decade. Disgusted by these figures (some authors, others podcasters and public intellectuals), I could no longer tolerate the voices of people who—either out of cowardice, dishonesty, naïveté, or all three—demonstrated a total failure to see what I, a lowly middle-class peasant, was so clearly capable of seeing. Thirsting for truth and desperate to find *anyone* uncompromised by the kind of biases, shortsightedness, greed, and stupidity which seemed poised to plunge America into a new dark age, I turned to the burgeoning world of YouTube livestreams. Ignorant to the media revolution that had long been developing outside the watchful eye of censorious hen-peckers and moral busybodies, I was quickly introduced to dozens of compelling programs, many of which regularly hosted fiery debates featuring thinkers from every corner of the intellectual and

---

ple mistake the man (Trump) and his movement (nationalism) for that specific moment in time in which it was possible for genuine Truth to be disseminated by an otherwise sterile and stultifying political circus. Trump, himself, is not an agent of awakening, nor is the continuation of Trumpism a guarantor of continued revelation. The significance of that disruptive political moment elevated many good people into a more sophisticated mode of consciousness, but only those capable, humble, or visionary enough to respond to the revelation. Such people will respond to future events of that magnitude, but there is no reason to believe that is a unique feature of Trump or Trumpism.

cultural sphere. Racists took on anti-racists; Communists debated the Fascists; Atheists wrestled with the Religious; and Nationalists took on all comers (while just about everyone beat up on the Libertarians). Academics and scientists took to the internet to participate in the kinds of conversations that would not be tolerated within the hallowed halls of their sacred institutions. Sometimes they debated other such enlightened folk, but often enough they were met by amateurs and laymen. It was through this medium that I was first exposed, in long form, to the second most infamous (or evil, depending on your point of view) man in the country at the time, Richard Spencer.

Prior to hearing him on the now defunct *Warski Live*, I considered Spencer little more than a political sideshow; from the few clips I had managed to watch in the preceding year, he seemed like a figure to be used conveniently by mainstream outlets to harm the *obviously* righteous and unimpeachable Trump campaign (and subsequent presidency). But by this point the veil had been lifted from my eyes, and my libertarian ethos had taken far too many hits to hold up against the unrelenting barrage of reality's psychic assault. On that late night in early January, Richard Spencer spent several hours verbally jousting with another prominent YouTube personality, Carl Benjamin (better known by his nom de plume *Sargon of Akkad*). More shocking than the fact that these two countercultural heavyweights agreed to appear side-by-digital-side was the far stranger fact that *I found myself agreeing with many of Richard's arguments*. He wasn't insane or evil, and he certainly wasn't some cartoonish buffoon. Rather, he seemed quite the opposite: affable, erudite, and highly compelling. Of course, Carl Benjamin's complete lack of success at engaging in any meaningful way with Richard's worldview only served to make Spencer look that much better. Nonetheless, Richard's appearance had achieved its intended effect on me. Slowly, and with more than a hint of trepidation, I set upon my perilous descent into the world of the Alternative Right.

In doing so, the depth of my ignorance was revealed in truly spectacular fashion. While it wasn't a religious experience by any stretch of the imagination, delving into the intellectual world of the alt-right did feel *a bit* like being spoken to by a burning bush or having a UFO descend into my backyard and making the acquaintance of little green men. I was introduced to alternative ways of thinking, texts I never knew existed, and whole ideological movements I was utterly and completely unaware of. Of course, I was wholly ignorant to their existence because nobody in polite society would dare mention such things if they even knew anything about them. For as long as I can remember, it had always been more important for me to know the truth, to know what was real and how things truly are as opposed to how we imagine them to be; it was that very impulse which drove me in this direction. I have no idea how regularly people experience *Oz* moments, where the curtain is pulled back and all is revealed, but when I started reading and listening to alt-right publications and broadcasts I had them virtually every week.

Intellectual journeys have always been my favorite kind; I have never been much of an adrenaline junkie, partly because I never felt the need to risk my life so I could go hang gliding or drag racing. A truly thought-provoking argument or idea can set my brain in motion long after its introduction (something that more visceral and participatory experiences rarely managed to achieve). But as it turns out, intellectual journeys are often more perilous than the kind that your average adrenaline junkie might pursue. People won't disown you for scaling a mountain, but *perhaps they will* should they catch you reading the wrong book. No one will hound you until you are unemployable for deciding to move to a different state or country, but they *just might* if they find out you spoke to someone who had been "cancelled" or unpersoned. Sure, your loved ones will worry themselves sick should you decide to do something foolhardy like base jumping, for instance, but intellectual and spiritual journeys can often be more threatening to those around you because they challenge ontological and epistemological certainties. And that is, in part, what the political is ultimately about—it is about establishing the boundaries of permissible exploration and interaction. The alt-right was just beyond that limit, though not for the reasons I was led to believe (a fact which I was quickly beginning to learn).

In a certain sense, very little truly changed; I had always been willing to traffic in taboos and consider ideas or positions that might otherwise be deemed unusual or even "dangerous". Chalk it up to my higher than average trait openness. What *had*

changed was that instead of opening a new door and finding myself greeted by a handsomely sophisticated *maître d'* sauntering
delicately around a well-decorated room with a freshly buffed
hardwood floor, this time I turned the knob only to tumble down
a long-since abandoned and badly dilapidated ideological and
sociopolitical staircase into the alt-right. I had started off as an
independent and loose libertarian, far from anything resembling
a hardcore ideologue. If anything, I was just right-of-center; I
had some romanticized notions of the American founders and
the Antebellum South, certainly, but I also held contemporary
left-wing views on drugs, race, and foreign policy. Yes, I voted for
Trump, but I saw the Trump presidency (like, I assume, many
others did), as a return to something like a classical Americana.
I wasn't an extremist—I was the average American voter. Different, yes, but in no sense was I a radical. (As I write this, old
memories of a warehouse office that a few friends and I convert-
ed into a recording studio come rushing to my mind. From time
to time, we would host friends for late-night parties and get-to-
gethers where we would talk about anything and everything of
interest. Friends and acquaintances who knew me as an *Edgelord
Trump Supporter*™ were surprised to find that my true thoughts
were totally reasonable and sound, if even a tad *banal*. The distance between their perception of me and the man I truly was
had collapsed entirely, vindicating my sense of being *utterly normal*.) In fact, it was the world that had become more extreme,
not me. But after that fateful night in my apartment watching
YouTube, not only was I introduced to foreign ideas, but many
existent ideas which had been floating around in my mind but
had not yet coalesced into a meaningful psychology were finally
given permission to be taken seriously.

These ideas were more like flirtations than legitimate cognitions; some having gestated for years, others, just a few months.
They were the kinds of thoughts one keeps confined to himself,
knowing that they would probably cause unnecessary trouble
were they to be spoken aloud. Accordingly, I set to work on a
path of transformative self-corrections by rearranging my life,
my relationships, and began working in earnest towards goals
and projects that I had pined for all my life (such as writing). In
a more personally meaningful sense, my turn toward online po-

litical activism occurred concomitantly with a turn toward radical self-ownership and self-representation. The only *extreme* or *radical* thing about me was the degree to which I began putting my concerns and welfare before that of others. There would be no more benefits-of-the-doubt, no apologies-as-preface, and certainly no more self-betrayals to the gain of others. There could be no disentangling my personal transformation from the decision to engage with the online political community. It was like my brain and soul had been struck by a lightning bolt of pure courage, imbuing me with the clarity and purpose necessary for striking out on a new path. Thanks to that broadcast I saw a potentially profitable way to advance my interests in psychology, philosophy, art, and fighting the good fight.

November 5th, 2018

Not profitable in the financial sense, mind you. To this day, the money I made from book sales and YouTube advertisements would not have covered a single month's worth of expenses. Besides, I had started a consultation practice as a hypnotherapist around the time I began podcasting and still had my work as an adjunct. I was getting by. Financial gain, while not unrelated, was considerably further down the list of motivations for participating in alt-right political discourse. I wanted to get to the bottom of things—the truth *beneath* the truths—you might say. And so, I did just that: November 2018, roughly two years after my broadcast career began and some ten months after my informal introduction to the alt-right, I began an interview series on YouTube.

In a certain sense this new project was a kind of psychological experiment, but in that way it was no different from how I'd approached most experiences in my life. For me, life itself has always been a bit of a science experiment and as such I have always approached it by asking myself a few important questions: *What can I learn from this? How is this challenging me? How can I challenge others? How can I reveal something as yet unseen or unknown?* I wanted to have the most thought-provoking conversations with the most interesting people I could possibly get my digitally enabled hands on. I would be a vehicle or a conduit through which truth and knowledge could pass, with as little judgment, reservation, or bias as a mere mortal could hope to achieve. And while I had consciously decided that the alt-right was the subculture that most closely represented my worldview, by no means did I want to limit myself to that identifier. How else could I develop a more robust understanding of the world— of philosophy, politics, the arts, *the human experience itself*—if I obstinately planted my feet, demanded punitively strict and unwavering adherence to a set of freshly discovered axioms, and locked myself in a virtual room with people who had made the same silent agreement? More than just impossible, it struck me as *wrong*.

Naturally, there were three major roadblocks to such an ambitious endeavor—I was an unknown with no social capital and thus was entirely reliant on the kindness of strangers. Moreover, I was a one man operation working from my Brooklyn apartment with only a wireless internet service and a small Twitter account to my name, which limited both my access to interesting people but also the degree of professional quality my program could offer. Most distressingly, I had decided that the most maligned, marginalized, socially unacceptable, and fringe subculture would be the one I called home. In many ways, this was not the best way to start a career, nor was it an intelligent way to keep the career I had worked for fourteen years to build. As much as these limitations posed potentially grave challenges, in other ways they also resolved them.

As fate would have it, people who aren't afforded the same kind of professional opportunities (media appearances, large publishing contracts, favorable press reviews) are remarkably accessible, and if treated with respect, *convivial*, even. Quickly, I learned that sometimes all you have to do is ask and you can get exactly what you want. In my first months of broadcasting, I had conversations with Dr. Kevin MacDonald and Dr. Sam Vaknin (both accomplished psychologists and highly regarded authors), and a host of other writers, independent scholars, and researchers all with utterly heterodox views of the world. Some were better known than others, but all of them were far more compelling than whatever polite society had offered me thus far. I would like to emphasize that these were *truly* heterodox figures, because so many of them were operating outside of the establishment, as opposed to the rash outbreak of public intellectuals (like Canadian clinical psychologist Jordan Peterson) who were self-servingly heralded as vanguard or dissident voices by the mainstream press. Self-fellating brainiac goon squads like the IDW (Intellectual Dark Web) had begun to emerge at roughly the same time, populated by thinkers whose only function was to create a caducean dialectic whereby average people who were seeking radical voices that actually challenged the institutional paradigm could be safely herded back on to the intellectual and cultural plantation—the very same plantation, by the way, which I had only very recently liberated myself from. The intellectual and integrity gap between the Weinsteins and Petersons of the world and those who would appear on my program (and those of my fellow travelers) was rather stark and only emboldened me to pursue this line of thinking with greater vigor.

Over time, I would host conversations with former and current presidential candidates, artists and musicians, mythologists, students of biology, physics, and theology, successful authors in the disciplines of history and political theory, investigative journalists, philosophers specializing in phenomenology, perennialism, post-structuralism, meta-modernism and nihilism, and representatives across the political spectrum including Marxists, libertarians, conservatives, identitarians (black and white), neo-reactionaries and neo-absolutists, transhumanists, and polite (if feckless) centrists. My broadcasts included conversations about family with both stay-at-home fathers and happy homemaker mothers. Less regularly, there were discussions about religion with Atheists, Orthodox Jews, and Christians. While a small number of my guests were decidedly controversial, many (if not most) were simply interesting and often successful (if untraditionally so) people who had something that I thought people needed to be exposed to.

You could call it open-mindedness or you could call it naïveté, but I had decided that playing the role of a willful and dispassionate interlocutor was the only way to get what I wanted out of my broadcasts. Coming from the tradition set forth by renowned 20th century clinician Carl Rogers and knowledgeable of research in the field of motivational interviewing (MI), I had developed a technique of openness, empathy, and curiosity which became essential to my approach. The dialectical techniques found in Rogers' work, and elaborated by researchers of MI, had proven to be successful in winning over my students and clients; applying this same strategy to my broadcasts allowed for my guests and broadcast partners alike to relax and open up. In short, it was a clear formula for success.

The initial program led to spin-off broadcasts that promoted my burgeoning foray into self-publishing. Later still, my first broadcast partner and I, after taking a brief respite to work on our respective projects, resumed our working relationship and dipped our toes (with a not-so-insignificant amount of success) into the pool of cultural analysis. We found a loyal audience who relished our discussions on popular works in contemporary film and music. All told, our broadcasts were regularly watched by an audience that numbered in the thousands (and in some cases *tens* of thousands), by viewers of all ages, male and female alike—and to my happy surprise—by people of *very* different political persuasions. In other words, my approach was proving to be the success I knew it could be. Soon, my comrade and I had attracted the attention of Mr. Evil himself, Richard Spencer, and after a few short months we became regular broadcast partners, and even friends. Of course, the partnership brought with it a higher profile, and for reasons owing to this new arrangement (though, not exclusively if I am being honest), I was beginning to attract attention from the wrong kinds of people.

November 5th, 2019

For better or worse, I have approached most things in my life with a kind of cavalier, devil-may-care attitude. While I *was* aware that what I was getting myself into carried potentially damaging consequences, I took what I considered at the time to be calculated risks (such as showing my face and using my real name, sans my surname). I felt that what I was doing was important and I wanted to be taken seriously. And as I said at the outset, I couldn't possibly have foreseen where my little podcast in a non-descript location somewhere outside of New York City would take me. As it would turn out, the calculated risks and free-wheeling approach, for all they did to advance my credibility, would in time reveal themselves to be grim miscalculations.

I feared being discovered by left-wing activists, but the great irony (and a testament to my political ignorance) was that the *enemy within* was a *far* greater threat to me and my work. It had been clear to me for a long while that the now tired accusations of racism, sexism, homophobia, and anti-Semitism were a form of political control designed to stifle dissent, but I was neither able to understand nor fully appreciate the implications of this fact until I began participating in political activism. By marginalizing the line of thinking I had chosen to pursue, the American educational and politico-media-complex had ensured that I would be forced into an intellectual and social ghetto rendering me incapable of meaningfully disassociating myself from the worst elements of the subculture. Politically speaking, the fog of war was thick, and for quite a while it was difficult to distinguish who was trustworthy and who was not. I would soon learn that just because you share a set of beliefs with someone doesn't mean you can trust them. Not only that, but I learned the hard way that just because you share those beliefs doesn't mean you share the same goals. Moreover, and I apologize if at this point I am getting a bit redundant, just because you *think* you share beliefs with someone doesn't mean that you *actually do.*

The alt-right was (and to some degree remains) the place to find some of the most courageous, intelligent, and talented people you'll ever meet—but it is also a den of thieves and scoundrels. Foolishly, I had gotten into bed with a group of snakes and paid the price for it. A tiny but vocal group had gathered all of the information on me they could find, and hand delivered it to their supposed mortal enemies—anti-fascist activists and their sympathetic friends working as journalists. Within the span of 48 hours, the story about a "*Far-right White Nationalist extremist*" who had "*infiltrated*" the New York college system, the underground music scene, and who was undoubtedly performing all manner of Mengelian inhumanities upon his poor, defenseless clientele was the top story in *The Gothamist*, *Newsweek*, and nearly a dozen other publications. Even *The New York Post* wanted to get a piece of the action. Close friends issued hand-wringing statements of disavowal through social media. Graduate school professors of mine opined about my "*dangerous insanity*", while former colleagues whom I had never met gave statements to the press declaring how they always knew I was *up to no good*. The situation was almost as hilarious as it was emotionally taxing. But it was not without its silver lining.

This rude awakening alerted me to a level of distinctiveness in the psychological foundations of political orientation, and ultimately to political affiliation. Since the moment of my initiation, I was more concerned with the '*what*' of this new political philosophy and worldview, and not the '*why*'. I admit that I had been somewhat disarmed by the media's continual haranguing about the supposed "threat of far-right extremism". Reflexively I had begun to doubt the existence of such a thing. The notion that there were hundreds of thousands, if not millions, of potential school-shooters and domestic terrorists was simply too hysterical to take seriously. And the fact that the people claiming such things made no distinction between truly troubled individuals and the third of the country that actually pulled the lever for Donald Trump only further disinclined me against considering their point of view. I was certain of the existence of left-wing extremism, as it was a reality I was faced with constantly. But while the hand-wringing concerns over "far-right extremism" didn't quite match my experience, there were in fact significant problems, and little was being done (or even could be done) to resolve them. From within the community, it was easy to issue thoughtless dismissals and hand wave away the more troublesome contingent within right-wing politics. They weren't likely to blow up a government building or shoot at a small congregation, but their behavior *was* detrimental to serious political activity.

Through this experience I had come to a more complete understanding of the American political scene; free-floating insights and observations made over the past three years had now locked into a singular gestalt of the American political animal. And with that, the genesis of a new approach to understanding American extremism was beginning to reveal itself. Just a few short months after my extracurricular hobbies were revealed to the public, I began to commit these new ideas to paper.

The Failure of Psychology and the Need for a New Political Gestalt

The discipline of psychology has much to answer for. After all, ideological overrepresentation, motivated reasoning, and the spirit of revolution found among many of the field's practitioners have brought us to this moment of mass hysteria and irrationality. And while the last decade saw attempts by prominent researchers and public intellectuals to advance our knowledge, challenge base assumptions, and reassure us that we could push through these trying political times, inevitably these same figures ended up reinforcing the prevailing myths and misperceptions of our time. The names are likely familiar to you—Jonathan Haidt, Steven Pinker, Jordan Peterson, Paul Bloom, and Christopher Ryan, to name a few—all intelligent and thoughtful scientists who have proven themselves utterly incapable of rupturing the psychopolitical paradigm that dominates America's collective mind. Certainly they are not the only ones, and neither do they deserve the totality of blame; if we turn back the clock we may consider a far greater number of individuals and even epochs in the history of psychology throughout the 20th century and into the early years of our new century, who all contributed to a fundamental misunderstanding of the human animal as a creature of creation and destruction.

The revolutionary spirit endemic to psychological movements of the 20th century was predominantly focused on liberating the human condition. Liberation can be a noble goal, to be sure, but recent history has clearly shown that the pursuit of this ideal merely gave way to an unending succession of quests for further liberty. In their zeal, torchbearers of this revolutionary instinct often failed to consider what the end result of their theoscientific machinations would be other than some vague and ill-defined utopian state of human Godliness. Freud's quoting of Virgil, *"flectere si nequeo superos, Acheronta movebo"* [*"if I cannot sway Heaven, I'll wake the powers of Hell"*, tr. Robert Fagles] has proven itself rather prophetic. At each and every turn, sub-disciplines such as social psychology, developmental psychology, clinical psychology, and even the generation of psychoanalysts and behaviorists who followed in Freud's wake all sought an erasure of limits, an aggrandizement of the self, and the overthrow of authority and ritual. Eager to depose the Gods of old, deicide became an end in and of itself.

None of the cultural developments of the post-war period could have been made possible without some team of psychologists theorizing, experimenting, and often, conjecturing their way into psychologically disarming the naturally evolved habits of the American people. Psychology, at least as much—if not more so—than any other social science, has served as the intellectual vanguard, the scientific attack dog which legitimized the sociopolitical developments that weakened the family, weakened the community, and weakened the country. An important argument which I will continue to make throughout this work is that no scientific fact or philosophical insight is born in a vacuum, and none of them are without their masters. They are the both the product of the State *and* the life's blood by which it might legitimize, nay, realize its own raison d'être. Such was the case during the Soviet era, when the Vygotsky-Luria Circle worked to realize a science of the Marxist and Soviet superman.[2] [3] A little later on, the marriage of State and University produced the collaboration between the OSS and members of the Frankfurt School who sought to resolve the problem of so-called totalitarian authoritarianism.[4] During the 1950's and 1960's, Dr. Ewan Cameron helped the CIA develop techniques of depersonalization using psychedelic drugs, electroconvulsive therapy, and looped audio recordings for the purpose of mind control (in which Ted Kaczynski would later be a participant, under the

2   Martin J. Packer, "Is Vygotsky Relevant? Vygotsky's Marxist Psychology", *Mind, Culture, and Activity,* Vol. 15, Issue 1, January 15th 2008.
3   "Vygotsky – a pioneering Soviet psychologist who derived his genius from Marxism", *Lalkar,* Issue July/August 2016 http://www.lalkar.org/article/2455/vygotsky-a-pioneering-soviet-psychologist-who-derived-his-genius-from-marxism.
4   Barry M. Katz, "The Criticism of Arms: The Frankfurt School Goes to War", *The Journal of Modern History,* Vol. 59, No. 3, September 1987, pp. 439-478.

"care" of Henry Murray).[5] [6] [7] Still more recently, it was revealed that in 2002, James Mitchell and Bruce Jessen collaborated with the CIA in the hopes of developing advanced interrogation techniques, thought to be vital for combating Islamic terror in the years following the 9/11 attack.[8] The history of psychology isn't wholly nefarious, but a great many psychologists played significant roles in the most heinous and tyrannical events of the last century.

Science is a tool of power, and thus the hard-won knowledge gained through the scientific method inevitably becomes a tool for State expansion and oppression, in addition to the other benefits it can provide. This should not be understood as an indictment of the discipline itself, but rather a reflection on how a scientific discipline, just like an individual, can decay, retard its own positive development, and impair the broader human ecosystem's ability to think and act in its own interest. A work such as my own is best understood as operating *against* this backdrop, as an attempt to steer us back in the direction of knowledge and truth. It is precisely this totalitarian tradition which my project seeks to overturn; however successfully or unsuccessfully I meet that goal is another matter entirely.

The scientist is society's scout; he maps the territory, gathers and evaluates reconnaissance, and then returns to his camp with fresh insights and knowledge to be used for the betterment of the people. Under the exponential totalitarianizing of the experimental disciplines, this is increasingly not the case. Where, in the past, it was more commonly the case that experimental and

5   David Remnick, "25 Years of Nightmares", *The Washington Post,* July 28th, 1985 https://www.washingtonpost.com/archive/lifestyle/1985/07/28/25-years-of-nightmares/cb836420-9c72-4d3c-ae60-70a8f13c4ceb/.

6   Alston Chase, "Harvard and the Making of the Unabomber", *The Atlantic,* June 2000, https://www.theatlantic.com/magazine/archive/2000/06/harvard-and-the-making-of-the-unabomber/378239/.

7   Robert D. Mather, "U.S. Government Mind Control Experiments", *Psychology Today,* April 26th, 2020 https://www.psychologytoday.com/us/blog/the-conservative-social-psychologist/202004/us-government-mind-control-experiments.

8   Julian Borger, "Guantanamo: psychologists who designed CIA torture program to testify", *The Guardian,* January 20th, 2020 https://www.theguardian.com/us-news/2020/jan/20/guantanamo-psychologists-cia-torture-program-testify.

philosophical inquiries led to an uncovering and a revealing of the unknown, it is now a fact that knowledge is diluted, hoarded, and weaponized for the purposes of State control. In our present circumstance, the psychologist is the eyes and ears of the State, feeding information through its institutional nervous system. Supposedly, it is through his diligent effort that as a collective we come to a better understanding of our nature, one which allows us to act more forthrightly, with greater wisdom, superior erudition, and toward a final result which betters the least among us as well as emboldens our greatest heroes. But under the modern psychologist's watchful eye, petty resentments have multiplied, and psychological dysfunctions have become a kind of minor deity to be worshipped rather than healed. Institutional psychology (and its siblings, psychiatry and social work) is among the first lines of defense against truly proper thought.

Bigotries and prejudices, human ailments which psychologists spent a great deal of effort during the past century attempting to understand and eradicate, have now become enshrined as a cultural pastime. Differences of opinion are no longer met with cautious optimism and curiosity but scathing hatred. Dissent directed at any of the prevailing norms is now seen as utter and undeniable proof of one's obvious moral hideousness and psychological dysfunction. The American mind has sealed shut like a steel trap, and one could be forgiven for fearing that it may never reopen. Interpersonal relations have never been more strained; married couples are regularly encouraged through the media (*and even their closest confidantes!*) to separate the moment one refuses to yield to the implacable and totalitarian demands of the other. Primary school educators are instructed to ferret out minor deviations and irregularities in the behavior of their students so that they may be exposed to a battery of dubious psychopharmacological treatments which will alter them in unpredictable and potentially damaging ways. Politicians are hand delivered studies by obscenely partisan institutions of diabolical intent, who, allegedly being tasked with such questionable responsibilities as "monitoring hate", are published by researchers who arrive at highly motivated conclusions which justify their a priori superstitions and vindicate their moral bugaboos. Our situation is an untenable one.

Cognizant of these facts, I have written this book with the hope that it will begin a process of rebalancing our collective consciousness. Armed with my academic training, clinical experience, and firsthand knowledge of the very groups which these studies and policies were intended to control, I humbly present a new analysis of political extremism. Moreover, I present a radical redefinition of extremism that aims to place the responsibility for our failings where they truly belong. In a way, I am engaging in the same tradition of liberation—not to undermine the psychological stability of the individual, nor to place more power in the hands of reckless and tyrannical institutions and advocacy groups, but to use my words like a crowbar to pry open the American mind and release the demons implanted there by generations of irresponsible scientists, talking heads, and policymakers.

I do not expect this book to solve all our problems overnight, and I certainly don't assume that I have solved these problems beyond any semblance of doubt. This text, if received as I believe it will be, shall begin a conversation of intellectual courage, moral fortitude and dialectical openness—the exact ingredients necessary to pull us out of these modern dark ages and allow our civilization to usher in an era of unprecedented psychological flourishing and cultural progress. A thesis such as mine would not likely pass the cynical inspection of a dissertation committee or peer review board. Undoubtedly, no mainstream publisher would dare reproduce this text en masse, either. These are not self-aggrandizing statements designed to impress you of my genius; neither are they intended to sway you to my position before having inspected the arguments for yourself. They are statements of pure reality. I entrust you with this analysis in the hopes that you will read it in the same spirit of benevolence and curiosity into which I entered in preparing and delivering this text for you. Embedded in this publication are the insights and analyses of over one hundred years of human brilliance through which I have poured; here I stand on the shoulders of giants, contributing my ideas and experiences in the hopes that in another hundred years from now, this text will be considered as vital and relevant to the project of human understanding and flourishing as those which preceded it. If I fail at that task, then the failure is mine and mine alone. However, I do not believe this endeavor to be a failure. Of the many potential cataclysms with which we are faced, and of all battles which we have taken up arms to fight, I believe this one to be the most grave and important of all. And with that behind us, let us in earnest embark on this journey together. May it be a fruitful and fortuitous one indeed.

BOOK I

Whose Extremism? Which Ideology?

Expressions of hatred, so vile and putrid,
Hesitate to be spoken, though when shared quite lurid.
Condemnations abound, intent to draw a boundary,
Only to constrain and confine, exposing the contrary.
Betrayed in the first, revealing their truest notion,
The greatest of acts—a complete devotion.

Myth, Mental Illness, and Political Extremism

We will begin this analysis by introducing some familiar concepts, carefully drawing them out so to as extract the greatest evidential power they may have to offer this work. Slowly their interconnectedness will become apparent, and by the end of this work, will hopefully prove irrefutable. I do not suspect that their application will evince much controversy (the very hypothesis of this book provides more than enough of that for the average reader); however there are several strains of contemporary thought which simultaneously deny certain aspects while overemphasizing others in their attempts to explain the relationship between political extremism, personality psychology, and mental illness. For those who are ideologically committed to certain ways of viewing the world and its inhabitants, these ideas shall prove controversial indeed. It is not my intent to discount the works of those who came before, but rather to reshuffle them in such a way that we might think about the problem of political extremism a little differently (and with a bit of luck, more constructively as well).

An unfortunate consequence of the medicalization and naturalization of the mind (and the body) has been to view cognitive dysfunctions and personality disorders almost exclusively in terms of biological causes. Chemical imbalances in the brain are responsible for mood disorders; certain alleles are to blame for intellectual and developmental disorders; irregularities in a given region of the brain provide the cause for condition X, Y, Z, and so on. In this view, material causes require material solutions: pharmaceuticals, surgeries, and a host of other purported remedies are therefore applied to the body. This perspective, while not incorrect, is certainly incomplete.

In those situations where thinkers dare to look beyond the biological, the tendency to consider environmental and even political causes will emerge. So, too, will these theorists turn towards explanations which emphasize various technological and cultural innovations (the omnipresence of visual and auditory stimuli), narcissistic industries (the arts, including fashion, music, and cinema), the nihilism of modernity, and the demands of changing work environments (affecting the individual's psychomotility, for instance), and the roles they play in contributing to the phenomenon of human dysfunction. To the credit of such thinkers, new disciplines emerged throughout the last century in an attempt to address these problems. Two novel therapeutic methodologies from the 20th century come to mind almost immediately: the Soviet experiment in engineering psychology and ergonomics (a science that would later migrate to the U.S.), which attempted to ease the stress of the worker so he might be more productive, and the work of Austrian psychiatrist Viktor Frankl who developed a style of psychotherapy known as logotherapy to help individuals discover meaning in their lives. Many philosophies of human suffering were born, and just as many methodologies to *end* human suffering were born in the 20th century. As different as they all were, they shared one thing in common: they all proved insufficient at achieving their stated aim. While each innovation in psychological research and theory promised to transform the world for the better, in the face of these advancements the problem of human suffering has only persisted.

This is not to say that the aforementioned theories (trauma, congenital disturbances of neurobiological processes, evolving technological and environmental demands, and considerations relating to the individual's political circumstance) are wholly incorrect or insignificant, but should we consider the explosion of mental health problems in industrialized and modernized societies—in particular over the last quarter century—as well as our failure to treat persistent psychiatric conditions, then we must admit that something is awry in our analysis. Thomas Szasz wrote of the myth of mental illness in 1974, but in this work, I would like to discuss myth *and* mental illness.

The *how* of human behavior throughout most of our history has been relegated to the domain of religion, in particular through the use of myth and parable to convey truths about our nature, and as such, to provide archetypes or models which we can then internalize and embody in our actions. Throughout our history these archetypes have provided the form for consciousness (we could also call that 'personality'), and the use of myth and parable has served as a kind of moral and ethical education. Myth and parable are among the oldest cultural technologies (likely second only to language) and have possessed the power to not only shape and order civilizations, but to guide the evolutionary process itself. During the period where religions and myths were held with sincerity, we regarded these societal tools with great care and as such they were not easily dismissed by past regimes; when new mythical systems were adopted, almost always for the purpose of political consolidation and expansion, the most successful societies either retained significant features of the existing system or wiped out any trace of their existence (including the people who held on to them). What we see in our current situation is a covering, an overlaying, of the existing mythic and parabolic foundation upon which America was founded. For all our modern cynicism, our rationalist scientific skepticism, we have not abandoned myth itself. We have merely stripped myth and parable of its higher values (e.g. truth, beauty, and order) and vainly appropriated them for our own power-seeking narcissistic impulses. An analogue to this may be found in Christopher

Caldwell's recent book *The Age of Entitlement*,[1] where he pointed out that America is presently divided between the founding
constitutional document and its mid-twentieth century legal replacement (brought about by the civil rights movement); we are
not only contending with dueling legal understandings, but dual
and incompatible understandings of our own mythical, historical, and parabolic origins.

Stepping afield of the technical and historical implications of
that statement and directly to its psychological consequences, we
can say that perhaps to a greater extent than people are a product
of their race, ethnicity, or geographical origin, they are the result of their mythological and parabolic inheritance. While these
materialist origins do reveal a great deal about who we are and
whence we came, they reveal nothing about who we can be. They
certainly tell us little about *how* we should be. It is in the stories
of our ancestors and our Gods, tales of our victories and our foibles—the very collective autobiography of our people—that we
draw our true strength, but more importantly, our true identity.
Given this truth, if a people can be ripped from their inherited
narratives (which are best understood as a true collective fiction
or ideology), or merely have their narratives re-written in a way
that is disempowering, then they necessarily become psychologically vulnerable to the slings and arrows of malevolent story-
tellers and cognitive colonizers. Once these new authors enter
the scene, new narratives may then emerge; such freshly adopted
tales provide a different set of ethical and moral codes, which,
as our present condition plainly evinces, do not foster the development of agency, maturity, and eusocial intimacy. Rather, they
engender quite the opposite.

Through this process, victims of this mythological theft become alienated from their own identities, thus producing a
kind of false consciousness and the development of an othered
self-concept. Natural instincts honed over generations of natural and sexual selection therefore become problematized and
confused. Conformity to a set of mythically ordered evolutionary behaviors (themselves finely tuned and highly adaptive) are
now indicators of repression, trauma, or worse, fascist tenden-

---

1 Christopher Caldwell, *The Age of Entitlement: America Since the Sixties*, (Simon & Schuster, 2020).

cies. Seen in this light, mental illness can be understood as the result of a conflict between a dysgenic mythos and the natural psychological tendencies which seek realization within an orderly mental and cultural framework. While it is not ideal to describe the resulting psychological deficits using the language of mental illness (a concept so bound up in pseudo-medical and pseudo-scientific complications as to be unwieldy in helping us to achieve greater clarity), understood in an uncomplicated and layman sense, it does give us a point of discursive origin—the dysfunction of human thought and action. Operating from the insights afforded to us by narrative theory—stated simply, the idea that storytelling is an essential component of human cognition—we would be better served to work with a parabolic and mythological conception of psychological dis-ease. When we consider the problem of political extremism (as this text does), we can now view the issue in a broader sense—one that does not place the responsibility of violence and terror solely on disenfranchised individuals or impersonal biohistorical processes, but on those members of society who possess the power to influence entire civilizations.

In short, the subversion of religious, national, and ethnic mythos grants a tremendous capacity for political and social control. Much of contemporary discourse is itself a fight over the rights to our foundational myths so that they may be used to combat the social and political ills of our time—namely racism, anti-Semitism, fascism, inequality, misogyny, colonialism, imperialism, and homophobia (to name a few). One such example of this contest for cultural supremacy may be found in the work of Donna Zuckerberg who wrote the book *Not All Dead White Men*[2] partly with the intention of de-fanging classic texts (such as those of the Stoics) who, in her view, served as a legitimating force that aided far-right misogyny. In a 2018 interview with *The Guardian*,[3] Zuckerberg was quoted as saying,

2 Donna Zuckerberg, *Not All Dead White Men: Classics and Misogyny in the Digital Age*, (Harvard University Press, 2008).
3 Nosheen Iqbal, "Donna Zuckerberg: 'Social Media has elevated misogyny to new levels of violence'", *The Guardian*, November 11th, 2018 https://www.theguardian.com/books/2018/nov/11/donna-zuckerberg-social-media-misoyny-violence-classical-antiquity-not-all-dead-white-men.

> The ancient world was deeply misogynistic—it was a time
> when there was no word for rape, feminism did not exist
> and women's actions were determined by male relatives.

Other choice quotes from the same interview bemoaned the fact
that white supremacists and racists:

> ...long appropriated the history, literature and myth of the
> ancient world to their advantage. Borrowing the symbols of
> these cultures, as the Nazi party did in the 1940s, can be a
> powerful declaration that you are the inheritor of Western
> culture and civilization"; that these texts were being "dis-
> torted and stripped of context;

And that furthermore,

> Classics are wrought with histories and narratives of op-
> pression and exclusion.

While universities make progressive attempts to broaden the
canon so students aren't simply reading one dead white man after another,

> the manosphere rebel against this. They see themselves as
> the guardians of western civilisation and the defenders of
> its cultural legacy.

One last statement from Mrs. Zuckerberg simply to punctuate
the point,

> By quoting Marcus Aurelius—as Steve Bannon is known to
> often do—Red Pillers perpetuate the idea that they, White
> men, are the intellectual authority under threat from wom-
> en and people of colour.

We can find countless examples of this phenomenon, though I
won't go into quite as exhaustive an investigation here (but a few
more will further illuminate the point I have already made). In
her 1976 work, *The Laugh of the Medusa*,[4] Feminist theorist He-

4 Helene Cixous, "The Laugh of the Medusa", *Signs,* Vol. 1, no. 4, (Summer,
1976), pp. 875-893.

lene Cixous reinterpreted the Perseus myth as an expression of male fragility and terror. In her own words:

> Too bad for them if they fall apart upon discovering that women aren't men, or that the mother doesn't have [a penis]. But isn't this fear convenient for them? Wouldn't the worst be, isn't the worst, in truth, that women aren't castrated, that they have only to stop listening to the Sirens (for the Sirens were men) for history to change its meaning? You only have to look at the Medusa straight on to see her. And she's not deadly. She's beautiful and she's laughing. Men say that there are two unrepresentable things: death and the feminine sex. That's because they need femininity to be associated with death; it's the jitters that gives them a hard-on! for themselves! They need to be afraid of us. Look at the trembling Perseuses moving backward toward us, clad in apotropes. What lovely backs! Not another minute to lose. Let's get out of here. (p. 885)

A pioneering moment in what would later develop into the discipline of Queer Theology, Hugh William Montefiore wrote in 1967 of Jesus Christ's obvious homosexuality. In a paper titled *Jesus, the Revelation of God*,[5] Montefiore wrote,

> Men usually remain unmarried for three reasons: either because they cannot afford to marry or there are no girls to marry (neither of these factors need have deterred Jesus); or because it is inexpedient for them to marry in the light of their vocation (we have already ruled this out during the "hidden years" of Jesus' life); or because they are homosexual in nature, in as much as women hold no special attraction for them. The homosexual explanation is one which we must not ignore. (p. 109)

Saint Sebastian, the early Christian saint and martyr who was killed during Diocletian's persecution of Christians has since enjoyed a second life as a symbol for the pain of closeted homosexuals. Richard A. Kaye wrote that,[6]

---

5   H.W. Montefiore, "Jesus the Revelation of God", in *Christ for Us Today: Papers read at the Conference of Modern Churchmen,* Somerville College, Oxford, July 1967 (SCM Press, London: 1968).
6   Richard Kaye, "Losing His Religion: Saint Sebastian as Contemporary Gay

> Contemporary gay men have seen in Sebastian at once a stunning advertisement for homosexual desire (indeed, a homoerotic ideal), and a prototypical portrait of a tortured closet case. (p. 105)

The *1619 Project*, begun by *New York Times* reporter Nikole Hannah-Jones[7] (and which recently was awarded the 2020 Pulitzer Prize for Commentary),[8] is another such example of narrative-based political action heavily dependent on myth as a means for influencing thought and action. The project argued, among other things, that the American Revolution was fought to preserve the institution of slavery on the freshly settled continent. While I do not intend to rebut the arguments and reinterpretations presented by Ms. Hannah-Jones, her arguments serve to underscore my position—myths make the people. Ayn Rand was alleged to have remarked positively at the release of the 1977 television series, *Roots,* arguing that it was an important work which provided African-Americans with a sense of myth and history, having lost this connection as a result of the slave trade. Clearly we can see what we may call mythic competition, as the story of the African slaves has been transported from a peripheral, though integral, part of American history to the front-and-center position it currently enjoys.

It would not be controversial to say that our knowledge of our own history is not as thoroughgoing as we would like it to be. The stories of our past are often shrouded in a great deal of mystery and intrigue. On this point, I would like to share a quote from Derrida delivered in his lecture "*Structure, Sign, and Play in the Discourse of the Human Sciences*" (who in turn was quoting Levi-Strauss),[9]

> The myth and the musical work thus appear as orchestra

Martyr", *Outlooks: Lesbian and Gay Sexualities and Visual Cultures,* (New York, Routledge, 1996).

7   Nikole Hannah-Jones, "The 1619 Project", *The New York Times,* August 14th, 2019, https://www.nytimes.com/interactive/2019/08/14/magazine/1619-america-slavery.html.

8   Dan McLaughlin, "The 1619 Project Wins a Pulitzer Prize for Agitprop", *Yahoo! News,* May 7th, 2020 https://news.yahoo.com/1619-project-wins-pulitzer-prize-103005628.html.

9   Jacques Derrida, *Writing and Difference* (Editions du Seuil, 1967).

> conductors whose listeners are the silent performers. If it
> be asked where the real focus of the work is to be found, it
> must be replied that its determination is impossible. Music
> and mythology bring man face to face with virtual objects
> whose shadow alone is actual... Myths have no authors.

And because myths have no authors, they can be seen as part of
the commons—belonging to the public domain—and therefore
subject to an unending sequence of reappropriations. An unwillingness to secure a *rightful* interpretation (or at least designating
an interpretative or priestly class of sufficient dutifulness and
loyalty), thus opens the populace up to powerful and unrelenting psychological manipulation. While one may appropriate any
myth for the purpose of empowering one group and demoralizing another, no matter what historical event one seeks to hijack,
all stories contain particular affective characters, the distortion
of which psychologically harms *both the empowered and the dis-
empowered.* The revised slavery mythos sets Black Americans in
the role of 'true' Americans and Whites in the role of oppressive
coattail riders. The narcissism of modern sexual identity allows
religious figures to be desacralized and reconfigured as counter-
cultural heroes for sexual minorities. Novel psychological and
sociological paradigms are cast retroactively upon classical texts,
thus removing their genius and necessitating their recontextu-
alization so as to accord with contemporary sensibilities. In all
such cases only one group truly benefits: the powerful. Not all
political power comes from the barrel of a gun; often we find the
pen to be just as mighty as the pistol.

The appropriation of myth has powerful implications for the
development of a secure identity, a point which I have hinted at
thus far but will elaborate more fully a little later in this text.
Mythical reevaluations are to a large degree the unavoidable
consequence of both cultural evolution *and* involution; the more
a people migrate from their formative circumstances, the greater
is the need for their myths and parables to be recontextualized
so they may make sense of new challenges and circumstances.
There may be a political dimension to this process, or it may reflect simple pragmatic necessities, sometimes both at once. In our
present situation it is difficult to deny the political motivations
behind the repurposing of Western and American mythology.

Whether owing to the desire to suppress political opposition, or as the logical result of a democratization of the arts whereby marginalized peoples seek to break the yoke of oppressive, supremacist, and phallogocentric narratives (an unquestionably revolutionary and political act), we see in all instances a will to power seeking its own exertion and preservation.

I spoke of the affective character central to any story. Often the most powerful emotions are negative ones, and so it should not surprise us to see that the most enduring and culturally transformative myths have, at their core, negatively affective narrative devices. Take persecution and suffering, for example. Both emotions being so central to the founding mythology of many Americans (be they English, African, Irish, Jewish, or otherwise) they provide a wellspring of resentment, angst, and terror to be drawn from and marshaled for reasons of political efficiency. By no means are these the only themes to be found in our myths, nonetheless they have proven the most successful and politically expedient for the achievement of control and subjugation. Consider the following realities of victimhood: The Jewish-American fears an inevitable persecution at the hands of his Gentile neighbor. The African American fears he will never free himself from the slavery of his Caucasian oppressor. The European American increasingly suffers under the weight of his own mythical tyranny, for increasingly his narrative is one of original sin, situating him as the sole agent of evil in the modern world. Woman, too, anguishes at her inability to escape man's cloying grasp. And as the revolution of human rights continues its march into the adolescence our new century, homosexuals and transsexuals find themselves similarly—and in their view, *most significantly*—suffering victimhood for the mere crime of existing. Resentment,[10]

---

10 The problem of resentment is one worth expanding upon, as it is central to many of the arguments I present throughout this work. Contemporary political discourse places a great deal of focus on the problem of resentment, and for good reason. However, it is usually regarded with a heavy dose of contempt. This, I believe, is a symptom of the technique of responsibilism which places the individual as the social unit tasked with resolving this problem. Again, this is true, but it is not the entire truth. Resentment emerges from loneliness and isolation, from abandonment and neglect, and ultimately is the fruit born of a failed and dying civilization. Resentment is something to be overcome, but it requires social (and in most cases, material) resources to do so. Many people never receive these resources. Resentment is a spiritual ailment, but the West is

that rich and eminently minable psychological resource, may be the prevailing feeling of our time; so long as this remains the case we will find ourselves helpless to improve our current circumstance and realize the grand ambitions of the last century.

If it wasn't clear before, the manner in which myth orders not only our moral and cognitive schemas, but our affective ones as well, should now be readily apparent. So, too, should the relationship between mental illness and political extremism begin to come into focus. The use of myth and parable to antagonize, demonize, and demoralize can only lead us down one path—violence. And when we consider that the punitively political use of storytelling is but one layer of the psychosocial scaffold, the one which orders the biological layers beneath it, a more comprehensive view of the problem ought to emerge. Having introduced the centrality of myth in the problem of political extremism, let us continue a little further down this path and discuss the effects which certain foundational ideas have on the contemporary American psyche.

Dispelling Popular American Myths

Having loosely introduced the importance of myth in the formation of man's mind as well as his civilization, I find it necessary to deflate certain misconceptions, or what we may even call *false* collective fictions. Here I am speaking of myth in the negative sense: if we are correct in accepting the existence of *true* collective fictions, then certainly we must accept the existence of their antipode. It is my contention that a set of political myths define our age and thus prevent us from gaining a clearer understanding of the situation at hand. Necessarily they must be dispelled before we may begin laying the groundwork for a truer understanding of the political scene and of the phenomenon of

---

bereft of spiritual healing. There is an element of narcissism or self-centeredness immanent to resentment, but this, too, is a cultural or civilizational problem. Preoccupation with the self is a central feature of American psychology. Compassion and brotherly love are the antidotes to resentment; to heal the psychic wound, others must be willing to push through their own transferences, their own feelings of contempt and disgust at the weakness and pettiness of the resentful other. Stronger, more self-assured individuals must take the burden upon themselves to lift the wounded up and restore them on the proper path.

extremism more broadly, for my later arguments are dependent on reconfiguring key beliefs we as Americans hold about our own way of life.

Let us begin with the myth concerning the fourth estate: the "free and independent press" is anything but. The function of the press is closer to that of an immune system; its purpose is to strengthen narratives that reinforce the power structure while simultaneously ignoring or misrepresenting counter-narratives. Media and the Press are extensions of the State and integral to the maintenance of cultural hegemony. *All* press outlets—be they mainstream or alternative—are perspectival by nature, and if we fail to understand just which perspective a given speaker is advocating for, then we will fail to evaluate the information which they present. This is hardly a novel claim, but even in the era of "Fake News" where the credibility of the American media complex is supposedly at its lowest, the ability of journalists and media personalities to influence the popular mind is probably stronger than it has ever been.

For the sake of brevity (and possibly, the reader's sanity), clear examples to this point will be restricted to significant events of the last twenty years. We may find it easy to recall NBC anchor Brian Williams's claim of the rocket-propelled helicopter attack in 2003 which nearly took his life—a claim which was only re-evaluated some twelve years later (and found to be utterly false).[11] While some rushed to his defense and others shifted the blame onto a broader American pathology of gutlessness and gluttony, most expressed horror at the trusted media man's complete lack of ethical regard. Perhaps, as Steven Almond suggested back when the story first made waves,[12] Williams' failure was in his overidentification with a certain masculine ethic (one which he clearly felt he lacked), and so he enthusiastically took on the delusion that he was participating in the very patriotic fervor which he was merely present to report on. It is a fool's errand to

11 Leslie Savan, "Finally, Someone pays for Iraq War Lies – Brian Williams", *The Nation,* February 12th, 2015 https://www.thenation.com/article/archive/finally-someone-pays-iraq-war-lies-brian-williams/.
12 Steven Almond, "Our dangerous macho delusions: Brian Williams' fraudulence – and our own", *Salon,* February 9th, 2015 https://www.salon.com/test2/2015/02/09/our_dangerous_macho_delusions_brian_williams_fraudulence_and_our_own/.

imagine we may have access to the man's motivations from afar, but it is not his motivations which should interest us. What is interesting is that Williams' lie took on a symbolic weight: his lie represented the lies of an entire industry, an industry which all too gleefully led Americans toward a perspective that was not their own. Americans were bombarded by the fourth estate and led toward a perspective that the hegemony already possessed but needed to be reciprocated before it could proceed. In his 2019 book *Hate Inc.*,[13] Matt Taibbi chronicled the series of lies perpetuated, in part, by the media complex that helped justify then President George W. Bush's desire to invade Iraq. In particular he singled out institutions such as *The Washington Post, The New York Times, CNN, ABC, PBS,* and prominent journalists including David Remnick, Jeffrey Goldberg, Ezra Klein, and Jonathan Chait, as being significant in their propagandizing for the war effort (though, to be certain, there was more than enough blame to go around). Many of those responsible for garnering popular support for the war are still working today and are *still* held in the esteem of millions of Americans.

Reporting of both the shootings of Trayvon Martin and Michael Brown were similarly rife with politically motivated misinformation, perhaps most significantly in the case of *NBC's* doctoring of George Zimmerman's 911 calls[14] and the perpetuation of the "*Hands up, don't shoot!*"[15] narrative which Glenn Kessler of *The Washington Post* would later include in an article of "the biggest Pinocchios of 2015" (a claim which would carry more weight were it not so frivolously juvenile).[16] The perpetuation of these falsehoods led to nationwide riots, racial strife, and the deaths

13 Matt Taibbi, "16 Years Later, How the Press That Sold the Iraq War Got Away With It", *Rolling Stone,* March 22nd, 2019, https://www.rollingstone.com/politics/politics-features/iraq-war-media-fail-matt-taibbi-812230/.

14 Michael Martinez, "George Zimmerman sues NBC Universal over edited 911 call", *CNN,* December 7th, 2012, https://www.cnn.com/2012/12/06/us/florida-zimmerman-nbc-lawsuit/index.html.

15 Jonathan Capehart, "'Hands up, don't shoot' was built on a lie", *The Washington Post,* March 16th, 2015, https://www.washingtonpost.com/blogs/post-partisan/wp/2015/03/16/lesson-learned-from-the-shooting-of-michael-brown/.

16 Nick Gass, "'Hands up, don't shoot' ranked one of biggest 'Pinocchios' of 2015", *Politico,* December 14th, 2015, https://www.politico.com/story/2015/12/hands-up-dont-shoot-false-216736.

of protestors and police officers alike. Now, over five years later, the clarion call of the activist and journalist class has become the mantra *du jour* for the corporate class as well. Failure to heed this call may cost one their job, their university enrollment, and potentially even their life. Without the amplification provided by the fourth estate, would the rest of society still have taken up this issue?

Trump's 2016 presidential campaign provided another such example of media distortion. Pundits including the likes of Nate Silver, Ross Douthat, Nate Cohn, and Bill Krystol (to name a few), got everything wrong from the moment he announced his candidacy.[17] Until the moment that Donald Trump was proclaimed the next President of the United States, the press would continue to get the story wrong (Josh Katz of *The New York Times*, for instance, gave Hillary Clinton an 85% of victory *the day of the election*).[18] Worse still, with each passing month, the ability of media analysts and talking heads to withhold their contempt for Trump and his supporters receded until any notion of journalistic integrity could no longer be plausibly accepted. The intervening years would provide many more opportunities for the media class to overplay the hand; from Russiagate to COVID-19, hardly a single story fell from their lips which wasn't tainted by ideological perspectivity and allegiance to the power structure. And at the time of this writing, the shooting of Ahmaud Arbery has all the makings of another event of media collusion and misrepresentation (May 10th, 2020). I hope that I am wrong.

But what can be said of the journalists themselves? Those who join the media complex to become journalists and media personalities are animated both by a certain set of ideas, as well as a particular temperament. Unfortunately, less can be said about the latter than the former, as a thorough psychological analysis of the archetypal journalist is not yet (to my knowledge) available. Some points of data do exist, which interesting as they might be, are best regarded as offering a frighteningly incomplete pic-

17 Katelynn Fossett, "16 worst predictions of 2016", *Politico,* November 6th, 2016,   https://www.politico.com/story/2016/11/2016-election-worst-predictions-230806.
18 Josh Katz, "Who Will Be President?", *The New York Times,* November 8th, 2016, https://www.nytimes.com/interactive/2016/upshot/presidential-polls-forecast.html.

ture. One study suggests a tendency toward hyperthymic temperament among those journalists who were recently psychiatric outpatients (Akiskai, Savino, Akiskaii, 2005).[19] Another study found among South African journalists a high need for power, sensation seeking, and binge drinking than those in the control group (Hirschowitz & Nell, 2010).[20] As relates to questions of mental fitness, the prevalence rate of post-traumatic stress disorder is higher among journalists than the general population, though this may be the result of certain occupational hazards (Aoki, Malcolm, Yamaguchi, 2012).[21] As for ideological data, an interesting study conducted by Thurman et al., found that left-wing journalists in the U.K. outnumber right-wing ones by 53%. Of those polled, 82% believe promoting tolerance and cultural diversity to be an important value. 96% claimed their personal values and beliefs informed their work. 66% said that journalism has lost its credibility.[22] The same study found a fairly significant disparity in the political identity of the journalists polled (see figure 1.5b).

19   Karen K. Akiskal, Mario Savino, Hagop S. Akiskal, "Temperament profiles in physicians, lawyers, managers, industrialists, architects, journalists, and artists: a study in psychiatric outpatients", *Journal of Affective Disorders,* Vol. 85, Issues 1-2, March 2005, pp. 201-206.
20   Rosaline Hirschowitz & Victor Neil, "The Relationship between Need for Power and the Life Style of South African Journalists", *The Journal of Social Psychology,* Vol. 121, Issue 2, March 8th, 1983, pp. 297-304.
21   Yuta Aoki, Estelle Malcolm, Sosei Yamaguchi, Graham Thornicroft, Claire Henderson, "Mental illness among journalists: A systematic review", *International Journal of Social Psychiatry, Vol. 59, Issue: 4, March 8th, 2012, pp. 377-390.*
22   Thurman, N., Cornia, A., & Kunert, J. "Journalists in the UK", *UK: Reuters Institute for the Study of Journalism,* 2016, pp. 12-13.

FIGURE 1.5a: POLITICAL AFFILIATION OF UK JOURNALISTS, DECEMBER 2015 (n = 603).

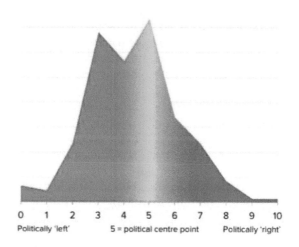

FIGURE 1.5b: POLITICAL AFFILIATION OF UK JOURNALISTS BY RANK, DECEMBER 2015.

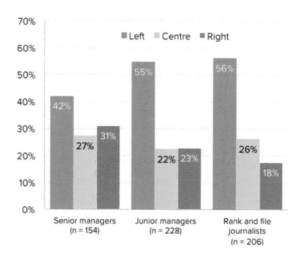

While these data do not directly correlate to the political scene in the United States, they do give us some measure of insight into the psychological and ideological makeup of your average journalist. There is, however, a measure of ideological symmetry to be found among American journalists. Findings by research-ers Hassell, Holbein, and Miles note that while there is no mea-surable liberal bias in political coverage, "*a dominant majority of journalists identify as liberals/Democrats*".[23] Lars Willnat and David H. Weaver found an 18% drop from 2002 to 2013 in the number of U.S. journalists identifying as Republican. While their survey found an overall decline in partisan identification (of the 1,080 journalists polled, 50.2% identified as Independent), only 7% identified as Republican.[24] In my view, further research into this area has not illuminated the political or psychological character of American journalism to any satisfactory degree and so I shall stop here.

At this point I must venture off into the realm of conjecture, as the paucity of definitive empirical data leaves me little choice but to draw my own conclusions on the matter. Mencius Moldbug tells us that "*Cthulhu always swims left*";[25] whether this is because of America's own foundational principles of liberty and justice for all, the cultural revolution starting with the Beat Generation of the 1950's and continuing onwards, the judicial victories of the 1960's that fundamentally changed our relationship with the law, or all of the above (the likely answer), one can hardly deny that the media industry itself has been and continues to be dominat-ed by progressive left-wing sentiment (or what has come to be known as neoliberalism). In some sense there is little meaning in pointing this out, as America has almost reached a point of total convergence between leftism (neoliberalism) and rightism (neoconservatism)—two ideologies birthed by the same mother, differentiated only by aesthetic and temperamental particular-

---

23   Hans J.G. Hassell, John B., Holbein, & Matthew R. Miles, "There is no liber-al media bias in which news stories political journalists choose to cover", *Science Advances*, Vol. 6, no. 14, April 1st, 2020.

24   Hadas Gold, "Survey: 7 percent of reporters identify as Republican", *Politi-co*, May 6th, 2014, https://www.politico.com/blogs/media/2014/05/survey-7-per-cent-of-reporters-identify-as-republican-188053.

25   Curtis Yarvin, "A Gentle Introduction To Unqualified Reservations", *Un-qualified Reservations*, January 8th, 2009, https://www.unqualified-reservations.org/2009/01/gentle-introduction-to-unqualified/.

ities. Points of disagreement between the two ideologies rarely scratch the surface of political discourse, instead opting to pedantically bicker over matters both optical and practical, thus limiting the scope of what can possibly be achieved. The theatrical nature of their dispute gives the impression of opposition, whereas on matters of political significance the two invariably march in lockstep.

Digressions aside, it is likely correct to say that this convergence is in fact the result of overwhelming cultural and legal victories secured by the left over the last half decade, which has dragged conservatism kicking and screaming along with it. That the two share an ideological foundation in individualism, expansionism, and progress offers the power of philosophical persuasion to the winning side (neoliberalism). Necessarily, the history of modern progressivism is one of over-turning an 'immoral' and 'authoritarian' order, of raising up the powerless and the marginalized, and of daring to challenge convention wherever it may be found. Left-wing journalists have inherited this worldview and carry it forward, secure in their belief that truth and courage are their most powerful weapons in the battle against oppression, conformity, bigotry. Whether their work requires them to oust corporate executives or grocery clerks is of little import for they are the attack dogs of American hegemony (a role which they relish). In the neoliberal journalist we see the importance of myth: leftists in the media complex are galvanized by a Manichean worldview with brave heroes, sinister villains, and a gallery of political saints and martyrs which grows with each passing day. Even if they live their day-to-day lives as secular humanists, they regard their politics with the same zealotry as a medieval crusader. So committed are they to their mythological worldview—that realer-than-real experience of their own lives—the journalistic class are totally blind to the material fact of their existence. Journalists, being ensconced in their bubbles of privilege and ideological conformity, imagine themselves to be speaking truth to power, when in fact they are merely reinforcing existing power structures. The illusion of the dispassionate and objective reporter or journalist is shattered when we understand that their True North is often found by simply taking note of which direction their ideological overlords happen to be pointing in.

Given this analysis we may say that the character of the left-journalist in particular is one of arrogance and gluttony, narcissism and pedantry, passive-aggressively confrontational, and possessing a uniquely religious quality of pettiness and vengeance-seeking. But it gets worse. At least as it relates to the digital press (where the profit margin is far slimmer, the barrier to entry is far lower, and the pressure to publish content is much higher), and in particular where these institutions themselves are defined in part or in whole by their commitment to certain neoliberal ideals (e.g. social justice, diversity, anti-racism, etc.), those who get hired are of the lowest quality and character. Often, they represent certain perspectives, though more accurately biological types, that are intended to enlighten the reader on different and unique points of view. Enabled by the progressive liberal, who in his narcissistic and navel-gazing obsession with authenticity loves to encourage the marginalized to 'speak their truth', we find these individuals guiltlessly unleashing their resentment upon the country, as 'their truth' so often translates to whatever real or imagined grievance they happen to be suffering from on that day. While their employment does not offer them much in the way of meaningful compensation, they out-earn others when it comes to catharsis, self-righteousness, and visibility. Really, these are easily controllable people; their hunger for power (itself fueled by identity-based pangs of anxiety and alienation) makes them ideal minions. And make no mistake, they are minions. Should we turn our attention to the papers of record, such as *The New York Times*, we find that circumstances are hardly much better (and if you disagree, I invite you to partake of staff editor Bari Weiss' appearances on *The Joe Rogan Experience*). Though reputable and antifragile news outfits *do* draw from a richer pool of talent, we invariably find the same tendencies toward therapeutic grievance mongering and institutional bootlicking. Psychologically speaking, the media classes (of which journalists are but one part) best represent that peculiarly American style of narcissism—equal parts self-aggrandizing and self-loathing, loud and lacking self-awareness, highly moral and yet highly unethical, and utterly antisocial to the core.

If I am correct in my analysis, then we can no longer suffer under the delusion that the press in any way retains the integrity it (rightly or wrongly) enjoyed in the previous century. Modern journalists and pundits tread a path so firmly beaten but at the same time imagine themselves to be courageous trailblazers. Often, they are petty and uncreative individuals who ply their trade by advancing system ideas through means that can only be described as literary violence. So because of their low status, low ability, poor character (and often, financial impoverishment), they are held in a near constant state of terror which they are able to inflict on others by way of the institutional support provided to them. This phenomenon finds its highest expression in those outlets of low repute, but it is certainly not absent should one turn their attention to more 'legitimate' propaganda outfits. Among those journalists, pundits, and talking heads that are better placed socially and financially we find a rather mundane and garden variety expression of narcissism, impulsivity, and self-aggrandizement. We may even find a measure of self-awareness, however, one that is dulled by drugs, alcohol, and financial coziness. Often, we see in them that familiar pattern of idealist-turned-cynic, of deflecting responsibility to *institutional* or *systemic* causes, telling us all the while that "*it's just a job, man*".

Several of these critiques are as true among right-wing outlets as they are of those on the left, though we will often find that their objects of cathexis—their fetishized obsessions—to be more in accord with their particular worldview (e.g. welfare recipients, debt-burdened university students, "communists", and so on). Racial and class antagonisms are not unique to one side or the other, and neither is the tendency toward the moral castigation of 'approved' social groups. Though, in an attempt to seek in-roads into the public consciousness, I have observed a greater tendency toward deliberate antagonism and juvenile titillation bordering on the verge of performance art. Such examples would include the failed smear of Elizabeth Warren in October of 2019, conducted by Jacob Wohl,[26] and perhaps even the entire careers of individuals such as Alex Jones and Milo Yiannopoulous. While it is easy to critique the conduct of mainstream

---

26   James Walker, "Jacob Wohl Mocked After Claiming Elizabeth Warren Sex Scandal, Says 2020 Candidate Had Affair with 24-Year-Old Marine", *Newsweek*, October 3rd, 2019, https://www.newsweek.com/jacob-wohl-mocked-after-claiming-elizabeth-warren-sex-scandal-says-2020-candidate-had-affair-1462895.

left-wing journalism, we would be remiss to ignore the fact that many prominent right-wing personalities merely affect a veneer of journalism so as to hide their otherwise evident sociopathic tendencies (a label that I would caution against using too broadly or too enthusiastically).

Theirs is a psychology of complete pleasure principle; gleefully promoting fantastical conspiracies about authoritarian overreach (such claims, while not entirely inaccurate, are compromised by belief in a dated paradigm), the release of their hypomanic libidinal energies overshadow any capacity for contemplative or reflective thought. Itching impulsively to play the part of the modern Paul Revere, conservative journalism is reflexively destined to clutch its anti-authoritarian pearls at the first sight of 'tyrannical governance'. Terror sells, but so too does confirmation bias and affirmations of the heroic and revolutionary American identity. Myopic fixations on 'real' political actors (be they shadowy super-sovereign governmental institutions or mythical Nazi billionaires hell-bent on the destruction of America) reduce these otherwise capable and intelligent figures to the level of a caricature. Mainstream right-wing journalism is every bit as hysterical and self-serving as its mirror opposite, only the object of hystericism differs for each. And because they are so hyperbolic and cartoonish, because they are slaves to an ideal which they are unable to reflect on critically, they in turn serve the role needed by true political operatives and institutions—that of a political boogeyman who may be deployed at any time for the purpose of controlling the frame of the political narrative. Certainly, more examples of this ethic of provocation-as-journalism exist, but I would prefer not to belabor the point.

The psychological tension which we might expect to find within the mind of the rightist media personality and the 'legitimate' news outlets to which they belong (such as *Infowars*, *Fox News*, and *OANN*) should be found in the friction between superego and id. The id, as we know, finds itself sublimated to the superego and thus toward symbols of American virtue. However, in accordance with the logic of mass media and capitalism these symbols are debased, trivialized, and sexualized, in a have-your-cake-and-eat-it-too psychology which satisfies the higher moral principle while also allowing for lower and more guttural urges to find a satisfaction of their own. The internet free-speech warrior, the Campus Conservative, the badass Gun Chick, the devout Christian, all of whom are actors providing a safe outlet both for political expression, but more importantly, for the satisfaction of essential psychological desires. Conservatives can be good law-abiding, flag waving, God-fearing Americans while still indulging in a bit of filth and violence (all the while never having to deal with the trouble of thinking about the consequence of their media consumptive habits). The tension which we might expect (taking a classically Freudian approach) dissipates, as the demands of the superego are flattened out in service of an immediacy which postures as ethos.

In their own ways, both the American right and left believe they hold a monopoly on truth and moral self-righteousness; the bifurcation of the political scene is, in effect, predicated on the bifurcation of the American mind. Both in fact *do* hold particular moral claims but owing to their reactionary co-dependence are unable to see where their perceived monopoly ends and totalitarian compensation begins. Issues of political and economic importance which would otherwise form the basis of a true political center (meaning, of importance to all members of American society) are necessarily split into the factions of conservatism and progressivism—two lovers who share the single umbrella of American neoliberalism. Though, to appropriate a lyric from Sting, it is often those who identify with the 'right' side of the umbrella who always end up getting wet. This is not an unimportant matter, as rightists, too, suffer a victimary complex. The conservative, that long-suffering wife of American political culture finds solace in the preponderance of the so-called alternative media sources which have sprung up in the last decade and a half. Lacking a champion to represent them in the arena of political media, the conservative unreservedly yields his agency to these warriors of free speech. This only reinforces his powerlessness, as so often these alternatives fail to provide any meaningful truth or praxis. As a further signifier of their impotence (their internalized sense of helplessness), the American right takes up political action only in a symbolic way; the Gun, the Flag, the Market, the Cross—all oversimplifications of the American identity which are too easily deployed as commodities by right-wing media. And so while the left-wing media monopoly serves, perhaps, to set the agenda and control the narrative, the right-wing co-monopoly becomes the playground where the conservative children are dropped off while their parents busy themselves with important adult work. Equal parts neurotic escapism and counter-narrative creation, popular right-wing reporting is an indispensable part of what Edward Herman and Noam Chomsky called "*manufacturing consent*".[27]

One final point before we move on from this discussion: most of the media any American will ever consume, be it digital, print, or otherwise, is effectively owned by six corporations—*National Amusements, Disney, Time Warner, Comcast, News Corp,* and *Sony.*[28] Institutional capture of this degree ensures that the populace will have to muster a truly Herculean effort if they are serious about truly being informed. This level of centralization allows the press to choose their preferred method for disarming political opposition; they can directly attack dangerous ideas or groups (dangerous in the sense that Foucault meant it—as in *dangerous to the establishment*) or they can simply choose not to discuss such matters at all. By the same token, it strengthens and reinforces those ideas which are necessary for the survival of the system by permitting, and even offering glowing praise for those ideas and in particular those individuals who champion such ideas. Since the press is only one aspect (albeit an important aspect) of the complex of control that shapes public opinion, navigating the line between giving oxygen to an idea or suffocating it must be done carefully. Miscalculations in their methods of antagonism and obfuscation can, and sometimes do, backfire.

The press succeeds on two fronts—its legitimacy as an institution and its monopoly on distribution. Even absent the former (which, according to a *Gallup* poll conducted in September of 2019 puts public support of the press at 41%),[29] the sheer monop-

---

27 Edward S. Herman & Noam Chomsky, *Manufacturing Consent: The Political Economy of the Mass Media* (Pantheon Books, 1988).

28 WebFX Team, "The 6 Companies That Own (Almost) All Media [Infographic]", *WebFX,* January 30th, 2020, https://www.webfx.com/blog/internet/the-6-companies-that-own-almost-all-media-infographic/.

29 Megan Brenan, "Americans' Trust in Mass Media Edges Down to 41%", *Gallup,* September 26th, 2019, https://news.gallup.com/poll/267047/americans-trust-mass-media-edges-down.aspx.

oly it enjoys means that victory is achieved merely by the existence of this monopoly. Little more can be said on this matter that has not been delivered more eloquently or insightfully than, say, C. Wright Mills or Noam Chomsky, so I will not attempt a further analysis beyond this point.

At this point I would like to expand on a point made earlier, for there is another myth that requires dismissal—that the ideologies of the American left (progressive neoliberalism) and right (reactionary neoconservatism) are in fact wholly distinct and antagonistic. At one point in American history, there were more divergent systems of belief represented by different factions, each vying for institutional control. That is (mostly) no longer the case, though there still is some degree of factionalism across the political continuum. By and large the American system works to create a broad center of consensus that will support system politics, while simultaneously pushing anti-system ideologies to the absolute fringe of the national conversation. Tight control of narrative framing affords the average American a belief (whether it is a volitional one, or merely one of resignation) in the inevitability the two-party system. In biological and psychological terms there are necessary distinctions to be made (a point which I will elaborate on more fully in the following chapter), but in truth both are system ideologies with a great deal of epistemic agreement, and as such uniformly share the same goals though they may achieve them through different methods. Axiomatically, both accept the primacy of the individual and share the belief that he can be improved or realized through the application of economic techniques. Both tend to view contemporary moral debates in terms of America's history with slavery and its participation in the Second World War. Both accept a linear, progressive view of history (that is to say, humanity always moves forward, improving along the way). Neither side fundamentally takes issue with America's imperial practices, especially if the military is used as a force for "spreading democracy". Curiously, both the right and the left exhibit a dual-mindedness about the exercise of authority for the purpose of resolving domestic issues (I will say more on this momentarily). While adherents of either side will strategically deploy a 'true' American identity when they feel threatened, both espouse a belief that Americanism itself is not bound in anything real, but rather is simply a result of the choice to live in America. Following this, both the right and the left will make moral exemplars *and* scapegoats out of ethnic, religious, and sexual minorities when they need to. Self-aggrandizement and self-flagellation, too, are key psychological features of Americans across both sides of the political spectrum. Americans march in lockstep when it comes to their habits of consumption, behavior, and thought. They even share the same moral vocabulary; cries of "*fascist!*" and "*Nazi!*" are bound to follow any heated argument, regardless of whether the individual thinks of themselves as conservative or progressive. Beyond the psychometric data used to differentiate them as biopsychological types, very little in fact separates the leftist from the rightist. As we will see in the second chapter, even extremism of both the left-wing and right-wing varieties shares a remarkable degree of overlap.

Lastly and perhaps most controversially is the idea that America's political woes can be reformed. As if evil itself could possibly be reformed. Americans of all political affiliations share a naïve hope in their heart—the dream of a great return—though depending on that person, the hope may find a slightly different expression. The capitalist believes America could "get back on track" if only the markets were permitted to function autonomously; the conservative thinks that everything wrong with the country could be undone by simply returning to some golden age in America's history; the White nationalist argues that all of America's problems would disappear if she were an ethnostate; the Christian's belief in Jesus Christ as America's salvation is beyond question; the communist's vision of a healthy America rests solely on the spilled blood of the wealthy; the atheist pines for the day when the American people become truly rational and empirical, and can thus free the country by abandoning all of their petty superstitions. I could go on. To understand the problem of political extremism is to understand that the problem *is* America. There is no *One Weird Trick For Restoring Your Democracy*. Economic reforms will not heal the country because reform presupposes that the system is desirable in *any* configuration. America is the tyrannical father who rapes and abuses, and in attempting to absolve himself of his wrongdoings, gaudily and shamelessly purchases the silence of his victims. America is the plundering vulture capitalist, the hectoring moralist, the arrogant tourist, the debauched sensationalist; it is the mercenary, the dilettante, the prostitute, and the chauvinist. The United States are a great many other things as well, and to give credit where credit is due, there are a great deal of nobilities which can be attributed to our nation. Philosophical Americanism, however, is something altogether different. Taken on the whole, considering America as an imperial force and as the wealthiest country on the planet, who is responsible more so than any other empire in human history for remaking the world in its image, the country can only be regarded as a dismal failure.

It is only the ideology of Americanism which can manage to rationalize away the failures of an empire as vast as our own. With vast technological and financial resources at our fingertips, and the benefit of being the only nation left standing in the aftermath of the Second World War, American leadership stumbled out of the gate and within a few short decades quickly saw its international lead disintegrate. It is in America that when the market collapses, banks and corporations recuperate their losses while the average American loses all of their wealth. It is because of America that wars are fought to spread democracy in regions that never again regain their autonomy or stability. It is in the wealthiest nation that you will find life expectancy decrease,[30] happiness decrease,[31] birth rates decrease,[32] while instances of drug abuse,[33] psychological disorders,[34] and suicides[35]

30   Steven H. Woolf & Heidi Schoomaker, "Life Expectancy and Mortality Rates in the United States, 1959-2017", *Journal of the American Medical Association,* Vol. 32, Issue 20, December 2019.

31   Helliwell, J., Layard, R., & Sachs, J. "World Happiness Report 2019", *New York: Sustainable Development Solutions Network.*

32   Brady E. Hamilton, Joyce A. Martin, Michelle J.K. Osterman, & Lauren M. Rossen, "Births: Provisional Data for 2018", *National Center for Health Statistics,* Report no. 007, May 2019.

33   William Wan & Heather Long, "Coronavirus has caused a huge spike in drug overdoses", *The Washington Post,* July 1st, 2020, https://www.washingtonpost.com/health/2020/07/01/coronavirus-drug-overdose/.

34   Jean M. Twenge, A. Bell Cooper, Thomas E. Joiner, Mary E. Duffy, Sarah G. Binau, "Age, period, and cohort trends in mood disorder indicators and suicide-related outcomes in a nationally representative dataset, 2005-2017", *Journal of Abnormal Psychology,* Vol. 128, Issue 3, March 15th, 2019, pp. 185-199.

35   Lea Winerman, "By the numbers: An alarming rise in suicide", *The Ameri-*

all increase. America, more so than any other nation, boasts the highest incarceration rate[36] and is among the nations with the most severe police violence.[37] [38] The country which first enshrined freedom of speech now suffers the pleasure of onerous censorship and hate speech laws. Annually, the United States gives billions of dollars in aid to foreign countries while tens of millions of Americans go uninsured, unemployed, and lack basic essentials, even housing. Not only has the cultural IQ of the West declined under America's tenure as leader of the free world (observed easily by comparing interview programs and day-time television shows of the last few decades with what is broadcast today), but the *actual* IQ of Western nations have been declining for decades. The Flynn effect, so named after the intelligence researcher James Flynn who found that the average IQ increased during the last century by about 3 points per decade, appears to have declined steadily in the West sometime between the 1970's and 1990's.[39] [40] In fairness to the U.S., while there isn't yet evidence to show a similar IQ decline as seen across Europe, other metrics of cognitive decline and impairment related to diet, obesity, and physical inactivity are apparent.[41]

The problems are endemic, and they have been boiling over for more than half a century. At this point, one could not simply attribute this to ignorance or error; a failure of this magnitude can only be described with a single word, and that word is evil.

can Psychological Association, Vol. 50, No. 1, January 2019, p. 80.

36   Adam Liptak, "US: Inmate Count in U.S. Dwarfs Other Nations'", *The New York Times,* March 23rd, 2008, http://www.mapinc.org/drugnews/v08/n417/a04.html.

37   "Police Killings By Country 2020", *World Population Review,* https://world-populationreview.com/country-rankings/police-killings-by-country.

38   Alexi Jones & Wendy Sawyer, "Not just a "few bad apples": U.S. police kill civilians at much higher rates than other countries", *Prison Policy Initiative,* June 5th, 2020 https://www.prisonpolicy.org/blog/2020/06/05/policekillings/.

39   Edward Dutton, Dimitri van der Linden, Richard Lynn, "The negative Flynn Effect: A systematic literature review", *Intelligence,* Vol. 59, November-December 2016, pp. 163-169.

40   Bernt Bratsberg & Ole Rogeberg, "Flynn effect and its reversal are both environmentally caused", *Proceedings of the National Academy of Sciences,* Vol. 115, No. 26, June 26th, 2018.

41   John Mirowsky, "Cognitive Decline and the Default American Lifestyle", *The Journals of Gerontology Series B: Psychological Sciences and Social Sciences,* Vol. 66B, Issue 1, July 2011, pp. 50-58.

This is to say nothing, by the way, of the degeneration of American ethics or morals (a fact so evident and commonly observed that it does not merit discussion here). Here we find another example of American political conformity, for as quick as rightists and leftists are to condemn the US regime when it comes to particularist claims, the willingness to seriously examine American identity itself, including its constituent parts, is simply lacking. Without a critical eye toward Americanness itself, we can neither hope to achieve a better understanding of our present circumstance nor develop a method for improving it.

Authoritarianism and Anti-Authoritarianism

At this point we arrive at another set of myths, though their significance merits a more concentrated analysis. Central to the modern American identity, to the problems the United States faces, and to our very discussion of false collective fictions, is the notion of democracy. Democracy, which in practice operates a whole lot less like a mechanism for political efficiency and a lot more like a blunt object to be wielded against one's foes, is to a degree predicated on stymieing the execution of political will by a central authority. Deeper than a mere political problem, the philosophy of democratization in all spheres continues to challenge Americans on a psychological level. This rejection of authority can be found at every level of contemporary American life to such a degree that one wonders whether anti-authoritarianism is itself a key psychological feature of the American population. I probably would not have given this idea very much consideration were it not for a broadcast on the NPI/RADIX YouTube channel that aired on April 8th of 2020. In that conversation, Richard Spencer discussed the cynical (if not outright hysterical) response of many Americans toward the federal government's handling of the COVID-19 pandemic. Forced business closures and a federally imposed lockdown drew considerable outrage, as many Americans looked upon Trump's response as a massive abuse of government power. While I was not unfamiliar with anti-authoritarianism conceptually, upon looking into the literature available on the matter, I was quite surprised at the volume of writings on the subject. Further investigation drove me to pursue this line of questioning even deeper. While his insight did give me pause, I believe I have arrived at a different conclusion than the one proposed on his program, as it seems evident to me that reducing the psychology of the governed to either simple authoritarianism (as was done by researchers such as Theodore Adorno in the mid-twentieth century) or simple anti-authoritarianism belies the fact that Americans struggle to find an actionable equilibrium between the two positions.

Before we analyze the psychological divide between authoritarianism and anti-authoritarianism in American consciousness, it would be prudent to consult the expert opinion on the matter. Noted authors on the subject of anti-authoritarianism including Bruce Levine, Noam Chomsky, and William Kreml,[42] generally agree on a definition of anti-authoritarianism which rejects both anarchic anti-authoritarianism as well as the kind of authoritarian submissiveness described by the likes of Theodore Adorno, Robert Altemeyer, and Erich Fromm. In the view of the latter (and those who accept their hypothesis), authoritarianism—meaning, the individual who is prone to fascistic sentiment, and thus will submit to authority—is defined by characteristics such as:[43]

1. Submission to legitimate authority,
2. Aggression toward minority groups and a predilection toward anti-Semitism,
3. Adherence to cultural values endorsed by authorities,
4. Blind allegiance to convention,
5. A tendency toward misanthropy,
6. A preoccupation with violence and sex,
7. Feelings of inferiority, and
8. Hostility toward creativity and artistic innovation.

While the psychological measurements devised to produce such findings (in particular the F-scale and the RWA scale) have been subject to much scrutiny, the conclusions drawn from these investigations have reached a degree of cultural saturation that no longer relies on the support of the academic community.

42 William P. Kreml, *The Anti-Authoritarian Personality*, (Pergamon, 1977).
43 Adorno, T.W., Frenkel-Brunswik, E., Levinson, D.J., Sanford, R.N., *The Authoritarian Personality*, (Harper & Brothers, 1950).

Contempt for politically authoritarian sentiment is now commonplace—not only among those well-situated members of the
American economy, but all the way down the socioeconomic
ladder as well. If authoritarianism was never central to American psychology, then at the least efforts of certain critical theorists certainly expelled any latent or residual tendency therein.
In the intervening decades, having exhausted opportunities for
experimentally measuring right-wing authoritarianism (and still
reluctant to examine left-wing authoritarianism)[44] [45] [46] [47] many
researchers pivoted from understanding the psychology of the
authoritarian to arriving at an accurate conceptual (and ethical)
model of anti-authoritarianism.

For Levine and Chomsky in particular, anti-authoritarianism
is not about a predisposition *against* authority, but rather, an antagonism toward *illegitimate* authority. To this point, I will quote
both. Chomsky has said that,[48]

> When you stop your five-year-old kid from trying to cross
> the street, that's an authoritarian situation: it's got to be jus-
> tified. Well, in that case, I think you *can* give a justification.

Levine echoes this sentiment,[49]

> Anti-authoritarians question whether an authority is a le-
> gitimate one before taking that authority seriously. Evaluat-

44   William F. Stone, "The Myth of Left-Wing Authoritarianism", *Political Psychology,* Vol. 2, No. 3/4, Autumn-Winter 1980, pp. 3-19.
45   Lucian Gideon Conway, Shannon C. Houck, Laura Janelle Gornick, Meredith A. Repke, "Finding the Loch Ness monster: Left-Wing Authoritarianism
in the United States", *Political Psychology,* Vol. 39, Issue 5, October 2018, pp.
1049-1067.
46   Sabrina de Regt, Dimitri Mortelmans, Tim Smits, "Left-wing authoritarianism is not a myth, but a worrisome reality. Evidence from 13 Eastern European
countries", *Communist and Post-Communist Studies,* Vol. 44, Issue 4, December
2011, pp. 299-308.
47   John J. Ray, "Half of All Authoritarians Are Left Wing: A Reply to Eysenck
and Stone" *Political Psychology,* Vol. 4, No. 1, March 1983, pp. 139-143.
48   Bruce Levine, "Curious "Anti-Authoritarian" Definitions and Divides",
Counterpunch, September 5th, 2019, https://www.counterpunch.org/2019/09/05/
curious-anti-authoritarian-definitions-and-divides/.
49   Bruce Levine, "Curious "Anti-Authoritarian" Definitions and Divides",
Counterpunch, September 5th, 2019, https://www.counterpunch.org/2019/09/05/
curious-anti-authoritarian-definitions-and-divides/.

ing the legitimacy of authorities includes assessing whether or not authorities actually know what they are talking
about, are honest, and care about those people who are
respecting their authority. And when anti-authoritarians
assess an authority to be illegitimate, they challenge and resist that authority—sometimes aggressively and sometimes
passive-aggressively, sometimes wisely and sometimes not.

Levine and Chomsky both make rational arguments in support
of a high-functioning and psychologically adaptive anti-authoritarianism. Of importance is the fact that their stance directly
opposes the chaotic anarchism which rejects all top-down and
hierarchically organized models of authority (a position more
commonly taken by communists, anti-fascists, and the anti-co-
lonialism movement more broadly).

Less directly related (though perhaps still worth noting), are
the findings of Cantoni, Yang, Yuchtman, and Zhang, who in a
2016 study set out to define the characteristics of the anti-authoritarian.[50] In a survey of over 1,500 university students in Hong
Kong, the team found that anti-authoritarians are

> More risk-seeking, more altruistic, more reciprocal, and
> have a stronger preference for redistribution in a series of
> real-stakes dictator games.

Furthermore, when examining the personality traits through an
application of the five factor model, their investigation revealed
that anti-authoritarians score higher on trait openness but lower on trait conscientiousness. The same group scored higher on
the Cognitive Reflection Test[51] but also reported lower average
GPA's. This was attributed to a pre-occupation with political
movements engaged in anti-authoritarian action. Cantoni et al
also noted that,

50 Davide Cantoni, David Y. Yang, Noam Yuchtman, Y. Jane Zhang, "The Fundamental Determinants of Anti-Authoritarianism", UC-Berkeley, unpublished,
November 16th, 2016.
51 The Cognitive Reflection Test is based on the work of Shane Frederick and
Daniel Kahneman; the CRT is a measurement of one's ability to access "system
2" cognition. Dual Process Theory, for which Kahneman is best known, posits
the existence of a layered cognitive mechanism wherein the individual may rely
on immediate and heuristic-based cognition (system 1) or effortful and analytic
cognition (system 2).

> Consistent with traditional, class-based models (e.g. Ace-
> moglu and Robinson, 2006), students from poorer house-
> holds and with lower anticipated future earnings are sig-
> nificantly more likely to be anti-authoritarian. Examining
> the demographic characteristics of students, one sees that
> older students are somewhat more anti-authoritarian than
> younger students, and that men are more anti-authoritar-
> ian than women. Interestingly, having a longer family his-
> tory in Hong Kong is not strongly associated with anti-au-
> thoritarianism.

It goes without saying that the historical, political, and biological differences that distinguish the United States from Hong Kong make any direction comparison or correlation in anti-author-itarian characteristics difficult, if not impossible, to do. None-theless, it would behoove us to consider how these observations might lead to *some* insight as we continue our analysis in this work. Economically favorable attitudes toward reciprocity and redistribution have long been features of American left-wing politics, and so perhaps the findings of Cantoni et al do provide us with some corroborative evidence to confirm certain widely accepted notions of authoritarian (rightist) and anti-authoritar-ian (leftist) attitudes (given the historical framing of the issue).

Having presented these arguments, I feel it necessary to let the air out of the theoretical balloon I have just provided. If we take the arguments I laid out in the preceding section as valid (that the left-right divide is an inaccurate and misleading politi-cal construct), then perhaps the authoritarian-antiauthoritarian divide, too, is fallacious and harmful to our understanding of contemporary politics. For example: under Obama, the Amer-ican right decried him as an authoritarian fascist (among other things, e.g. crypto-Islamist, communist, etc.) As we have seen throughout the Trump administration, the left has levied similar condemnations. What does this tell us? Are Americans hopeless-ly confused? Is every political actor a fascist or a fascist-in-dem-ocratic clothing? I believe that we can confidently say *yes* to the former, but *no* to the latter.

What we have is the reality of democracy in action—one side of the political machine running roughshod over the other, at least until the temporarily dispossessed one gets their turn to abuse the governed. More significantly, the democratic process (or more accurately, the belief in a process where individuals are selected based on characteristics of moral and technical excellence to represent their constituency in accordance with a set of legal and philosophical precepts) obscures the *true* nature of authority, thus facilitating the interminable confusion in the minds of Americans as to what constitutes authority, and when precisely (if ever) it becomes "fascistic".

Auctoriphobia, or the fear of authority, clearly emerges out of this confusion. Not only does it emerge out of this confusion, but it also emerges as a result of the tragic and violent history of the preceding century; wars that claimed the lives of tens of millions, technological developments that stoked fears of ecological collapse, and the erosion of national infrastructure, to offer a few examples, have provided sufficient justification for anti-authoritarian sentiment. As a result of these events we are now confronted with two important questions as relates to authoritarian and anti-authoritarian positions: what constitutes legitimate authority? (a question of perception) and how ought one conduct themselves in relation to authority? (a question of agency and ethics) To orient ourselves in a healthful and psychologically adaptive way—that is to say, with clear-headedness and a maximum of free will—we must be able to understand this problem in a new way.

As I stated at the outset, the fundamental tension in the American political mind is of that between the authoritarian impulse and the anti-authoritarian impulse. So should it be, as the question of authority is the most important question in virtually any human endeavor. Authority, which for all intents and purposes might as well be another way of saying *agency*, is a matter of *right* thought and *right* action implemented in the *right* circumstance. It stands to reason, then, that authority is often about having the *right* person in charge. Without oversimplifying this problem inappropriately, we might say that he who possesses the will to act makes himself the authority. Beneath that will lies courage, and so we may also say that authority is a game of confidence.

(To use a silly example, in an episode of *Star Trek: The Next Generation,* chief medical officer Beverly Crusher and captain Jean-Luc Picard are stranded on an alien planet with no clear way to escape back to the starship *Enterprise*. At the outset of their adventure, the two are transported to the planet's surface in a diplomatic effort to make first contact with a new alien race, but through some technological mishap end up in a prison where electronic devices are implanted in their necks, linking them telepathically. Upon making their escape, Crusher senses that Picard (ostensibly leading them to safety, and ultimately, back to their ship) does not actually know what he is doing. Still, Picard feigns confidence, as his role as a leader is dependent on the ability to project an aura of authority so that his crew (in this case, just Dr. Crusher) is willing to follow. A brief exchange occurs in which Picard reveals that he does not always know exactly what to do but acts as though he does in spite of this fact.)

We see then, with the aid of this admittedly low-brow example, that a hidden dimension of authority is confidence. Of course, authority can be secured through other means; hereditarily, meritocratically, anti-socially, to name a few. Already, we are becoming aware of the perceptual problem of authority, as not all people view each method as a legitimate path to the throne. And even when a political actor rises to a position of authority through a conventional and generally accepted means, subjective perception may still deign to invalidate him.

In the home, in the classroom, at the market, and at the ballot box, Americans have struggled mightily with the question of authority. Parents fail to exercise their rightful authority over their children; teachers do not discipline their students; hedge fund managers, investment firms, and executive boards routinely engage in unethical and illegal conduct but frequently go unpunished (often, in fact, they are rewarded); and to the degree that Americans engage in the political process (which is far less than they "ought" to), we find that they support the same policies and the same actors time and time again. Embedded in this problem of authority is the secondary problem of discipline. This is not to put the blame squarely on individual shoulders, as in each instance we find top-down initiatives which undermine the responsible exercise of power. Nonetheless, the point remains. We can therefore say, and with a great deal of recent historical proof attesting to this fact, that Americans are deep in the throes of a crisis of legitimacy. With neither the information necessary to make a proper evaluation of authority, nor even the capacity to adjudicate existent (or potential) information, we have been cast adrift in a sea of hopelessness and despair. What we *do* have, however, is fear, anxiety, and resentment—and lots of it. Supposedly unified by our shared American values, our freedoms, and our love of democracy (though not in actuality), the line between friend and enemy grows murkier with each passing year. Though it should be said, there are things which unite us, just not in any productive or eusocial way. We are united by the increased feeling of unease and uncertainty we experience, not just toward our present sociopolitical circumstance, but toward our very lives. Here we see the problem of relation to authority, as our seemingly foundational antagonism toward the will to act renders us impotent in virtually every arena of American society. Everywhere Americans look, they see failures of authority (often enabled by the *very same authorities*), thus producing a conceptual collapse whereby failures of authority anywhere become failures of authority everywhere. Without anyone to show us *how* to act, we struggle to devise constructive courses of action for ourselves. Absent a rightful authority, agency and ethical conduct collapses.

It has been said of scientific experimentation, though I know not by whom, that "*everyone is a conservative in the area they are most knowledgeable.*"[52] This was meant to express the deep hesitation specialists in a given field of study have toward making grand extrapolations from the data they uncover. Their expansive knowledge affords that rare gift of foresight; one can only stretch a set of data so far before it reaches its natural limit. Co-opting this statement and applying it to the realm of the political, I would add the following "*...and an authoritarian in those areas where they are least knowledgeable and most fearful.*" Take the issue of gun control, for example. Well-practiced and disciplined acolytes of the pistol or the rifle generally seek to retain control of their ability to act on this privilege and to preserve the culture of liberty around firearms, while those with less experience often seek swift and decisive action to limit it. It follows that ambiguity and uncertainty may be critical psychological motivators behind the desire for authoritarianism. In other words, when we sense

52   cf. Robert Conquest's first law of politics ("everyone is conservative about what he knows best").

the possibility of danger, authoritarianism suddenly becomes a lot more attractive. But authoritarianism is not simply an expression of powerlessness or fearfulness; it is a recognition of the need for a central force which can act judiciously, particularly (though not exclusively) in those circumstances where there *is* insufficient information, and thus requires cool and measured action. Perhaps we *could* say that the ambiguities (which inevitably crop up around important social issues like barnacles on the side of an ocean tanker) *demand* a capable authority, one who will not engage in endless and doubt-filled discussion, thus problematizing necessary actions and prolonging suffering. The *correct* attitude towards authority is one that recognizes it as both an inevitable and necessary feature of social organization. Authority and authoritarianism are too often used as synonyms for oppression and violence and are therefore used to indicate the badness of a person, party, or ideology. Rarely do we think of it as the *solution* to our problems. Once more, we suffer a problem of perception.

Let us think a little bit more about this dichotomy between conservatism and authoritarianism. Conservatism to a great degree is an instinct toward retention, often an impotent and stationary impulse, and as Freud noted,[53] possibly even an instinct toward self-annihilation, or a reaching back to a state of non-existence. Certainly, American conservatism's inability to confront the problems of change and expansion indicate a death of one kind or another (something that modern conservatives are increasingly aware of). Authoritarianism thus is progressive; it is a willful and vital stance which seeks assertion, dominance, security—yes—but more importantly a securing of desire, of *some thing*, be it an object or a goal. It is not merely a means for securing one's own welfare or the welfare of the group, rather authority is the psychosocial means by which we may express our will. The juxtaposition of these two instincts—(1) the instinct to conserve, or preserve in stasis and (2) the instinct to progress and secure desire—remain a psychological and political problem that has not yet found resolution within the American mind. Necessarily this tension produces an ambivalence whereby the pursuit of something as novel as "*life, liberty, and the pursuit of happi-*

---

53   Sigmund Freud, *Beyond the Pleasure Principle* (1920).

ness" is met with an equal force of *"no, not too much of any of these, please."* A society such as ours, built on ideas like breaking from tradition, limitless expansion, and geographic conquest is itself an expression of the paradox of authority and non-authority. Even a cursory reading of the disagreements between America's neophyte aristocratic order reveals this fact. A commonly understood insight of psychology is that the stand-off between two opposing impulses creates a mental fissure by which action is rendered impossible and will is denied. Such is the circumstance with which we are presently confronted.

For now, let us turn away from the abstract and look at the problem of anti-authoritarianism and how it is expressed differently by our two subjects, the conservative and the progressive. A fundamental and mutual misunderstanding made by conservative and Republican types as well as progressive and democrat types (who both draw their historical and philosophical worldviews from the same liberal foundation) is that—from both perspectives—the other appears as a totalitarian despot, who, being unreasonable, dishonest, and stupid, seeks the domination and eradication of the other. Both fail to recognize, particularly as their anxieties are intensified by interested parties in the politico-media complex, that they are both sons of the same father. Both see undue privileges bestowed upon the other, and each seeing themselves as solely and uniquely suffering the oppressive tyranny of their oedipal persecution. A Jungian analysis applies here, too; the hostile brothers that they are, the conservative and progressive enjoy a sibling rivalry par excellence.

The conservative liberal is the yin to the progressive liberal yang, not being fundamentally distinct from one another in any politically meaningful sense, merely separated at birth. For the progressive, the exercise of authority (for example, in the classroom or in the bedroom), stifles and necessarily suspends the realization of identity and the pursuit of happiness. And for the conservative, an interventionist authority (perhaps at the gun show or in the marketplace), suspends autonomy, and self-reliance, themselves necessary for the pursuit of happiness. Both seek permissiveness in those areas where their identities find realization and their values find expression. Government, or the father, is never seen as a wise king, instead, he is always and forever the mad tyrant. Where the conservative and the progressive lock hands, however, is in the righteous use of authority against external opponents—the Russians, the Chinese, the Iranians. Authority expressed within the domestic boundaries is an insufferable oppression, but when directed outwardly, it is felt as a gleeful nigh-orgasmic expression of a will to life. "*Yes, he may be a tyrant, but god damn it if he isn't our tyrant.*"

Building on the ideas set forth earlier in this chapter about the mythic formation of the mind, the conservative has a peculiar antagonism toward authoritarianism predicated on his own mythologized self-concept. The conservative, ever the rugged individualist, is therefore *fiercely* opposed to collectivism. Being that the conservative is fundamentally liberal in his self-concept and his relation to the world, authoritarianism represents the final result of collectivism, to which he as a liberal is fundamentally opposed. His opposition is rooted in the fear of self-destruction, of becoming absorbed into the horde, the mass, if collectivist authoritarianism were to emerge. The right-liberal (conservative), who most clearly has inherited the frontier myth of the American man, is unwilling to sublimate his internal drives to an order which would threaten his petty frontier psychology—understood here as having the meaning of a smaller, more individualist and self-serving ambition. Originally, the frontier was a place of limitless expansion—a physical terrain fraught with uncertainty and great danger. It was a real place where the true test of man's conquering spirit could be found. But that place no longer exists. Still, the myth lives on. The ideology of the conservative frontiersman, not cleanly extinguished, has been abstracted from the physical terrain and transposed into the space of concepts and intangibilities (the free market, the stock trade, etc.) The market is the new conservative frontier where much can be gained and much can be lost, but at a comparatively lower cost. No longer will the conservative lose his wife, his children, or even his own life, but rather he may lose his accumulated wealth and—should the danger prove sufficiently great—other material (his home, private property) and social (status, respectability, prestige) goods. Though the right-liberal may tell us that collectivism and authoritarianism are morally wrong because of an a priori philosophical justification, if we scratch the surface we find that the true cause may be found in the threat posed to his tenuous self-concept and his grandiose social ambition. And, of course, because we cannot truly assume that the American Girondin is in fact a monolith who may be reduced to a singular motivation, we may assume other factors exist which could explain his anti-authoritarianism. Perhaps he shares the historical anxieties associated with authoritarianism which are more clearly typified by his Jacobin brother (as we shall see in the following paragraph).

The progressive on the other hand—sensitive primarily to concerns regarding social welfare and guided by his self-imposed moral responsibility to those with fewer protections—regards authoritarianism as a danger for its supposed historical implications (persecution and genocide). Authoritarianism being something that only an evil person participates in, the progressive looks to history and sees those great villains, Italy and Germany specifically, as proof of this belief. For the progressive, authoritarianism is not a true ideology or political system, but rather a collective hysteria predicated on the irrational scapegoating of a benevolent minority. His moral axiom (protect the little guy) thus indicates to him that authoritarianism is wrong because it is rooted in the unjust persecution of endangered minorities. In the case of Germany, those minorities were homosexuals, gypsies, Jews, the mentally and physically infirm, while in modern America, what constitutes an endangered minority is far more expansive (women, Muslims, immigrants, Blacks, Hispanics, etc.) The historical factors at play (and the veracity of said historical claims) are of little consequence; what matters is *that someone is being persecuted.* By the progressive's own logic, for centralization to occur and a politic of authoritarianism to settle in, there must be a scapegoated minority, and they must be extinguished for the good of the collective. Authoritarianism is the means by which the mad tyrant, empowered by his brainwashed thralls, exercises his deranged will.

So while the conservative fears erasure of the self, the progressive fears erasure of the other, who owing to his otherness is ontologically 'first' or 'higher'. We might observe this in a Christian way, that because the last shall be first, the authoritarian must always be denied. This relation to the other is interesting as it clearly differs in conception between the conservative and the progressive. A number of studies conducted in the last twenty years attests to this difference. In 2008, Oxley et al observed differences in threat sensitivity, noting that,[54]

> In a group of 46 adult participants with strong political beliefs, individuals with measurably lower physical sensitivities to sudden noises and threatening visual images were more likely to support foreign aid, liberal immigration policies, pacifism, and gun control, whereas individuals displaying measurably higher physiological reactions to those same stimuli were more likely to favor defense spending, capital punishment, patriotism, and the Iraq War.

It should be noted that the researchers did not label the collected policy positions as Conservative or Liberal due to their relatively limited testing of political ideology (for example, they did not assess for positions on economic issues). Sinn and Hayes (2016)[55] compared Jonathan Haidt's Moral Foundations Theory[56] against the Evolutionary-Coalitional Theory and found that the "*individualizing*" (harm and fairness) moral foundation of liberals was better understood as a "*universalizing motive*" that consisted of a "*broader set of moral commitments*" and a "*broader sociality than ethnocentrism*", while the "*binding*" (authority, respect, purity) moral foundation of conservatives was better characterized as an "*authoritarian motive*" typified by threat-sensitivity and outgroup antagonism. Inbar et al (2011)[57] found a positive rela-

54   Douglas R. Oxley, Kevin B. Smith, John R. Alford, Matthew V. Hibbing, Jennifer L. Miller, Mario Scalora, Peter K. Hatemi, John R. Hibbing, "Political Attitudes Vary with Physiological Traits", *Political Science*, 321:5897, September 19th, 2008, pp. 1667-1670.
55   Jeffrey S. Sinn & Matthew W. Hayes, "Replacing the Moral Foundations: An Evolutionary-Coalitional Theory of Liberal-Conservative Differences", *Political Psychology*, Vol. 38, Issue 6, December 2017, pp. 1043-1064.
56   While Jonathan Haidt's Moral Foundations theory does offer us a great deal of insight into the psychological dimensions of political action, I do find that it misses the mark to a great extent. His research has demonstrated that left-liberals respond more strongly to the moral foundations of Care and Fairness, while right-liberals are activated by all five dimensions of the MFT (Care, Fairness, Loyalty, Authority, and Sanctity). I believe that when we account for the particular cathected ideal, image, or object, that there is no difference between left and right liberals in the MFT.
57   Yoel Inbar, David Pizarro, Ravi Iyer, Jonathan Haidt, "Disgust Sensitivity,

tionship between disgust sensitivity and political conservatism, which held when controlling for demographic variables as well as the "Big Five" personality traits. And finally, in 2017, Mendez[58] reviewed personality, evolutionary and genetic, cognitive, neuroimaging, and neurological studies, arriving at the conclusion that

> Evidence [exists] for a normal right-sided "conservative-complex" involving structures sensitive to negativity bias, threat, disgust, and avoidance.

To the best of my understanding (and there exists a *not-so-inconsequential* amount of literature to the contrary), the conservative has a stronger sense of self-preservation, aversion to contamination by pathogen, and is therefore more troubled by issues potentially caused by the other (such as immigration, diversity and inclusivity mandates, marriage equality, etc.) Therefore, ontologically speaking, the other is second because—for reasons of self-preservation—the conservative must be first. With full view of both conservative and progressive lines of reasoning, we arrive at a differing-yet-convergent psychological justification for anti-authoritarian sentiment.

But *is it true* that Americans are genuine anti-authoritarians? We must understand that the most important aspect of this entire phenomenon is how a liberal worldview requires compartmentalization and rationalization among its adherents; fullblown, decadent, and permissive 21st century liberalism doesn't ask the individual to sublimate himself, much less repress any aspect of himself. *All* ideas are given equal weight, *all* values are sanctioned, *all* actions are laudable, *all* pursuits are capable of commoditization, and *all* modes of being are *good*. Of course, these cannot all be true simultaneously, nor can such a worldview be sustained indefinitely. And thus, compartmentalization and rationalization become necessary as the limits of the natural world collide with liberal ideology. The sociopolitical realities of

Political Conservatism, and Voting", *Social Psychological and Personality Science*, Vol. 3, Issue 5, December 6th, 2011, pp. 537-544.

58   Mario F. Mendez, "A Neurology of the Conservative-Liberal Dimension of Political Ideology", *Journal of Neuropsychiatry and Clinical Neuroscience,* Vol. 29, Issue 2, Spring 2017, pp. 86-94.

war, sex, race, religion, family, class, and their intermediated negotiations increasingly puncture the thin veil of liberal thought,
especially as America—for all its technological and material
splendor—diminishes in global significance. Without the prestige and comfortable living standard afforded as a result of being the uncontested leader of the free world, the house of cards
noticeably begins to lose its stability. As these tensions emerge,
neurotic and obviously contradictory justifications fill the gaps
like cheap glue.

In truth, the authoritarian is the shadow in the soul of the
American liberal (conservative and progressive alike). And while
it may be the force that performs acts of evil, this does not pre-
clude either type from identifying with or enacting residual or
latent authoritarianism when a situation of sufficient self-servingness emerges. As has been pointed out earlier, there are times
when life demands acts of authoritative will from us. It is an
unavoidable result of living as material beings that must suffer,
and toil, and strive in this world. The solution to this severing of
the conscious from the unconscious finds itself in the execution
of some ego defense which resolves the dilemma. Whether it be
through denial, compartmentalization, rationalization—some
technique will be applied which soothes the pain of self-betrayal.

There is also, of course, the fact that political and philosophical identities are no different from the mask worn by attendees
of a masquerade; they are a form of role play which facilitates the
navigation of social realities. So in those circumstances where
we are not talking about the true believers who have a deep psychological need to explain their inconsistencies to themselves,
we see that in both the conservative and progressive type a kind
of childishness—the childishness of one who has been caught
in a lie or some other impropriety who, upon being discovered,
merely declares "*you got me!*" and laughs at the silliness of having been taken seriously in the first place. Not everyone treats
the idea as an object of the real; far from it, they are regarded
by many (if not most) as a fanciful and irreverent device which
is more a problem of life than a means through which will and
action can find their realization. This psychological fact complicates the ideals of democracy and egalitarianism, and in fact, fatally undermines the liberal worldview. Taking this into account

we can characterize psychological and political liberalism itself as a Kleinian phantasy, a device of the mind through which the individual can interact with the world, but always at a distance, and always with the aid of a litany of ego defenses.

And so, once more I ask, is the average American anti-authoritarian? The answer is that every man serves a master, even if that master resides within his own mind. It is on irrational grounds that we choose our authorities, no matter how coherent or logical the contrivances we make may be. America's ongoing crisis of legitimacy has perhaps created a fair-weather anti-authoritarian sentiment, but it is in the wind to be certain. Different American institutions have burned all their credibility in the minds of different sects of America; those institutions that manage to retain their credibility only do so, again, in compartmentalized ways. Left-liberals revere the institution of science, but not in its entirety. Particularly for more extreme liberals and progressives, whole disciplines (e.g. behavioral genetics) are written off entirely. Right-liberals revere the institution of the church, but not in its entirety. The Christ that exists in the minds of many Christians today could not be any farther from the man found in the New Testament. There is nothing Christian about the prosperity doctrine, and yet, many right-liberals conveniently reject the anti-materialism of Christianity in favor of the abundance afforded by capitalism. When Obama was in office, many right-liberals suddenly became cynical, data-crunching statisticians who took the government's reports on unemployment and job growth with a rather large grain of salt. This was not so when Trump took office. Many left-liberals were riotous zealots in their opposition to George W. Bush's warmongering. Not so when Obama took office. Even *NPR*[59] in 2011 and *The Washington Post*[60] in 2013 took notice of this fact, asking "*where did the anti-war Left go?*" Americans are not anti-authoritarian; they merely want *their* authorities.[61] Only now the country is too big, too bloated, and too

59   Linton Weeks, "Whatever Happened To The Anti-War Movement?", *NPR*, April 15th, 2011, https://www.npr.org/2011/04/15/135391188/whatever-happened-to-the-anti-war-movement.

60   Brad Plumer, "How Obama demobilized the antiwar movement", *The Washington Post*, August 29th, 2013, https://www.washingtonpost.com/news/wonk/wp/2013/08/29/where-did-the-antiwar-movement-go/.

61   Thomas Costello et al reach a similar conclusion in the as-yet-unpublished

divided to provide a universally legitimate authority figure.

Individualism, Anarchism, and Sociopathy

Yet another piece of the puzzle must be laid on the board before we may begin our analysis of political extremism in earnest. Thus far, we have discussed the importance of myth and narrative on shaping human cognition. We then took that argument a step further and used it to dismiss the false and obscurantist myths which retard our political understanding. Having accomplished that, we began to inch our way forward to the issue of extremism by broaching the question of authority. Central to our questioning of authority was the notion of the individual and the ways in which the individual seeks to retain his status as such in the face of collective power. It is from this point that we must continue our investigation, as there is much more to be said about the ideology of the individual, his relation to society, and the ways in which contemporary neoliberal individualism sets the stage for extremist ideology and action.

Many great minds have written, in one way or another, on the Western tradition of individualism (for instance: Geert Hofstede, F.A. Hayek, Kevin MacDonald, Max Stirner, Ayn Rand, John Dewey, and Max Weber, to name a few), and the dialectic of the individual versus the collective has been a subject of intense study across multiple disciplines, including sociology, anthropology, and psychology. It is not my intention to analyze or critique the writings of past thinkers on this matter, but rather to take for granted that the ideology of the individual exists; not only that it exists but that it exerts powerful influence on the American way of life. Scholarship on this subject is vast, and a thorough investigation of these works both exceeds the

study: "We conduct quantitative tests of LWA's relations with a host of authoritarianism-related variables, based on a priori hypotheses derived in part from right-wing authoritarianism's well-established nomological network, and use a behavioral paradigm to show that LWA and social dominance orientation (but not right-wing authoritarianism) predict aggression towards threatening ideological opponents over and above political ideology. We conclude that a shared psychological "core" underlies authoritarianism across the political left and right." Thomas Costello, Shauna Bowes, Sean Steverns, Irwin Waldman, Scott O. Lilienfeld, "Clarifying the Structure and Nature of Left-Wing Authoritarianism", *PsyArXiv*, 11, May 2020.

scope of my work and would deter the clarity of the arguments which I intend to present. Suffice it to say, the disposition of the Northwestern peoples who conquered the American continent, in conjunction with the selective pressures which attracted different ethnic groups to this country once it had been settled, established individualism as the American modus operandi. This has been further concretized by the emergence of a neoliberal economic model which Michel Foucault argued in his 1979 lectures on biopolitics, transformed workers into *"entrepreneurs of themselves"*.[62] Many other factors contributed to this phenomenon; the quintuple threat of (1) particular strategies of urban planning, (2) the changing nature of labor, (3) advancements in technology and mass production which encouraged individualistic modes of travel (a car in every driveway), (4) the application of Freudian innovations in the disciplines of marketing and advertising, and (5) changing attitudes of representation in popular media. We could even go back several centuries into the past and examine how aspects of Enlightenment philosophy (emphasizing utility, rationality, and skepticism) and Protestant theology (the doctrine of sola scriptura) established the preconditions for our modern preoccupation with the individual. All of this to say that we as 21st century Americans celebrate the mythos of the individual like no other nation. Even now as I write this, in the middle of a government-mandated lockdown to control the spread of the Coronavirus, the primacy of the individual is being championed in opposition to these collective measures.

It is a common critique, made by many thinkers and writers far greater than myself, to remark on the follies of our contemporary infatuation with the individual. Nonetheless I shall continue this grand tradition, though before I do, I feel it necessary to speak of its virtues as well. I would argue that without the Western ideal of the individual, our exceptional contributions to the musical lexicon could not have been possible. While I am no musicologist, the West's elevation of the genius of the individual must have been necessary to produce great works by composers like Beethoven, Wagner, Chopin, Dvorak, and Debussy. America, the foremost frontier of the individual, proved a fertile

62 Michel Foucault, *The Birth of Biopolitics: Lectures at the College de France, 1978-1979,* (Picador, 2010).

breeding ground for many of the great European composers (like Dvorak, Rachmaninoff, and Stravinsky) to forge a daring and new path, unburdened by Old World tradition. Later developments like rock and electronic music also owe their genesis to the Western man's predilection toward individuality. Romantic love is doubtlessly indebted to individuality, as well. The ability to choose your loved one based on attraction to their unique qualities is certainly a feature of the Western individualist ethic. So, too, does upward social mobility require a respect for individual autonomy at the expense of class structure. Other examples include our tradition of private property, intellectual curiosity, etc. We owe a great debt to the ideology of the individual, for without it none of these things would be possible.

Having said this, any system of thought or disposition can expand beyond its natural proportions and thus produce unimaginable and tragic calamity. Such is our present circumstance; the mythos of the individual has transformed into a cult of individuality, an extremist cult which threatens social organization at every level of American society. Individuation, being necessary for normative psychosocial development and whose absence would prevent the birth of a sovereign identity, is ironically *denied* by the cult of individuality. It is only through the collective (family, community, nationhood, the State) that true individuality can be developed because these institutions amply provide the necessary social resources. Those resources, of course, include basic human actions like love, discipline, responsibility, mentorship, labor, and creativity. Absent these ingredients, what actually emerges is narcissism, neuroticism, and pathological conformity (and from these seeds grows the true foundation of political extremism). The individuals who will be analyzed in chapter two—those who can truly be called extremists—are best understood as *anarchic conformists*, individuals who have unconsciously accepted the prevailing ideological paradigm of their time (hence their conformity) but who rage against it on the level of conscious awareness (hence their anarchism). But we shall get to that discussion in due time.

Extreme individualism is psychologically indistinguishable from sociopathy. Sociopathy as a concept is poorly defined within the disciplines of psychiatry and psychology, and owing to its operational weakness, is greatly abused by the lay public (and sadly, professionals especially). Often conflated with other somewhat nebulously defined terms such as "anti-social" and "psychopath", here "sociopath" should be understood as an individual with an impoverished social feeling often exhibited by the following characteristics:

1. Impulsivity,
2. Weak ego defenses,
3. Narcissism,
4. Irresponsibility,
5. Callousness, and
6. Attachment-related anxiety

The intensity of these characteristics may vary from individual to individual, and in more severe cases may even rise to the level of a clinically diagnosable personality disorder. Informed readers may take note of the overlap between my characterization and existing Cluster B personality disorders as defined in the fifth edition of the Diagnostic and Statistical Manual of Mental Disorders. I am intentionally averting the use of explicit diagnostic criteria, as it is my contention that these behavioral features are the direct consequence of contemporary Western Individualism. Or to be more specific, these dysfunctions of the intimate and social feeling are directly reproduced by our materialistic and imperial American culture.

(As an aside, how else could we explain the morbid cultural fascination with such characteristics as psychopathy, antisocial conduct, and sociopathy if they were not reproducible by Americanism itself? Were they merely fringe contingents of American society, they would be identified as such and held to an equal regard. It is not just their titillating and salacious aspects (which are so often exaggerated and mass-reproduced by visual media), but rather their omnipresence and immediate relateability which keeps Americans preoccupied with these psychological types.)

The degree to which individual Americans vary in the presentation of these characteristics is dictated by congenital factors, be they strictly genetic, owing to deficits in prenatal development, or both. Subsequent social experiences factor into the development of this phenomenon as well. We would be best served, then, to view this problem as the microsocial manifestation of larger macrosocial trends (hence my usage of the phrase 'materialistic imperial culture'). Mark Fisher makes a similar though not identical argument by linking the rising rate of mood disorders to American economic policies of the last half century,[63] so I do not believe my position is without merit or precedent. Not being a strict materialist (Fisher was an avowed Marxist), it is my contention that the deteriorated state of the American psyche could be more directly linked to the spiritual crisis America suffers, though it may be difficult to disentangle the political from the religious.

Taken individually, nearly all of these characteristics are predictive of overall cognitive and behavioral instability and are strongly associated with poorer life outcomes. Impulsivity has been shown to be correlated to alcohol abuse and dependence,[64] gambling,[65] and risk for STD infection.[66] Poor attachment styles are clearly indicated to be a risk factor for suicide),[67] as well as depression and eating disorders.[68] As for the other features I described above, we may look to the long history of psychoanalytic thought which has much to tell us about the problems of narcis-

63   Mark Fisher, *Capitalist Realism: Is There No Alternative?* (Zero Books, 2009).
64   Robert D. Rogers, Frederick G. Moeller, Alan C. Swann, Luke Clark, "Recent Research on Impulsivity in Individuals with Drug Use and Mental Health Disorders: Implications for Alcoholism", *Alcoholism: Clinical & Experimental Research*, Vol. 34, Issue 8, August 2010, pp. 1319-1333.
65   R. Andrew Chambers & Marc N. Potenza, "Neurodevelopment, Impulsivity, and Adolescent Gambling", *Journal of Gambling Studies,* Vol. 19, March 2003, pp. 53-84.
66   Richard Charnigo, Seth M. Noar, Christopher Garnett, Richard Crosby, Philip Palmgreen & Rick S. Zimmerman, "Sensation Seeking and Impulsivity: Combined Associations with Risky Sexual Behaviors in a Large Sample of Young Adults", *The Journal of Sex Research,* Vol. 50, Issue 5, March 28th, 2012, pp. 480-488.
67   Arielle H. Sheftall, Charles W. Mathias, R. Michael Furr & Donald M. Dougherty, "Adolescent attachment security, family functioning, and suicide attempts", *Attachment and Human Development,* Vol. 15, Issue 4, April 8th 2013, pp. 368-383.
68   Giorgio A. Tasca, Leah Szadkowski, Vanessa Illing, Anne Trineer, Renee Grenon, Natasha Demidenko, Valerie Krysanski, Louise Balfou & Hany Bissada, "Adult attachment, depression, and eating disorder symptoms: The mediating role of affect regulation strategies", *Personality and Individual Differences,* Vol. 47, Issue 6, October 2009, pp. 662-667.

sism and a weak ego. Any combination of these traits is sufficient to produce psychological and social impairments; often enough, these characteristics co-occur. And in the grand tradition of psychoanalysis (as well as those thinkers profoundly impacted by that discipline), we must look beyond the individual, beyond his immediate environment, for the clearest understanding of this particular ailment.

Having provided a definition for extreme individualism (we could also call it sociopathic individualism) and presented enough examples to show the dangers inherent to such a condition, I would now like to dig a bit deeper and apply a more analytic method. The extreme individualist demonstrates a curious ability to transcend feelings of guilt with regards to pursuing the upper limits of his sensation seeing and narcissistic self-exploration. Similarly, theirs is an absence of shamefulness for transgressing against existing social and moral norms; in fact, they have a particular mission, one could say, to push against existing mores and norms so they might expand what is possible for the individual. It is not that these individuals lack feelings of guilt, shame, or empathy, but rather that the normal social feeling has been overcoded by the particularly American culture of narcissistic self-obsession which provides new moral and ethical dictates to those subsumed within it. Some percentage of the population will flourish in this environment as it is their natural condition (new estimates place the number upwards of 6%);[69] others will simply adapt to changing circumstances while the rest of us simply tolerate it.

Such individuals must be accepted for *who they are*, even if who they are is insufferable to those around them. Our very recently developed culture of non-judgmentalism, itself a pretext for the erasure of any system of mores (disguised as liberation and freedom) should be considered the primary cause for this phenomenon. For the extreme individual, immorality is that which crosses them and them *alone*. Whatever cause they may take up is very rarely out of a sense of duty or philanthropic spirit, but for the purpose of self-aggrandizement. In this way,

---

69   Bill Eddy, "Are Narcissists and Sociopaths Increasing?", *Psychology Today*, April 30th 2018, https://www.psychologytoday.com/us/blog/5-types-people-who-can-ruin-your-life/201804/are-narcissists-and-sociopaths-increasing.

moral causes are therefore a way of signaling class allegiance (or anxiety). Something is *wrong* if it suppresses their individualist pursuit, or the moral universe which provides justification for their status and pleasure seeking. Often, we find that their relationships are self-serving and unfulfilling. Resulting from their attachment anxiety, they struggle with intimacy and pursue destructive and highly libidinally charged trysts. Relationships are ended or avoided altogether the moment they threaten the extreme individualist's narcissistic self-concept. He rushes headlong into danger because it is *his right* to do so. Consequences are rarely, if ever, considered because to imagine the potential outcome is nearly the equivalent of denying the impulse (which is unacceptable to him). Duties are quickly shirked, assuming they are ever taken up in the first place. His language is coarse and his rhetoric brutally to the point. Everywhere he goes he must be himself, expulsive to the absolute limit, because *it his right to be as such*. For him, being an American means to be an imposition at all times. The foreign policy of the American empire doubles as a social policy for the extremist individual.

What is typically meant by sociopathy (a condition of narcissism or antisocial personality disorder, sometimes mislabeled as psychopathy), though it does exist in the population to some degree (Martha Stout places the number at 4% of the population;[70] ASPD is estimated around 4%;[71] NPD and psychopathy at 1%),[72] as I have defined it is observed in far too high a degree to be viewed as anything other than the result of larger cultural trends. It is not unreasonable to say that America is itself a culture of sociopathic individualism. The pathology of the sociopath, the psychopath, or the antisocial type, is an aberration. Very often these are low-functioning types, sufferers of brain trauma and highly dysfunctional family circumstances, and thus struggle in vain to succeed or adapt to the environment around them. A great number of true psychopaths and clinically diagnosable

70   Martha Stout, *The Sociopath Next Door* (Harmony, 2006).
71   Kimberly B. Werner, Lauren R. Few & Kathleen K. Bucholz, "Epidemiology, Comorbidity, and Behavioral Genetics of Antisocial Personality Disorder and Psychopathy", *Psychiatric annals,* Vol. 45, Issue 4, April 2015, pp. 195-199.
72   Kimberly B. Werner, Lauren R. Few & Kathleen K. Bucholz, "Epidemiology, Comorbidity, and Behavioral Genetics of Antisocial Personality Disorder and Psychopathy", *Psychiatric annals,* Vol. 45, Issue 4, April 2015, pp. 195-199.

individuals with ASPD end up in prison (psychopaths making up 25%[73] of the prison population and ASPD estimated between 40-70%).[74] Their sensation seeking and higher than average level of physiological arousal necessitates a zero-sum kind of competition for pleasures whereby they must take from others in order to be satisfied. It is he, as an individual, who is flawed. With extremist individualism, these people are not necessarily malicious by disposition, but rather are operating within an ideological framework that advances over time, encouraging a narcissistic limit-pushing which is systemic. Both types may find avenues of success and both can find absolute failure. It is not to say that one is superior or better adapted than the other (or worse, even), but to draw a distinction between what we consider dysfunctional psychological profiles and the ways in which culture can mass reproduce features which are minimally occurring within a people group. America's culture of transaction and domination, of immediacy and short-sightedness, of ruthless pragmatism, could produce little else in its population. The speed with which recently migrated peoples conform to this system surely indicates the verity of this fact.

This kind of sociopathic individualism produces the antisocial extremist of both varieties discussed in the second chapter of this book. Cutthroat institutional immorality found in such industries as journalism, business, politics and media will both attract the rarer sociopath,[75] but also 'turn' those who enter into

73   Kiehl KA, Hoffman MB, "The Criminal Psychopath: History, Neuroscience, Treatment, And Economics", *Jurimetrics,* Vol. 51, June 16th, 2011, pp. 355-397.
74   Jari Tiihonen, Marja Koskuvi, Markku Lahteenvuo, Pekka L.J. Virtanen, Ilkka Ojansuu, Olli Vaurio, Yanyan Gao, Ida Hyotylainen, Katja A. Puttonen, Eila Repo-Tiihonen, Tiina Paunio, Marja-Riitta Rautiainen, Sasu Tyni, Jari Koistinaho, Sarka Lehtonen, "Neurobiological roots of psychopathy", *Molecular Psychiatry,* February 21st, 2019 https://www.nature.com/articles/s41380-019-0488-z.pdf?origin=ppub.
75   According to the September 23rd 2016 edition of *The Telegraph,* an Australian study found that 1 in 5 corporate executives were psychopaths (Jonathan Pearlman, "1 in 5 CEOs are psychopaths, study finds", September 13th, 2016, https://www.telegraph.co.uk/news/2016/09/13/1-in-5-ceos-are-psychopaths-australian-study-finds). The study on which the above article was founded examined 261 senior executives in the United States, finding that 21% had clinically significant levels of psychopathic traits. It is worth noting that psychopathy can be adaptive in some circumstances, and does not always lead to adverse or antisocial outcomes (see N. Schutte, G. Blickle, R. Frieder, F. Schnitzler, J. Heu-

these systems. Whether that means they behave in more socio-pathic ways, or are simply willing to subordinate themselves to sociopathy, is of little consequence to the larger problem. Much is made of the notion of systemic racism, and how ideologies of racial supremacy and otherness can insinuate themselves into those who join the system whether they existed previously or not. We ought to also discuss institutional or systemic sociop-athy in the very same way, so as to better understand how in-dividuals can, over time, adopt increasingly damaging attitudes and behave in ways that betray the integrity of the social order. Whatever biological or evolutionary factors presage this condi-tion, they pale in comparison to the power a moribund culture has to erode the moral and social feeling.

Anarchy, therefore, is simply the political application of this extremist brand of individualism. The same characteristics of the extreme individualistic sociopath (as described above) are found in the political anarchist. True political extremism, as I will define in the following section, is anarchic, individualistic, and endemic to both wings of the American political machine. Universal features of this individualistic anarchist are common-ly known, though I will reiterate them here: the anarchist rejects natural hierarchical human structures, centralized authority, and the natural competitive process by which individuals de-termine the hierarchy. He rejects any principled and strategic resolution to political or social dysfunction and will accept only the most extreme propositions for resolving them (often, this means "resolutions" are achieved through violence). The lower functioning he is, the more likely he is to make politically insig-nificant targets the object of his violence. Virtually nowhere else will you find a stronger embodiment of Carl Schmitt's concept of "*absolute enmity*" than in the antisocial and extremely indi-vidualistic anarchist. But once more, I must leave this point to be explicated further at another time, for I have one additional

pel, "The role of interpersonal influence in counterbalancing psychopathic per-sonality trait facets at work", *Journal of Management*, Vol. 10, Issue 4, 2016, pp. 1338-1368; Lilienfeld, S.O., Waldman, I.D., Landfield, K., Watts, A.L., Rubenzer, S., & Faschingbauer, T.R., "Fearless dominance and the U.S. presidency: Impli-cations of psychopathic personality traits for successful and unsuccessful polit-ical leadership.", *Journal of Personality and Social Psychology,* Vol. 103, Issue 3, 2012, pp. 489-505).

comment to make before closing off this discussion.

A curious phenomenon that has crept upon the West slowly, only to emerge all at once, is this notion of oikophobia. In psychiatric terms, oikophobia describes the deranged fear one has toward their house, or the commonplace items one might find inside it. But in the sense in which I am using the term, oikophobia is not so much a clinical phenomenon as it is a cultural one. Americans are tired of themselves, tired of the neighborhoods that they grew up in, and tired of the entire system of inherited beliefs and values within which they are entrenched. I do not believe this has any meaningful bearing on issues of the political insofar as violence or extremism is concerned, but it is nonetheless tied into issues of individuality, abundance, familiarity, and radical choice affordances. Disdain for the suburbs (though, perhaps this is justified), for the quiet life of the family, for the repetitiveness of a normal life—these are all common features of the oikophobic American. Among well-situated members of the bourgeois and petit-bourgeois, oikophobia takes a decidedly more hostile turn, as it manifests in a hatred for rural America, the bible and rust belts, what are commonly referred to as "flyover" country. These antagonisms have great political ramifications but are nonetheless confined to the upper classes (and those who would fain join them).

Our fascination (if not obsession) with the other is so much a part of this phenomenon that it is difficult to not see these phenomena as codependent. With so much access to the world, unparalleled at any other time in human history, it is easy to see why such a development might emerge. International travel is available to more people for a lower cost than ever. Academic achievement, too, is now in the reach of entire groups of people who would never before have been permitted entry into a graduate program. The life of a cultured, well-traveled, and sophisticated cosmopolitan has all the sex appeal that being a run-of-the-mill mid-Westerner doesn't. Naturally, it helps that large parts of this country have been economically and culturally hollowed out—when there's nothing to justify sticking around, who wouldn't want to get the hell out of dodge? The fear of the average, of the typical, of the normal, is now a central feature of the American psyche. Everyone wants exhilaration. We can only conclude that this is the result of a fatigued and weary American spirit, one that can only be kept on life support through the continual administration of narcotics and environmental novelty. And, of course, we are sustained by the vicarious joy of the other. If the self-disgusted feeling can be permitted to metastasize as it has in America, is self-destruction not a logical impulse? Would it become, in a sense, defensible to push over that which is already on its way to collapse? Nietzsche made this very point well over a century ago, and while it may not be morally defensible, it is certainly easy to understand.

What is Extremism? Who is an Extremist?

Here we begin our first examination of the problem of political extremism, albeit in somewhat of an oblique fashion. The question of extremism will be investigated more deeply in the following chapter, where I examine it as a feature of both left- and right-wing political movements. For now, I will wrest the concept of extremism away from its current partisan definition and resituate it into a new context which will allow us a clearer understanding of the phenomenon. Through achieving greater clarity on the matter, we will be in a superior position to evaluate our present circumstance, prevent further catastrophes of a political nature, and organize along more coherent and efficacious lines. As long as political discourse can be reduced to monomaniacal fixations with bygone political movements (e.g. communism, fascism) or long dead historical figures (such as Adolf Hitler or Joseph Stalin) then conversations between differing parties will never achieve healthful resolution. This is not a predicament that corrupts only American voters, but the lack of political holism is endemic to the media and legislative classes as well. Our country is gripped by a collective trauma wrought by the tragedy of the 20th century and facilitated by naïve and malevolent actors of the present century, which is why, now more than ever, it is critical to reclaim political language for ourselves. Because of this grand obfuscation we are unable to see what is novel about our current age; routinely we see measured perspectives regarded with intense suspicion, as if they were nothing more than cleverly erected Trojan horses devised to sneak totalitarian evil into the country. By reversing the linguistic damage committed against political schemas we may open a new line of discursive inquiry, and perhaps pull our civilization back from the brink.

Americans struggle to think through many social and political questions largely because of the heavily confused moral language we bring to our dialogue. It is not possible to understand the true nature of political extremism when those with the largest voices and the most influence engage in what we may call *the politics of misrepresentation*. The goal of such a strategy is to dismiss potential opposition through marginalization and vilification. Misrepresentation sustains the continuity of cultural and political hegemony and is therefore a primary feature of media-amplified psychological warfare. Let us then define this phenomenon: the politics of misrepresentation (PoM, henceforth) consist of 1) the maligning of intent 2) a demand for hyper-accountability (holding an individual or group responsible for acts that are unreasonable or cannot be justified; or to say this in a simpler way, holding one's interlocutor to a higher moral standard than would be typically expected), 3) outright libel or slander, 4) projection, and 5) an unwillingness to disclose one's own true belief or objective. With a media apparatus as extensive as America's, implementing a PoM ensures that the society itself is pliable, easily controlled, and perpetually misinformed. Not even alternative media platforms are protected against this; invariably alternative media outlets will conform not only to the aesthetic style of institutional media, but so too will it adopt the attitude toward broadcasting, its moral norms, and even its lexicon. This is partly the result of intense censorship (forcing commentators and writers into a claustrophobic state of anticipation and conformity), but also the desire on the part of supposed alternatives to appropriate for themselves the kind of professionalism and dignity that institutionally supported broadcasters enjoy. More important to this conversation is the fact that partisanship is the norm for American discourse. Inherent to partisanship *is* the PoM; one must distinguish himself from his opponent and in doing so, he must establish in no uncertain terms the correctness of his position and the absolute incorrectness, if not moral insanity, of his opponent. It is as Cioran said, "*Natures capable of objectivity in any and every situation give the impression of abnormality. What has been broken or perverted in them? Impossible to know, but one divines some serious problem, some anomaly. Impartiality is incompatible with the will to affirm oneself or quite simply with the will to exist. To acknowledge another's merits is an alarming symptom, an act against nature."[76]* (p. 94). Partisanship is the norm because the anti-partisan is forever locked out of the conversation. And in those rare moments where he is permitted to speak, he runs the risk of having his words turned against him, or worse, appropriated by the partisan himself. To be anti-partisan, or simply intellectually honest, is to doubt—and doubt is the antithesis of the will to power.

Our conception of extremism is itself a result of highly partisan institutions, in particular, the Anti-Defamation League and the Southern Poverty Law Center (ironically named, as the former traffics almost exclusively in defamation while the latter can in no way be seen as concerned with the problem of economic inequality in the South). I single these institutions out because of the central role both play in monitoring 'hate groups' and facilitating censorship, particularly on the internet. If you visit the SPLC's website, there are precious few mentions of left-wing hate groups, excepting for their inclusion of "Black Separatist Groups" in a report published on February 15th, 2017.[77] Listed on their website under the 'Ideologies' tabs are the following:

- Alt-Right
- Anti-immigrant
- Anti-LGBTQ
- Anti-Muslim
- Antigovernment movement
- Black Separatist
- Christian Identity
- General hate (a somewhat nebulous—and brief—collection of ideologies, though disproportionately 'right-wing')
- Hate music
- Holocaust denial

76 E.M. Cioran, *Drawn and Quartered,* (Arcade Publishing, 1979).
77 Mark Potok, "The Year in Hate and Extremism", *Southern Poverty Law Center,* 2017 Spring Issue, https://www.splcenter.org/fighting-hate/intelligence-report/2017/year-hate-and-extremism.

- Ku Klux Klan
- Male supremacy
- Neo-Confederate
- Neo-Nazi
- Neo-Volkisch
- Phineas Priesthood
- Racist skinhead
- Radical Traditional Catholicism
- Sovereign Citizens Movement
- White Nationalist

Virtually every group listed is right-wing affiliated in some way or another, with the lone exception of those groups listed under "General hate" (still being disproportionately right-wing) which seem to be included due to accusations of anti-Semitism (e.g. the Nation of Islam). Although, in the interest of investigative honesty, the SPLC also recognizes two New York institutions, the Jewish Defense League based in Brooklyn, and the Jewish Task Force, from Fresh Meadows (the inclusions of which I could not help but laugh at). The Aryan Brotherhood is included as well, despite boasting an official membership of about 300 (and some 15,000 unofficial members) and operating predominantly within the prison system. Curiously, the Black Guerilla Family (with associates numbering more than three times that of the Brotherhood, roughly 50,000) is *not* listed by the SPLC as a hate group. Conspicuously absent from their list of hate groups is Antifa—a so-called anti-fascist movement that has not been able to stay out of the news following Donald Trump's election. Since 2015, Antifa have been a scourge across the nation, one that has been allowed to continue its campaign of violence largely undeterred. Whether their political action takes the form of disrupting legal political demonstrations, assaulting people with deadly weapons, harassing employers with the intention of getting people fired for holding politically incorrect views, under the judgment of any sane person Antifa would surely warrant inclusion on a list purported to monitor violent extremists and hate groups. To this day, no such action has been taken.

In pursuing a campaign to end extremist violence, the SPLC is responsible for perpetuating the very same thing. Consider the case of Floyd Lee Corkins, who wounded a security guard in an attempt to murder employees of the Family Research Council back in August of 2012. According to Carol Cratty of CNN, Corkins had *"told the FBI he planned to kill as many people as he could at the research council and then smash the [Chic-Fil-A] sandwiches in their faces."[78]* He was later sentenced to 25 years in prison. Having listed the Family Research Council as an extremist anti-LGBT group some ten years ago, Corkins *"...told FBI agents that he used the SPLC website to determine that the FRC was anti-gay, prompting Perkins (President of the FRC) to claim that the SPLC had "given a license" to Corkins' attack because it had named FRC an anti-LGBTQ hate group starting in 2010."[79]*

While endangering the lives of those listed on their website is awful by anyone's assessment, we should not dismiss the less immediately dangerous tendency of the SPLC to define its "hate groups" in such liberal terms. Nathan J. Robinson of *Current Affairs* wrote on this very issue, saying:[80]

> In fact, when you actually look at [their] hate map, you find something interesting: Many of these "groups" barely seem to exist at all. A "Holocaust denial" group in Kerrville, Texas called "carolynyeager.net" appears to just be *a woman called Carolyn Yeager.* A "male supremacy" group called *Return of Kings* is apparently just a blog published by pick-up artist Roosh V and a couple of his friends, and the most recent post is an announcement from six months ago that the project was on indefinite hiatus. Tony Alamo, the abusive cult leader of *"Tony Alamo Christian Ministries," died in prison in 2017.* (Though his ministry's website still promotes *"Tony Alamo's Unreleased Beatles Album."*) A "black nationalist" group in Atlanta called "Luxor Couture" appears to be an *African fashion boutique.* "Sharkhunters International" is *one guy who really likes U-boats* and

78   Carol Cratty, "25-year sentence in Family Research Council shooting", *CNN,* September 19th, 2013, https://www.cnn.com/2013/09/19/justice/dc-family-research-council-shooting/index.html.
79   "Family Research Council", *Southern Poverty Law Center,* https://www.splcenter.org/fighting-hate/extremist-files/group/family-research-council.
80   Nathan J. Robinson, "The Southern Poverty Law Center Is Everything Wrong With Liberalism", *Current Affairs,* March 26th, 2019, https://www.currentaffairs.org/2019/03/the-southern-poverty-law-center-is-everything-thats-wrong-with-liberalism.

takes small groups of sad Nazis on tours to see ruins and relics. And good luck finding out much about the "Samanta Roy Institute of Science and Technology," which—if it is currently operative at all—is a tiny anti-Catholic cult based in Shawano, Wisconsin."

The SPLC has a longer, more sordid history of ethical quandaries beyond the unintended consequences described above. In 2019, Morris Dees (co-founder of the SPLC), Richard Cohen (then President), and other high-ranking executives were forced to resign amid allegations of sexual harassment and racial discrimination. Dees' profile was swiftly removed from the SPLC's website immediately following the controversy. The *Los Angeles Times* reported that two dozen employees signed a letter to management, concerned with allegations of "*mistreatment, sexual harassment, gender discrimination, and racism.*"[81] By some accounts, the level of discrimination and hypocrisy which only came to light in the past year had been part of the SPLC's culture for decades. As reported by Dan Morse back in February of 1994,[82]

> Outside the Southern Poverty Law Center, a stunning civil rights memorial honors those who died to give blacks more opportunities. Inside, no blacks have held top management positions in the center's 23-year history, and some former employees say blacks are treated like second-class citizens. "I would definitely say there was not a single black employee with whom I spoke who was happy to be working there," said Christine Lee, a black graduate of Harvard Law School who interned at the Law Center in 1989. Only one black has ever been among the top five wage-earners at the center, and he was one of only two black staff attorneys in the center's history. Both said they left unhappy.

Morse goes on to say that,

> According to internal memorandums, staffers have accused

---

81 Matt Pearce, "Southern Poverty Law Center fires co-founder Morris Dees amid employee uproar", *The Los Angeles Times*, March 14th, 2019, https://www.latimes.com/nation/la-na-splc-morris-dees-20190314-story.html.
82 Dan Morse, "Equal Treatment? No Blacks in Center's Leadership", *Montgomery Advertiser*, February 16th, 1994, https://rkeefe57.wordpress.com/montgomery-advertiser-series/.

Morris Dees, the center's driving force, of being a racist and black employees have "felt threatened and banded together." Charles Ogletree, a black Harvard Law School professor who knows blacks who've had negative experiences at the center, said he no longer recommends his students take internships there.

Bob Moser, a former staffer at the SPLC shared some experiences of his own at the time of Dees' dismissal:[83]

In the days since the stunning dismissal of Morris Dees, the co-founder of the Southern Poverty Law Center, on March 14th, I've been thinking about the jokes my S.P.L.C. colleagues and I used to tell to keep ourselves sane. Walking to lunch past the center's Maya Lin–designed memorial to civil-rights martyrs, we'd cast a glance at the inscription from Martin Luther King, Jr., etched into the black marble—"Until justice rolls down like waters"—and intone, in our deepest voices, "Until justice rolls down like dollars."

And the justice *still is* rolling down like dollars. Despite the pillorying it has endured over the last year and a half, the SPLC's net assets grew another $52 million (from $493 million to $545 million) according to their latest financial statement.[84]

But it doesn't end there: just a year before Dees' exit, the documentary *Alt-Right: Age of Rage* was released, and one scene in particular drew quite a bit of attention. The scene in question featured Mark Potok (then a senior fellow at the SPLC) and a pair of unusual charts hanging conspicuously in his office. Both detailed the changing racial demographics of the United States and Europe. Ominously, the chart of the United States was titled *"Non-Hispanic Whites proportion of population"*, tracking the declining White population of America from 1920 to 2015. What possible motivation could a group concerned with violent

83 Bob Moser, "The Reckoning of Morris Dees And The Southern Poverty Law Center", *The New Yorker,* March 21st, 2019, https://www.newyorker.com/news/news-desk/the-reckoning-of-morris-dees-and-the-southern-poverty-law-center.

84 Steve Sailer, "Scandal-Plagued SPLC's Net Worth Still Grew $52 Million to $545 Million", *The Unz Review: An Alternative Media Selection,* April 30th, 2020, https://www.unz.com/isteve/scandal-plagued-splcs-net-worth-still-grew-52-million-to-545-million/.

extremism that disproportionately targets, White, Christian, and right-wing groups and individuals have for monitoring the racial make-up of Western nations? These facts go beyond mere partisanship into something altogether more sinister, and ought to deeply concern anyone with a conscience.

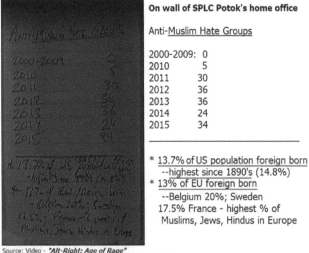

On wall of SPLC Potok's home office

Anti-<u>Muslim Hate Groups</u>

2000-2009:	0
2010	5
2011	30
2012	36
2013	36
2014	24
2015	34

_____

* <u>13.7% of US population foreign born</u>
  --highest since 1890's (14.8%)
* 13% of EU foreign born
  --Belgium 20%; Sweden
  17.5% France - highest % of
  Muslims, Jews, Hindus in Europe

Source: Video - *"Alt-Right: Age of Rage"*
https://www.youtube.com/watch?v=664yE9daTxk   (@ 23:05 minute mark)

And what may be said of the ADL, that other bastion of courageous verity? We may say it is a metaphysical principle of certainty that whenever an individual or group undertakes a world-transformative mission of moral excellence that their true intention probably has more to do with the opposite of goodness and nobility. This is particularly true when that mission is aided by State and Capital. The Anti-Defamation League, which was founded in September of 1913 in response to the (still) hotly debated conviction of factory owner Leo Frank (who had been found guilty of murdering child laborer, Mary Phagan), is now one of the most powerful institutions in the country, having the ear of public schools, police departments, and major corporations such as Google and YouTube (both owned by Alphabet Incorporated). In fact, in 2017 the Anti-Defamation League became part of YouTube's Trusted Flagger program, itself an attempt to combat the spread of fake news and hateful content on the social media platform.[85] This led to claims of anti-Conservative bias, thus provoking a Senate Judiciary Hearing on internet censorship in the summer of 2019. The hearing itself did not achieve anything of significance, though the Trump administration would hold summits with prominent Conservative activists shortly thereafter.

As with the SPLC, we find that the ADL employs a broad and highly elastic definition of "extremist", a label that continues to strain credibility. In 2017, the ADL published its annual *Murder and Extremism in the United States*,[86] claiming that white supremacists and far-right extremists were responsible for 59% of all extremist related fatalities in that year. The ADL also claimed that virtually every terrorist murder in 2018 was linked to far-right extremism, and moreover, that far-right related murders were three times as high as those attributed to Islamist extremists in the past decade.[87] (Similar claims were made in their most recent publication.)[88] This was argued as definitive despite the inability to identify extremism as a motivation for each killing. According to a 2019 article published by the website *American Renaissance*, of the sixty-nine deaths attributed to extremism in a

85   Whitney Webb, "YouTube To Censor "Controversial" Content with ADL Assistance", *Mint Press News*, August 7th, 2017, https://www.mintpressnews.com/youtube-censor-controversial-content-adl/230530/.

86   ADL, "Murder and Extremism in the United States in 2017", *An ADL Center on Extremism Report*, https://www.adl.org/resources/reports/murder-and-extremism-in-the-united-states-in-2017.

87   ADL, "Murder and Extremism in the United States in 2018", *An ADL Center on Extremism Report*, https://www.adl.org/murder-and-extremism-2018.

88   ADL, "Murder and Extremism in the United States in 2019", *An ADL Center on Extremism Report*, https://www.adl.org/murder-and-extremism-2019.

report published by the ADL tallying extremist related deaths in 2016, only three could reasonably be attributed to white supremacist extremists, with only a single murder being attributable to racial motives.[89] The authors of the article found that of the eighteen murders attributed to white supremacists in 2017, only two were judicially found to be true examples of white supremacist terror. Gregory Hood and Jared Taylor (the article's authors) found similar discrepancies, to put it politely, in the ADL's 2018 report, arguing that, "[o]f course, when the media wrote about the 2018 report, they didn't distinguish between "right-wing" and "white supremacist," implying that every killing was similar to the attack on the Tree of Life Synagogue: a planned, racially or politically motivated killing by a venomous white man." Dan Feinreich, a political writer for *The Times of Israel*, similarly took issue with the ADL's publication, arguing that:[90]

> The ADL claims that "white supremacists in the US regularly commit murders in support of their hateful cause, but their violence — and thus the danger they pose to the country as a whole — extends far beyond that," and includes "rivals, spouses, children, and acquaintances." Nonsense. People commit murders for a variety of reasons, mainly because of mental issues or a difficult childhood. Having mental problems may cause some people to join white supremacist groups. However, there is no evidence that having white supremacist thoughts or joining a white supremacist groups can be directly attributed to acts of violence. Not every white supremacist is violent, and there are many violent people who are not white supremacists. The report includes no examples of left-wing extremist murders and only one incident of Islamic extremist murder. Did the COE conduct extensive research to determine if any left-wing or non-white murderers had extremist connections?

Troubling as all this may be, we find that the ADL's problems

---

89   Gregory Hood & Jared Taylor, "Media Promote ADL Propaganda on 'Extremist Terrorism'", *American Renaissance,* April 10th, 2019, https://www.am-ren.com/commentary/2019/04/media-promote-adl-propaganda-on-extremist-terrorism/.

90   Dan Feinreich, "The ADL Murder and Extremism Report is a fraud", *The Times Of Israel,* January 29th, 2019, https://blogs.timesofisrael.com/the-adl-murder-and-extremism-report-is-a-fraud/.

go back much farther than the last decade. FBI files obtained by the Institute for Research: Middle Eastern Policy (which were released under the Freedom of Information Act) seriously injure the ADL's credibility.[91] One FBI report showed that, in 1941, an ADL operative named Arnold Forster was arrested at Madison Square Garden for using illicit press credentials to disrupt an anti-war rally. According to the report, the ADL had brought

> tremendous pressure to bear on Commissioner Seery and the Mayor's Committee on Press Cards to drop the Forster incident.

In 1951, the ADL brought information from an investigation of the Arab League and activities of Egypt and Saudi Arabia to the FBI. Then director John Edgar Hoover wrote on November 23rd, 1951 that,

> material which the Anti-Defamation League has been channeling to this Bureau in the past is now believed by the officials of the League to be absolutely unreliable.

Most embarrassingly, that same year (1951), the ADL had sought the freedom of suspected Soviet spy Morton Sobell, only for Sobell to admit in 2008 that he was, in fact, spying for the Soviet Union. At one point, the FBI proposed investigating the ADL as an Israeli foreign agent after it was discovered that three ADL undercover operatives infiltrated the Organization of Arab Students, intent on taking over the group. The FBI reported that the:

> investigation conducted by ADL, using code name sources, pretexts such as local news reporters … recruiting of Jewish refugees from organizations such as HIAS (Hebrew Immigrant Aide Society) to infiltrate the OAS in NYC. Of course, there is no evidence to indicate this information is compiled on behalf of a foreign principal, however, it is felt incredible to assume it is not furnished to an official of the

91   Institute for Research: Middle Eastern Policy "FBI files reveal ADL's long history spying on peace, pro-Palestinian and Arab diplomat groups", *Cision PR Newswire*, May 16th, 2013, https://www.prnewswire.com/news-releases/fbi-files-reveal-adls-long-history-spying-on-peace-pro-palestinian-and-arab-diplomat-groups-207706361.html.

Government of *Israel*...

An FBI-conducted interview of undercover ADL operative Roy Bullock in 1993 revealed that he had improperly obtained social security numbers and drivers licenses from San Francisco Police Department officer Tom Gerard. Bullock and Gerard infiltrated and obtained information on Pro-Palestinian and anti-Apartheid groups as paid agents of the ADL and South African intelligence services. This discovery prompted the ADL to promise not to collect confidential information in the future (as well as pay tens of thousands of dollars in damages).

Clearly, we can see a history of unethical conduct from the ADL, but where does it stand on the question of partisanship? While we explored this problem earlier, I would like to provide a few more pieces of information to solidify my argument. Ostensibly, the ADL began as an institution dedicated to the protection and preservation of the Jewish people and their rights; however, under Jonathan Greenblatt's leadership (beginning in 2015) many have taken notice of the ADL's left-ward drift. Writing in December of 2016 for *The New York Post*, Alex Van Ness argued that,[92]

> Under Greenblatt, the ADL has rightly taken a strong stance against anti-Semitism stemming from Internet trolls associated with the "alt-right" — but he's also largely ignored anti-Semitism spawning from the left. Notably, the ADL has downplayed the anti-Semitic nature of the Boycott, Divestment, and Sanctions Movement — the ultimate goal of which, its founder has openly admitted, is the destruction of Israel. The ADL has also promoted the Black Lives Matter movement, for example, by creating school lesson plans that promote it, despite BLM's support for BDS and open hostility toward Israel. Just recently, Greenblatt accused American Jews of living with white privilege.

An op-ed from the same publication, written in September of the same year called the ADL *"another J Street—an arm of the Democratic Party's stable of pressure groups."*[93] But why? Green-

92   Alex VanNess, "Jonathan Greeblatt is destroying the Anti-Defamation League", *The New York Post,* December 9th, 2016, https://nypost.com/2016/12/09/jonathan-greenblatt-is-destroying-the-anti-defamation-league/.
93   Post Editorial Board, "The Anti-Defamation League turns anti-Israel, pos-

blatt had criticized recent comments made by Israeli Prime Minister Benjamin Netanyahu, where he claimed that the Palestin-
ian desire for a Jew-free state amounted to "ethnic cleansing".[94]
The editorial quoted former executive editor of the *Commentary*,
Jonathan Tobin, as saying

> for Greenblatt to re-position ADL from its former centrist
> position as a mainstream address for pro-Israel activism to
> one that is now in open opposition to the democratically
> elected government of Israel is a sea change of enormous
> importance . . . This is a betrayal of ADL's long and honor-
> able legacy as a group that sought to speak for the interests
> of the Jewish community as a whole and respected the right
> of Israel's people and their leaders to make their own deci-
> sions about security.

Isi Leibler, who at one point served as the vice president and
board of trustee's chairman of the World Jewish Congress, criticized Greenblatt for "*tilting the ADL policy away from its primary
mandate of combating anti-Semitism and steering it toward partisan social action issues.*" Furthermore, Leibler argued that, "*the
ADL board has knowingly empowered*" Greenblatt, whose "*outlook is not only liberal but effectively represents an echo chamber
of left-wing Democratic politics*".[95]

It cannot be said that these institutions concerned with political violence and extremism are looking at these situations
with clear eyes and an open mind. Quite the contrary, as I have
demonstrated they are manifestly, perhaps hysterically, partisan.
And yet they have massive national *and international* influence
in shaping public discourse, policing strategies, education, and
legislative policy. But this phenomenon is widespread, not merely localized to a handful of supposedly non-partisan, non-gov-

sible hush money from a Clinton ally & other notable comments", *The New York
Post*, September 15th, 2016, https://nypost.com/2016/09/15/the-anti-defama-
tion-league-turns-anti-israel-possible-hush-money-from-a-clinton-ally-oth-
er-notable-comments/.
94   Isi Leibler, "Fight on campuses, don't condemn Israel's prime minister", *The
Jerusalem Post*, September 15th, 2016, https://www.jpost.com/Opinion/Fight-
on-campuses-dont-condemn-Israels-prime-minister-467845#/.
95   Isi Leibler, "Fight on campuses, don't condemn Israel's prime minister", *The
Jerusalem Post*, September 15th, 2016, https://www.jpost.com/Opinion/Fight-
on-campuses-dont-condemn-Israels-prime-minister-467845#/.

ernmental institutions.

Once again, we turn our attention to the major press outlets courtesy of a series of charts compiled on Twitter by Zach Goldberg, a doctoral candidate in political science at Georgia State University studying "*The Great Awokening*". Pulling the charts below from the *LexisNexis* (a corporation that uses computer-assisted legal research, and boasts one of the world's largest databases for legal and public-records related information) and sharing them in a pair of threads on May 28th, 2019 and March 30th, 2020,[96] a most curious pattern emerges:

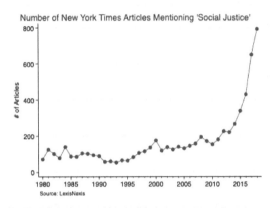

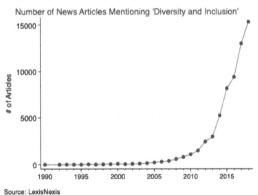

Source: LexisNexis

---

96 https://twitter.com/zachg932/status/1133440945201061888?

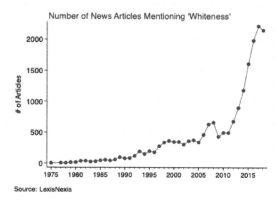

Source: LexisNexis

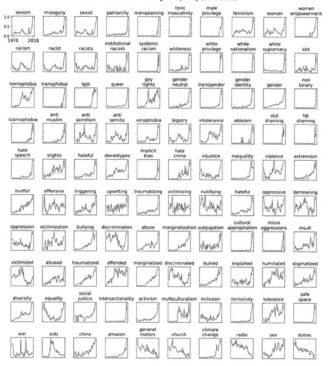

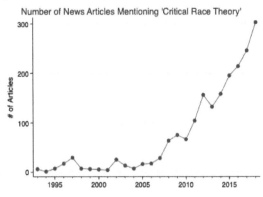

Source: LexisNexis

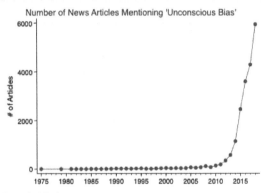

Source: LexisNexis

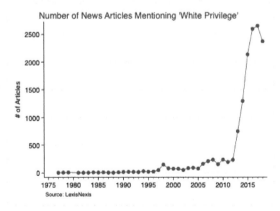

Source: LexisNexis

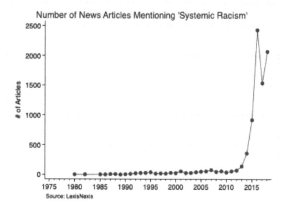

Number of News Articles Mentioning 'Systemic Racism'
Source: LexisNexis

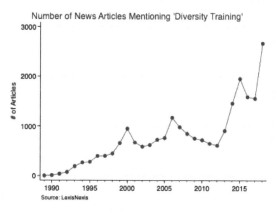

Number of News Articles Mentioning 'Diversity Training'
Source: LexisNexis

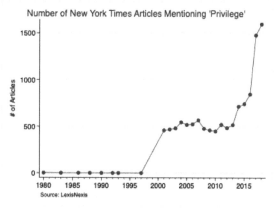

Number of New York Times Articles Mentioning 'Privilege'
Source: LexisNexis

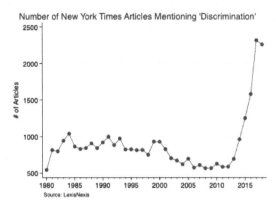

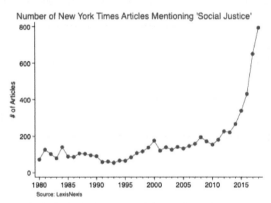

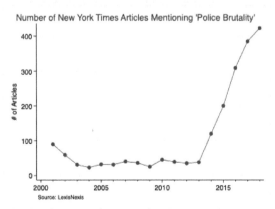

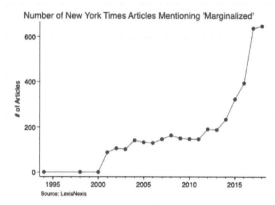

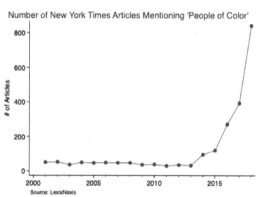

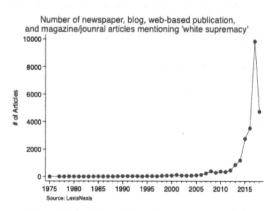

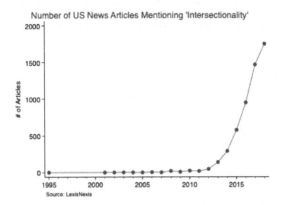

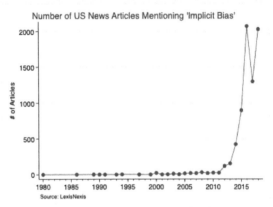

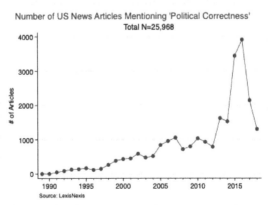

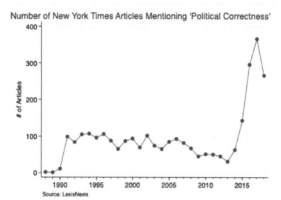

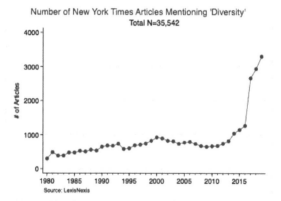

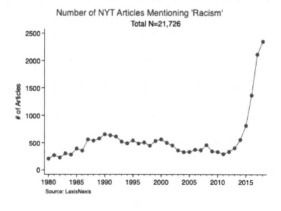

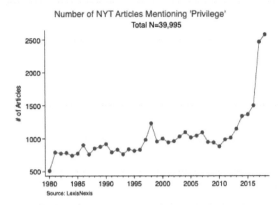

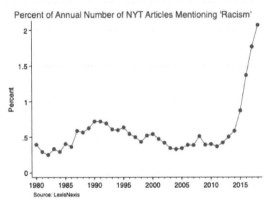

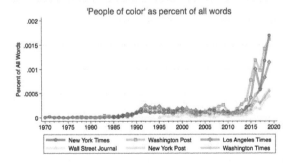

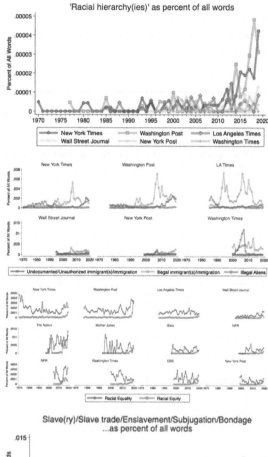

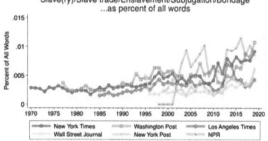

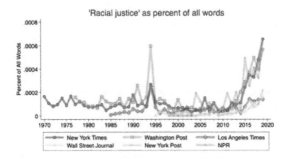

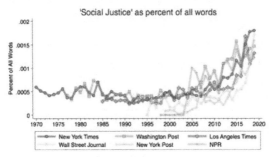

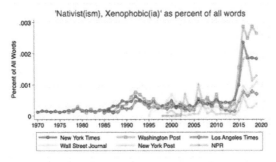

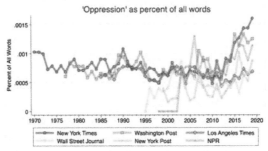

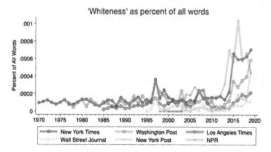

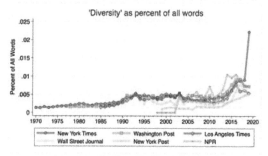

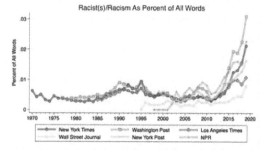

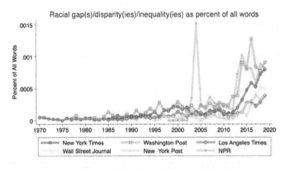

Racial gap(s)/disparity(ies)/inequality(ies) as percent of all words

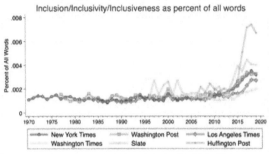

Inclusion/Inclusivity/Inclusiveness as percent of all words

In the last decade, roughly the period in which the ADL claimed the threat of white supremacy rose to alarming rates, the language of the top press outlets radically shifted in favor of extreme intersectional neoliberal ideology. One can only conclude that, institutionally, the ideology of the intersectional left rose to prominence, not white supremacy. Ideological white supremacists, nationalists, immigration skeptics, racists, and patriots (who are all regarded as indistinguishable from one another and thus equally evil) hold no sway in the media, the government, and are hard pressed to locally organize. The other conclusion that one may draw from these findings is that fixating on grievance politics and extremism is a lucrative endeavor—one that will find you in the good graces of the establishment. As it turns out, *the extremism is coming from inside the house!*

It is the establishment that *wants* to mimetically reproduce the threat of rising hatred, intolerance, and violence as a way to achieve social and political control. What we begin to see, then, is the true nature of extremism: that it is a phenomenon known in some circles as the HLvM (high and low versus the middle). First developed by French philosopher Bertrand de Jouvenel, this model of power relations provides us with the clearest understanding upon which we may construct a theory of the political. Adapting de Jouvenel's theory for our own purposes, we have the myth of extremism as perpetuated by the upper classes which are then fed to the lower classes (rank and file anarchists, anti-fascists, activists in the university system, etc.) who will take on the myth as a call to action with the kind of religious zeal not seen in most truly religious people. Caught in the middle, as it were, are the working classes and other members of the recently dubbed precariat—people who are economically vulnerable to the changing winds of a rapidly evolving techno-informational labor environment. The implementation of this strategy serves as a pincer attack from above and below, designed to squeeze the center out of political existence.

What, then, is extremism? And just who exactly is an extremist? From the point of view of the establishment, any paradigm which challenges it is by definition extremism, and so extremists are those people who stand in opposition to those ideologies and institutions which enjoy legitimate power. Critics of global finance, open borders, multiculturalism, radical individuality (feminism, identity politics, etc.), scientism, institutionalized art and media, and the sexual revolution—being chief among them—are the modern day heretics of the American empire. Merely alluding to such critiques is sufficient (in the eyes of the establishment and everyone who has been ideologically or economically captured by it) to be dubbed an extremist.

We would be mistaken to believe that establishment actors are necessarily, uncompromisingly, opposed to reactionary or even radical critiques; it should be noted that the flexible nature of neoliberal governance is such that, out of one side of its mouth, hegemonic powers can decry these worldviews while out the other side strategically deploying them to serve its own purposes. In a single presidential campaign, Vermont senator Bernie Sanders can be a respectable statesman *and* a vilified antagonist of all that is good and holy. Racism can simultaneously be condemned at every level of the social order, and then permitted when strategically aimed at domestic and foreign enemies. Extremist energies can be created out of whole cloth, or they can be appropriated and commoditized to stabilize and re-center political power. In one sense, extremism is nothing and everything all at once; the state operates by a kind of morally relativistic will to power that is not meaningfully committed to any particular individual, group, or ideology. The state's flexibility is its strength, because power (if we could say such a thing) *wants* to be consolidated. And the powerful want to consolidate it on their terms.

Ultimately, we must admit that a radical political force always exists in its true form as that which could deter or delegitimize the domestic and foreign aims of the American imperial order. While state antagonism can be created or captured, there is always a measure of *true* hostility to hegemonic power that is not merely aesthetic or status-oriented and therefore must be denied if the hegemonic institutions are to retain their monopoly on power. We may call them radicals; individuals and groups who are outside of the existing order but who seek strategic and eusocial resolutions to the problems of the day. As far as the establishment is concerned however, lawful and peaceable radicals are no different from the violent school-shooter, the rioter, the unhinged lunatic—they are extremists one and all.

Extremism, in my view, is something altogether different from the establishment conception which we are now so familiar with. My definition may come as a surprise, for it requires a kind of cynical discernment that is willing to see the contemporary social order without bias or rose-colored glasses. Those readers who are initiated into this way of thinking may find little that shocks them. Political extremism is not necessarily about any particular ideology or objective, but rather a set of biopsychosocial predispositions and an overall attitude of hostility toward eusocial practices and conventions. What is political extremism? It is the instantiation of the death principle, of *Thanatos*, as per Freud. The extremist stands in diametrical opposition to the radical who seeks life, and for whom destruction is a controlled and methodical tool wielded for the purpose of greater creation (a conception of the death instinct that is more in alignment with Sabina Speilrein's interpretation). I will elaborate on this idea at the close of this chapter but let us continue discussing the identity of the extremist. Seeing as the extremist isn't genuinely ideological in any meaningful sense—invariably he may be guided by *some* principle or idea (better described as a fixation), though it is altogether superficial and easily discarded—he cannot be said to have a proactive will. Thrown into chaos, he is relegated to the status of eternal reactionary for the chaos he seeks to sow in the world is merely a reflection of his internal sense of disorder.

It has often been remarked that the fascist is one who takes complex feelings of inferiority and persecution and marshals them toward an external process of order creation. This description would be more apt for our purposes, although with a minor twist. Our extremist is one who takes his subjective chaos and simply desires to reproduce it on a mass scale. As with authoritarianism, extremism is bound to neither left- nor right-wing ideology but is equally distributed across the political spectrum and shares a similar structure wherever it is found. American extremism in the 21st century is a HLvM phenomenon; it is not something conducted solely by the low-functioning untermensch or the mentally ill, but the high-functioning and well-situated socialites as well. The absence of a positive social feeling is often the precursor to extremist thought and action; whether it's the willingness to betray the shared social reality in favor of some solipsistic abstraction (e.g. an open border immigration policy instead of social programs for the working class, synthetic technologies and artificial intelligence instead of pro-natal policies, the market instead of the environment, etc.), crude identitarianism that seeks punishment of the other rather than reconciliation (e.g. maladapted White nationalism, retributive intersectionality, violent Zionism, and similar genocidal sentiments), or self-obsessed careerism and status advancement, all are defined by the aggrandizement of the self and the antagonism of the other. Together, these traits constitute the foundation of 21st century American extremism.

We may identify fear, resentment, and despair as the major emotional motivations used to direct emotional and political energy in service of extremist narratives. The circumstances which are themselves responsible for generating such a fervently toxic psychology are lamentable (intergenerational trauma, physical and cognitive handicaps, impoverishment, persecution), but best resolved in the clinician's office and not the editor's office, the faculty lounge, or the floor of the Senate. Whereas the cure for such spiritual and psychological ailments may be found in self-overcoming, forgiveness, and the relinquishing of anger, the response of the true political extremist is to shun sociality itself and to escalate violence (or the potential for violence) to a fever pitch. He condemns being itself, finding existence unworthy and unjustifiable; he is filled with the most venomous cynicism and nihilism—the kind which is simply beyond the imagination of the average person. Not all extremists are necessarily drawn to direct violence, but in their poisoned minds they see justifications and rationalizations for violence of every kind. Any target can be made a deserving victim, regardless of the truth of the circumstance.

Extremism of this kind is temperamental first, and not ideological.[97] One can adopt radical positions which are achieved through logical or empirical investigation, and in that sense, adopt an extremist stance (relative to the prevailing ideology), but ultimately these are still people engaging in the social order, engaging in civil society, if only in their own way. Writing books, organizing conferences and guilds, creating art and participating in politics—they get married, have children, and generally concern themselves with the world of the here and now (while maintaining an eye toward the future). Antisocial extremism, the kind of extremism which, as fringe as it is, ought to genuinely worry people (for its existence is not only in part a consequence of the failings of contemporary system politics, but is also cultivated and nourished like an infant child) is a rejection of the world as is, and is a yearning for the world as they would have it be. Theirs is a world *for them and them alone*. Unable to sublimate their lower urges, to negotiate with people *even modestly* unlike themselves, the true extremist can only live as a dominator, however impotent and petty his pursuit of conquest may be. It is important to remember that the extremist often lacks a real ideology or worldview. What he has is sentiment—a sentiment of total rejection and hatred. Extremists are governed by contempt as well; not just for his supposed political enemies, but for

97   Meysam Alizadeh, Ingmar Weber, Claudio Cioffi-Revilla, Santo Fortunato, Michael Macy, "Psychological and Personality Profiles of Political Extremists", *Computation and Language*, April 1st, 2017.

those who would work to slow his antisocial and accelerationist aspirations. The extremist says, *"either I get exactly what I want or I'll burn everything to the ground."* Higher-functioning and genetically gifted types will find success in working toward their individual projects, as their natural abilities allow them to more deftly navigate social realities, though they still find themselves unable to restrain their more tyrannical impulses. Lower-functioning extremists are caught between two poles; they pine for each and every situation to be either a stunning success, or a guaranteed and exponentially increasing failure. The extremist is principled in his *lack* of principles. This of course is not to somehow privilege rationality over affectivity, but rather to say that the habits of thought and emotional regulation, or lack thereof, are utterly disordered in these individuals.

The extremist fixates on the object of hatred, which may be conceptual but is just as (if not more) often personal. Certainly, legitimate and coherent grievances exist, however the target of their impotent rage and frustration takes on a decidedly personal face—fathers, mothers, schoolteachers, rival classmates, ex-lovers, even God himself. Their fixation takes on a quality of delusion, as the true circumstances rarely match up to the rationalization or analysis provided by the extremist. When they do, a healthful psychological adaptation or insight toward the fixated object is never developed. The extremist is a cultist, a political theologian of a kind. His beliefs are neither rational nor scientific, but instead are rooted in experience and then mythologized. The mythos of the extremist is integral to the reinforcement of their beliefs; they self-mythologize their actions and place themselves in the center. Extremists adopt the position of a god—a supreme actor with perfect moral agency. In that sense, extremism is political psychosis, a psychosis that is often the product of estrangement and alienation, tragedy, addiction, and neurobiological weakness. In other words, these people are primed to develop antisocial tendencies. While it is only a minority of a minority who ever become dangerous in any proximal way, nonetheless only a dedicated minority are necessary to destroy social cohesion.

And so the university professor who betrays his role as shepherd of his academic flock, the journalist who uses his platform to spread maladaptive ideas or destroy the lives of those he views as contemptible, the media personality who engages in dishonest and destructive speculation and reckless cheerleading, the tech guru who indulges in post-human fantasies, the capitalist who sacrifices his workers livelihood for greater earnings, the physician who trades his role as healer for that of political activist—they are all, no more and no less, every bit the extremist that the school shooter and the online anti-fascist/racist are. Certainly the latter are more obvious and visible in their ability to tear the social fabric apart, but it could easily be argued that it is the *invisible* damage that at once sets the stage for such craven acts of resentment and violence while simultaneously securing hegemonic extremism for generations to come that is significant in its own right. It is precisely their unaccountability, their prestige, the belief in their absolute necessity which places them on equal footing with the more commonplace extremists, whom we recognize plainly as such. We commonly think of extremism, just as we do of revolution, as a bottom-up process of organic emergence. This could not be further from the truth; pathological and antisocial extremism from on high breathes life into the lungs of those down below. Their relationship is symbiotic. Taken as a whole, they form a complex and interconnected matrix of antisocial extremism that serves as a bulwark against true, psychologically developed and eusocial progress.

Extremism (as I have defined it) operates to direct social anxieties towards targets which can be easily manipulated and away from legitimate sources of angst and tension. Stories of only marginal interest or significance become major cultural moments because they allow for the power structure (by way of the press, various political operatives, or even the entertainment industry), to manipulate, distort, and imbue these events with the necessary narrative structure to give form and shape to the lie. The use of image and framing arrests the imagination of the populace. In capturing their imaginations, their political energies are also arrested. Individuals who are susceptible to this then take on the consciousness of the political order, and take it as a moral duty to at the very least abstain from exploring the issues deemed extreme and to ostracize those considered to be extremists. The more emboldened will seek out extremists and attack them physically or otherwise. But the mere suggestion of a position or an actor as extreme is enough to create a ripple effect. Guilt by association therefore becomes another weapon of the establishment. Call it the *political scarlet letter*; it is a mark that renders one a pariah. And because fear of ostracization is a prime motivator in the average person (as Lawrence Kohlberg's work in the area of moral reasoning has shown us), individuals will thus police their own thoughts and social interactions. The tool of oppression therefore shifts from external to internal, a far more effective means for stifling dissent and manipulating political consciousness. Moreover, they will police those around them, reinforcing the taboo that such extremists are dangerous. Taboo is integral to the claim of extremism. Average people do not fear being wrong, or philosophically and intellectually inconsistent. The average person fears social censure; he fears a disruption of employment. He fears, *deeply fears*, an inability to find romance and friendship. Many Americans are intimately familiar with the inefficiencies of bureaucracy and the outright immorality of electoral politics and thus merely seek to eke out a quiet life of modest satisfaction, anonymity, and political insignificance. Even as the ideology of neoliberal governance finds ever more baffling ways to complicate the lives of the average person, he still seeks to adapt to it, for the cost of doing otherwise is simply too high.

Political control is not about agreeing to a mere set of facts, or making decisions about impersonal and uninteresting issues such as the price of a given tax, or about whether more money ought to be spent on infrastructure or education, issues which are entirely pragmatic and beyond the realm of the personal. To control the political is to have absolute moral authority and, therefore, social control. And as far as we can tell morality and sociality evolved together; a monopoly over political axioms has ontological and theological implications. Political control dictates what is "true", which god(s) to worship, which myths and traditions to honor, matters of social etiquette, and a whole set of other critically important philosophical questions with far reaching implications for human relations. Identity itself is constructed on the conscious and unconscious assumptions one makes about the world and one's place within it; political control then permits the privileging of certain identities over others, granting or denying them the primacy of their very existence, as I shall elaborate this more fully later.

In summation, we are caught between two competing understandings of the extremist. The first, a self-serving definition which aids the program of hegemonic power, and the second (more useful understanding) which allows us to recognize, for the first time, who truly threatens our welfare and the future of the American project. Is every member of every institution an extremist? No. Should we view every institution with a radical doubt and skepticism that prevents us from stealing truths wherever they may be found? To this question I must also say, emphatically, *no*. In fact, the tangible absence of credibility found within contemporary American institutions is itself reproducing this radical doubt, pushing people into paradigmatic niches which struggle with credibility issues of their own. The plurality of alternative institutions (media, academic, etc.) that have emerged in response to the gate-keeping and self-discrediting habits of the establishment are themselves producing as many additional problems as they do solutions to our present conflict. Americans walk a precarious tightrope at all times simply to navigate the failing landscape we have constructed for ourselves. While I cannot offer concrete and exact resolutions to this problem, by redefining the problematic aspects of this equation I am able to provide some clarity, and hopefully a possible first step to my readers that will help them in their journey. We are progressing, bit by bit, ever closer to that final analysis of the extremist, and ultimately to a *possible* answer to the challenge of political extremism. But before we reach the conclusion, I must tease out a few more details of the extremist ideology.

Ideophilia and Extremism

The history of the concept we call "ideology" stretches back to the work of 19th century Enlightenment philosopher Antoine Destutt de Tracy—and at least in its initial usage—was intended as a discipline devoted to the study of ideas.[98] In de Tracy's con-

---

98 Van Dijk, T.A., "Politics, Ideology, and Discourse", *Discourse in Society,* 2006, pp. 728-740.

ception, one may speak of the ideology of capitalism or idealism, for instance, and understand that they signify a comprehensive and internally consistent matrix of ideas and beliefs designed to give us an epistemological and ontological understanding of the world and its subjects. However, de Tracy's support of American republicanism (which his notion of ideology, it has been argued, was intended to defend)[99] not only saw him fall out of favor with Napoleon Bonaparte, but marked the beginning of a long philosophical trend which transformed the meaning of ideology into something wholly negative and obstructive toward social and intellectual progress.

This trend was amplified to great effect by thinkers in the Marxist tradition beginning with Karl Marx and Friedrich Engels, perhaps achieving its zenith as a derogatory and slanderous term thanks to the efforts of luminaries such as Guy Debord and Theodore Adorno. When we hear someone utter that damnable word, we understand that it is not intended to indicate a system of thought or a valid worldview, but rather a vehicle for the reproduction of falsehoods. As we know, it was Marx who asked why it was that people acted against their better interests. His answer was that ideology made them that way. No longer an organized philosophy or worldview capable of offering a coherent explanation of reality, in Marx's view ideology was something hideous and perverse; ideology was a political device that distorted thought rather than facilitated it. Most importantly, it was a device of the powerful to maintain their control over the powerless. We may examine the ideologies which propagate contemporary antisocial extremism (e.g. abolition of law enforcement, left-liberal "environmentalism", Randian selfishness, vulture capitalism, bourgeois socialism, anti-racism, ethno-narcissism, etc.) and find that they more or less match this description. The Marxian formula, *"we do something yet we know not why we do it"* is true, but only in a partial way. Yes, we act in accordance with a certain ideology, unaware that we were formed within it, or primed to be supplicated to it. This occurs on a level below conscious awareness, but it is not *merely* unconscious. One can speak of the problems of false consciousness and ideology, how-

99   Emmet Kennedy, "'Ideology' from Destutt De Tracy to Marx", *Journal of the History of Ideas*, Vol. 40, No. 3, July-September 1979, pp. 353-368.

ever I think we have yet to look under the hood, so to speak, and examine the true psychological factors at work. In this section I shall take a step further and present new terminology which shall make a sharper distinction between ideology as it was originally described and how we know it now to be.

Using this understanding as a foundation, I propose a new concept, one which may help us to understand the psychological causes that produce such crippled cognitions. Contemporary American discourse is not blessed with a plurality of gifted thinkers, capable of navigating different worldviews and presenting sophisticated arguments. What we have are barren minded and sophistic dilettantes incapable of producing new ideas, and fit only for absorbing stultified and regressive slogans which can be easily deployed as loudly and obstinately as possible. Worse still, many who dominate industries of thought are themselves *ideophiles,* that is to say, they are individuals whose worldview can often be reduced to a singular, highly fetishized notion or appetite, enlarged by affect and self-aggrandizement, advanced not for the purpose of knowledge or truth or greater social unity, but often for petty retribution and status seeking.

At the heart of any ideology is always some a priori irrationality. I use irrational in the sense that its primacy or centrality cannot be justified in any logical or dispassionate sense; it is adopted and then spun into a system of thought because the thinker *wants* to adopt it. It is important to him not for any mathematical or philosophical reason, but because of its nearness to his heart. He desires it to be true and then makes it so with the aid of his rational faculties. For one to be able to rationalize some desire they must first possess a command of language, just as with ideology, where the irrational precedes the rational, so too does desire precede language. This is a well-known psychological fact demonstrated by theorists in both the constructivist school (like Jean Piaget) and within psychoanalysis (particularly Sigmund Freud, Melanie Klein, and Jacques Lacan). Before we can think, before we develop the schemas necessary for categorizing experience, we have desire. Desire propels us to engage with the world around us through a sequence of "*circular reactions*" (Piaget's term for the repetitive chain of reflexes used by the infant) until ultimately we develop the motor and linguistic competencies necessary for autonomous goal-oriented behavior. Thus to understand ideology we must understand that it is the end result of a process that began with desire (the irrational), proceeded with language (the rational), and develops into a complete system of thought that allows the individual to engage meaningfully with others and the world around him. Even before we have desire, we have temperament; we are primed by the influence of heritable biological and prenatal or environmental factors which set the table for all potential desires. Naturally, ideology is limited in its ability to permit us an objective view of existence, but this limitation is itself a human reality, and not a condemnation of ideology as such. The problem arises (which has led me to develop the concept of ideophilia) whereby ideology's foundation, the desire which is seeking satisfaction, is maladaptive or psychologically dysfunctional. Ideophilia, being defined as an ideological fixedness, is preceded by the Lacanian *objet petit a*, a loss caused by imposition which is transformed into an unattainable desire, just as ideology is preceded by a desire capable of being satisfied (that is, when properly conceived).

Given this negative connotation of ideology, which perhaps has justifiably emerged due to the sheer faultiness and capacity for destruction which false ideologies have demonstrated in the very recent past (and continue to do so), some have taken to prophesize a new age of post-ideological (or anti-ideological) thought which would liberate consciousness and usher in a new golden age of progress. This is not possible, and the belief in such a possibility betrays a fundamental psychological misunderstanding. Post-ideological thought is itself an illusion and an admission of one's naïveté and, perhaps even, sloppy thinking. One may step outside of a mental framework to better evaluate it, but there is always a return (or even, a progression). Ideology is an unavoidable feature and not a bug of human cognition, one that is necessary for giving a systematizing form to thought. The degree to which one claims to be free of ideology is the degree to which one is governed by the unconscious and is thus incapable of the necessary reflective analysis of one's own priors. In such cases what we often find is an internalized and unchallenged acceptance of the predominant strain of thought. An übermensch or free spirit such "thinkers" are not. The identity of the "free thinker" (a kind of synonym for, or an antecedent to, post-ideological thinking) is an illusory and intoxicating myth that allows one to feel powerful, distinct, and most importantly—superior. But it is only an illusion, or better still, a cognition of consent; it functions as a moral permission slip, allowing whoever possesses it to simultaneously roll around in the mud while still carrying the air of a king upon stepping out of the slop.

That some people adopt an ideology for reasons of conformity, social advancement, or as a psychological defense against trauma or dissonance is not a strike against ideology, but a testament to the adaptive power of the mind. The important question is not whether ideology is legitimate or not, but rather whether it is indicative of a true capacity for systematized thinking, or just mental scaffolding, cobbled together after the fact so as to maintain some rudimentary, if crude, order of the mind. Ideology is the global positioning system of the mind; it tells us what ideas or conclusions are important and which we may discard. So, too, does it tell us whom to trust and whom to dismiss. Ideology is negentropy manifest, and thus relentlessly dedicated to the conversion of the chaotic world of that which is external to us into something more phenomenologically sensible (our internal psychophysiological reality).

We would be right to be concerned by those individuals who are cognitively at risk, one could say. The more neurotic and cognitively inflexible one is, the more one is susceptible to ideology as psychological totalitarianism.[100] For these individuals, ideology ceases to be a mechanism for the development of systematized thought and instead becomes a trap of paranoia and conformity, designed to limit information processing rather than expand it. Its new function is that of a defense mechanism, tasked with protecting its host against all manner of existential horror. Such traumatized minds require the utmost certainty, which is precisely what psychological totalitarianism offers them. Ideology of this kind indicates to us the lack of agency, the impotency, which these types struggle with. Slaves to their own psychologi-

---

100   To clarify, I do not use totalitarianism in any political sense, but to express the potential for consciousness to become expansive and oppressive. Here, psychological totalitarianism or totalitarian consciousness should be understood as a process of aggressive domination and delimitation of the boundaries of thought, affect, and experience.

cal deficiency, they are powerless on their own. However, in their slavishness is found the capacity for power as a tool of the establishment. Though they may not be capable of creative power, their innate Dionysian madness makes them useful vessels for the strategic application of disorder. Weak people (or to put it more politely, people with low agency and high neuroticism), make for perfect tools of the powerful and the malevolent—they are natural born sycophants.

And so, we may now return to this notion of *ideophilia*. Setting aside factors of congenital predisposition, trauma, and sociopolitical machinations, we may say that—psychologically speaking—extremism has its roots in the myopic and fetishized idealization of some singular idea, concept, or notion. These individuals become fixated, psychologically arrested, and out of their arrested fixation erect a solipsistic worldview where all social and political issues may be reduced to a single cause. The desire of the ideologue may be placed in its correct position, understood and accepted as something that is finite and must be couched within the frame of some attainable and justifiable end. It requires visionary thought capable of establishing a multiplicity of goals, each understood as unfolding into the next as part of a grand plan. The desire of the 'correct' ideologue (or non-ideophilic thinker) has a limit, a pleasure which can be satisfied without producing an erratic remnant or leftover (Lacan's idea of *jouissance*). He pursues ends which can be made tangible and concrete, which are time-bound and finite, and which he is capable of articulating. Ideophilic desire is precisely the opposite; it is a desire that is never fully sated, which always demands more and thus harms the ideophile.[101] For the ideophile, the desire continually grows with time, requiring satisfactions of ever greater intensity—he goes beyond the pleasure principle into a

---

101 The desire of the ideophile is transgressive in a pathological and antisocial way. Transgression in and of itself is not necessarily destructive; play, for example, is often transgressive. Limitations are often established only after one has trespassed upon a territory which was not previously known. Transgression, in a sense, is innovative—a creative force. Therefore, we can imagine any number of circumstances where transgression can be consensual, even if only in an implicit fashion. Titillation and shock are fully human and utterly *typical* features of our psychology. But it is the peculiarly narcissistic expression of transgression which marks the character of the ideophile.

pleasure bordering on self-annihilation—as the object of his desire is an abstract signifier, or a signifier without a signified, an ineffable Other which only exists in the realm of the Symbolic (for example, the ideophile pursues "justice", "equality", "world peace", concepts wholly divorced from any true linguistic or conceptual basis and therefore unrealizable). If we take the Lacanian position that desire emerges from a lack, the ideologue is able to integrate this lack into himself (as he is capable of autonomous individuation) while the ideophile is in a perpetual state of psychological disintegration, and must continually draw upon the completeness of others to temporarily fill or alleviate his sense of absence.

In writing this, I am reminded of the phrase first popularized by feminist Carol Hanisch, "*the personal is political.*" Intended as a call to action, the slogan was used to argue that issues of personal relevance to women (e.g. abortion, sexuality, childcare, etc.) could only be resolved through collective action. Matters of personal importance were not something to be viewed as trivial, or local only to the individual, but necessitating society-wide political resolution. This mantra, though it emerged at a time of great tumultuousness, has endured and has since been appropriated for liberation movements of all types—not merely the second-wave feminism which spawned it. Owing to Hanisch (and the other activists who took this slogan up, of which there were many) grievance politics have become the norm, not the exception. Here we see a clear example of ideophilic thinking, where political conflicts can be reduced to one's woman-ness, or black-ness, or Jewish-ness, or white-ness, etc. Similarly, the ideophile's desired political solutions are themselves reductive and fetishized: more liberty, less government, no discrimination, more firearms, and so on. Ideophilic thinking is the opposite of holism; there is no need to view social and political issues in terms of a complete gestalt, and in fact, nuanced and holistic thought are directly antagonistic to this mode of thinking.

Setting aside the various critiques and alternative definitions of the term ideology, let us suppose for a moment that something like a "true" ideology—that is, a high-functioning and psychologically adaptive ideology—exists. Functional ideological thought *ought* to help give meaning to a person's existence, allow him to evaluate information, to orient him toward productive social engagement, open creative or intellectual opportunities, and *should* have proper explanatory power that allows him to formalize his life's history—to conceptualize his past, understand the present, and make relatively accurate predictions about the future. A proper system of thought (ideology) *ought* to facilitate individuation and social integration. Perhaps this is an abuse of the word, but insofar as we may contrast it to ideophilia, we may at least better understand how the "closed thinking" of the ideophile hinders anything approximating healthful psychosocial development. Rather, it resembles the monomania one might typically expect from the obsessive-compulsive or the paranoid schizophrenic. A "proper" ideology should provide one with insight into the inner workings of others; a consistent system of thought should help one reasonably determine cause and effect, and so on. But in the case of the ideophile, which we may think of as a degraded ideology, or perhaps more accurately a defense mechanism,[102] the external world and all its trappings are twisted so that they may conform to his fragile self-concept.

What then fractures (or outright prohibits the development of) one's self-concept? Under liberal techno-capital—with its concomitant forced associations, its repressive desublimations,[103] and its casual habit of traumatization—any sense of certainty, stability, and meaningful identity is denied, thus creating a void in the minds of Americans, making them vulnerable to ideophilic thought. This absence of identity and certainty are necessary byproducts of modern civilizational development; put *very* simply, modernity produces complexity, which in turn produces uncertainty, which then leaves the door wide open for the mass promulgation of extreme ideologies. What else, really, can one do when he is thrown into a sea of chaos without so much as a life preserver? He will look for the strongest horse; he will look for one who can speak to his suffering and provide an answer to

102   And if it is just an overly elaborated ego defense masquerading as an ideology, then it necessarily follows that its function is to patch up a dissociated and dysfunctional identity, rather than to construct an outwardly facing worldview free from the projection—as much as such a thing is even possible—of internal psychological conflicts.
103   A term coined by Herbert Marcuse to describe the culture of instant gratification afforded by modern society.

all his terrifying questions. Similarly, the absence of meaning, stability, and purpose, resulting from neoliberal capitalism's abolition of pro-social and traditional values, means that exposure to strong ideologies (and stronger ideologues) will empower the individual, leading him inevitably to fanaticism and extremism. And where does that path start? With few exceptions, this process begins with one simple idea. Director Christopher Nolan understood this well and skillfully implemented this concept in his 2010 film, *Inception*. In the film, Dom Cobb (played by Leonardo DiCaprio), a mentalist and professional thief uses the dream world to extract information from—or implant in—the mind of his targets. Of inception, Cobb says, *"An idea is like a virus. Resilient. Highly contagious. And even the smallest seed of an idea can grow. It can grow to define or destroy you."* Still later, Cobb tells us that *"Once an idea has taken hold of the brain it's almost impossible to eradicate. An idea that is fully formed—fully understood—that sticks; right in there somewhere."* Here Nolan is describing the reality of a mind gripped by ideophilia, utterly arrested and unable to free itself.

Having described the genesis and structure of ideophilia, I will now discuss the kinds of ideas which are seized upon with such zeal. Ideophilias always find their center in existential and interpersonal anxieties. Plagued by simple questions, *"who am I?"*; *"where do I belong?"*; *"where do I come from?"*; *"where am I going?"*; *"what will I leave behind when I die?"*; *"why do I suffer?"*; *"why must I be different?"*; *"why must I be alone?"*; *"why am I faithless?"* These are by no means trivial queries; far from it. They are among the most important questions one might ask of oneself. However, 21st century American *anti*-society does not offer any meaningful answers. More importantly, the means for finding such answers have either been obscured, lost to time (vis-à-vis the New World's hostility toward long-practiced rituals) or re-territorialized and directed toward the accumulation of profit. Patently insufficient (and not to mention psychopathic), man and woman alike are left spiritually hollow, angry, bitter, and self-loathing. Negative affect thus forms the core of the ideophile's cognitive matrix, which is why we find them impenetrable to and unmoved by reasoned argument. Before he is a fanatic, the ideophile is first and foremost *a victim*. Recognition of this fact is an important first step in consciousness transformation; however, it is all too easy to linger in this space, which is precisely what ideophiles do. And so, while they may imagine they have overcome their existential suffering, in truth they remain mired in it, and repeatedly re-invest in their pain, doomed to an endless cycle of repetition compulsions. The fetishized or fixated notions which then make up the foundation of the ideophile's worldview are disguised from themselves, and represented as their opposite (in Freudian terms, a reaction formation): fear becomes worship, vengeance becomes justice, hatred becomes love, etc. Unhealed psychic wounds and confusions about the true nature of existence, having been paved over with a megaton of propaganda, still seek a resolution—an acting upon. Which they do, but only through the incentives and frames provided by the establishment.

I write this now, on May 31st, 2020, after nearly a week of riots have ravaged major cities all around the country and threaten to reproduce themselves around the world. Triggered by the highly publicized death of George Floyd (allegedly at the hands of Minneapolis police officer Derek Chauvin), ideophiles tell us not only that White supremacy led to his death, but that White supremacists are organizing these riots in every city they take place. Ideophiles tell us about well-funded and highly organized White nationalist cells and how they are currently being activated in order to smear the good reputation of anti-racist and anti-fascist activists. Joy Reid of *MSNBC* and Mike Cernovich, author of *Gorilla Mindset,* have both taken to Twitter (on the same day, no less) to tell us how their political enemies are White supremacists. There couldn't have been a more synchronistic time for me to write this section, as ideophiles across the political spectrum are tripping all over themselves to identify White supremacy as the cause of all the problems occurring at this particular moment in history. This is a perfect crystallization of every argument I have made thus far—how the ideophile is utterly incapable of viewing the world as it is, but rather through a monomaniacal lens which grotesquely distorts their perception.[104]

104 A few additional thoughts on the subject before I depart. Narcissistic distance allows one to believe and disbelieve, to disbelieve and still act. The object from which one's ideology is taken may not be a wholly perfect representation

Sigmund Freud, Sabina Spielrein, and the Death Instinct as Political Will

In our discussion of the extremist's identity, I spoke of how the life instinct and the death instinct find their expression in the will of the political actor. I am now prepared to discuss this point more fully. It is my view that all political actions, whether it be intentional, eusocial, rational or aimless, antisocial and irrational, are essentially expressions of the death instinct. We are left then with a most important question—whose conception of the death instinct describes each kind of political action?

While the death instinct[105] has become known as part of Freud's project, it originated in the work of Sabina Spielrein, a one-time patient of Carl Jung and later a colleague of Freud's who would go on to become an accomplished psychoanalyst in her own right. She introduced the concept of the death instinct in 1912[106] which inspired Freud to develop the idea more fully eight years later. Though Spielrein's work shows her to be more in line with the Freudian tradition of psychoanalysis than the Jungian one, there is a clear distinction between how Spielrein and Freud conceptualized the death instinct—one that has critical implications for the argument I am presenting here.

In Freud's work, the death instinct is the home of aggressive and destructive impulses, seating it in direct antagonism to his notion of *Eros*, or the life instinct. *Thanatos,* the impulse towards aggression, is a force that jeopardizes civilizational development and therefore must be thwarted by a cultural superego. Aggres-

---

of their belief, and in fact, there may not be *any* representation of that ideology which justifies their identification with it, nonetheless it is their narcissism which permits them to take it on all the same. Ideophilia is permissiveness; it is an avenue for satisfaction of the id. This psychological explanation lends credibility to Zizek's turn of the classic Marxian line, *"We know what we do is false, yet we do it all the same."* Conscious buy-in to an ideology, which is a choice in one sense, but a false choice in another, nonetheless dismisses ideology as a wholly unconscious process. Consider the myth of the vampire, who can only be allowed into one's home by choice; an ideology can only enter one's soul through some level of volition, of conscious acceptance.

105   It was given a variety of names by the different psychoanalytic thinkers who employed the concept: Wilhelm Stekel termed it *Thanatos,* Paul Federn called it *Mortido,* and under Edoardo Weiss it went by the name *Destrudo.*

106   Sabina Spielrein, "Destruction as the Cause of Coming into Being", *Journal for Psychoanalytic and Psychopathological Research,* Vol. 4, 1912, pp. 464-503.

sion is tamed by the guilt-producing superego, though at great cost to the individual; Freud saw this social massaging of man's psyche as the cause for his suffering. Of course, aggression is never dispelled completely; rather it may be sublimated into the pursuit of a higher purpose or expressed in more proximal and self-destructive ways (e.g. interpersonal conflict, drug addiction, etc.) However, as Spielrein's argued in her seminal paper, human beings are torn between a static desire to remain as they are and a dynamic one to reproduce, but that the reproductive instinct contains an aspect that is destructive of oneself as well as creative. In pregnancy, there is creation but also destruction—a child is born, but the woman's body is ravaged in the process. Psychologically as well, her life as a pre-maternal feminine character is gone forever, but out of that death comes her life as a mother. Self-overcoming similarly follows this pattern of destruction–creation; every change in our identity demands that we say farewell to who we once were. And so, in contrast to Freud, Spielrein's concept of the death instinct found it in service of creation, rather than standing in opposition to it. In this view we understand that the death instinct is essential and necessary if radical transformation is to occur.

The Freudian model of psychology maps best when overlaid upon the highly dysfunctional, and in particular highly neurotic, class of human animal. As a universal theory of human psychology, Freudian theory leaves much to be desired. This should not be a surprise as Freud's career was in large part dedicated to the phenomenon of neurosis (a fact recognized, and even regretted by many who followed in his wake), particularly of the upper class, Jewish, and female kind. The death drive as described by Freud quite nicely describes the psychology of the antisocial extremist, regardless of political affiliation. Theirs is a kind of uncalculated, visionless yet vaguely utopian attempt at political engagement that simultaneously denies productive vitality and the will to life while directing their energy into denying the will of others as well. It is one thing to make a project out of refuting one's own existence, but to marshal one's own will and resources to stifle the attempts of other people, in particular people with whom one is not even in direct conflict, crosses the psychological threshold from mere dysfunction into petulant antisocial

conduct. Extremism is distinct from moderate and radical political action in that it has no creative aim. *Thanatos-as-extremism*
is an act of pure destruction, a project with no true goal, and
is therefore self-serving in the final analysis. The feminist who
seeks the abolition of all men, the anarchist who seeks the destruction of all hierarchies, the White nationalist, Wahabbist, or
Zionist who desires the termination of his racial enemies[107]—all
of these expressions of extremism (to say nothing of those I have
not mentioned) are clear examples of a political manifestation of
the death instinct as per Freud.

Spielrein's model clearly indicates to us the *true* psychological
model, i.e. the healthy and adaptive psychological model for understanding the dialectic of creative and destructive impulses as
it relates to our discussion of political engagement. It should not
surprise us to realize that it would take a woman to understand
this phenomenon with such clarity; woman better understands
the role destruction plays in the birthing of something new, as
her own body is transformed by the miracle of childbirth. *Destruction-as-becoming* is in fact the psychological foundation
for radical, visionary politics whereas extremism as defined in
this book is resentful; radical politics are revolutionary while extremist politics are retributive. For the radical, destruction is a
means to an end. A new political order can only arise from the
ashes of one that has just been put to rest. And to clarify, I am
speaking of a *civil* destruction—the death of morally failed systems, not individuals. The extremist seeks the death of peoples,
the destruction of property, and the disruption of all life-giving
and order-preserving institutions. Whether we speak of Brenton
Tarrant who senselessly murdered 51 people while injuring 49
others in March of 2019, James Hodgkinson who attempted to
murder Republican legislators in June of 2017, or any number of
other tragic events, they all can be reduced to a single psychological fact: the extremist manifests the Freudian death drive for his
own dysfunctional purposes.

As I write this on June 3rd of 2020, extremists (allegedly members of Antifa, but possibly federal agent provocateurs as well)
have left crates full of bricks in every major city where riots are

107 This is not to suggest that all who identify as such *do*, but rather to highlight that tendency among extremists.

currently taking place. Though they claim to protest peacefully against a tyrannical order, the past week has seen churches, businesses, police stations, and private residences ransacked and destroyed. All the while, radical political actors (both of the "left" and "right", who in my estimation, comprise the true "center" of American politics) are urging civility and advocating for novel solutions which, if faithfully enacted, could not only provide the means to redress the grievances of the past but finally propel our stagnant country forward.

Extremists of the higher and more socially integrated types (e.g. journalists, self-styled analysts, organizers and activists, educators) use their political capital not for personal and societal redemption, but rather as a weapon to punish those individuals and groups who (in fact, or in an archetypal fashion) have wronged them, while the lower and less socially integrated types (e.g. NEETs, the economically displaced, the genetically compromised or otherwise mentally ill), who, having finally found a sense of community by networking with people of similar experience and background, use their small window into the political to stymie creative and novel thought by enforcing the narrow boundaries of ideology that permit the existence of their newfound community.[108]

Now let us return to the matter at hand: the powers of critique

108   A brief digression from my main point before we continue; it is interesting to note the symbolic acuity which extremists possess. Possibly owing to the presence of higher than average neuroticism (as defined by the Five Factor model, a greater capacity for negative affect), they more keenly pick up on the archetypal cues which give away their opposition long before they have been revealed as such. I have observed (and in the past puzzled over, though no longer) the speed with which I was identified as a "rightist" by my left-leaning colleagues and friends, despite not having conceived of myself as such. Perhaps it has more to do with their psychoticism (as defined by Hans Eysenck, here having the meaning of aggression and interpersonal hostility) that their biological need to sniff out threats finds its mark so easily. Though perhaps I am being too charitable, and the causality is in the other direction. Brad Verhulst who co-authored a paper in 2012 that claimed conservatives scored higher in psychoticism than liberals (a fact which was proven to be true *in the reverse*) may tell us that the sheer intensity of their psychological dysfunction creates the enemy rather than identifies them. I would like to offer a caveat here by saying that it is not necessarily the case that left-liberals are in general more likely to be extremists, though, perhaps the last six or seven years of constant anti-fascist street violence may suggest otherwise.

and destruction are indeed mighty, but they are also abilities that mostly anyone can wield. Aggression and force are powers that can be wielded without impunity—they require neither sophistication nor erudition. It is only when destruction has a teleological framing, when it is used purposefully and ethically and with a desire to bring about a greater and more fulfilling event that it can be justified psychologically, morally, or philosophically. Might *can* (and often does) make right, but in valorizing such a tactic one is left with no moral or intellectual defense when it is *he* who must succumb to the might of another. Sheer aggression and force-of-will alone must not be seen as the tools for individual and civilizational transformation; to do so would only beget a cycle of senseless brutality, thus extinguishing the very things that make us human—our compassion, our ability to defer and to negotiate, and our ability to step outside of the dispassionate cruelty of Darwinian selection. Once again, I can only marvel at how the events which are currently taking place, the riots all around the country, attest to this psychological reality. Anti-racist and anti-fascist activities, who despite their violent modus operandi, have largely avoided any serious moral investigation precisely because of the strength of their moral argument (though, to be fair, it is a moral argument which enjoys the support of corporations, the media, and the dominant political structure). Setting aside the power analysis which may invalidate this argument, in the eyes of millions of Americans who believe wholeheartedly that racism and discrimination are moral evils, and who believe that our system of law enforcement is deeply flawed—when they see individuals (whether they are formally affiliated with Antifa, Black Lives Matter, or are simply acting out of their own accord) senselessly destroying private property, and in some cases attacking and even murdering those around them, their formerly unwavering support suddenly finds itself questioned. Destruction for its own sake is not a cause that right-thinking and psychologically well-developed people can support.

In a situation such as ours where a visionary politician or activist presents a more vital, moral, and comprehensive model for political action, we should expect to see marginalization, character assassination, and accusations of "*dangerous extremism*" follow shortly behind them. Massive social resources will then be marshaled to socially, economically, and legally attack them. A bipartisan effort will emerge to morally reframe their arguments while never articulating or rebuffing them, all while a litany of "experts" will be called upon to provide "*The Truth*". Though Freud was right to tell us that our cultural superego works to suppress aggression, we must also recognize that a morally decayed and power-hungry society will provide "legitimate" avenues for aggressive impulses to find their expression. America may decry sexism, but it will strategically permit open misogyny when the interests of the powerful are threatened (e.g. Tulsi Gabbard's 2020 presidential campaign, Ann Coulter when she broke ranks with Bush era neoconservatives, etc.) Homophobia is condemned, unless of course it is directed at a political enemy (e.g. political cartoons depicting Vladimir Putin and Donald Trump engaging in sordid homo-erotic acts). And when a visionary thinker emerges to provide us with a radical new paradigm, so too should we recognize that they will become an acceptable target for our repressed aggressive impulses by the same people and institutions that would otherwise condemn such actions. In doing so, creation *itself* is under attack, not just those brave individuals willing to embrace *destruction-as-becoming*. Extremists in both the upper and lower crusts of American society harm our collective ability for radical transformation, and dramatically impoverish our collective consciousness through these casual acts of society-wide traumatization.

How a Society Becomes Extreme

Up until this point I have addressed the problem of extremism in piecemeal fashion, opting to discuss the phenomenon incrementally. While I still have not presented my full analysis of the extremist's psychology, we now have a common language and framework by which to approach the problem. At this point you should be aware of the forces complicit in the problem of extremism, but we have not yet discussed in detail the psychological methodology which these actors employ. It is now time to do just that.

Once more applying the Jouvenelian model, we understand that extremism is a top-down phenomenon, originating among the powerful and then floating downstream through the various institutions of power and influence. It is a widely held belief that revolutions (be they political, intellectual, artistic, and so on) arise organically from the bottom, but many a great scholarly work[109] [110] utterly demolish this faulty assumption. Nothing that has ever occurred, whether we speak of the American Revolution, the Bolshevik Revolution, Mussolini's or Napoleon's rise to power, to use some recent examples, without the patronage of the upper classes. The extremist capture of the United States is no exception. Before we may begin I must credit many of the insights provided in this section to the work of Polish psychiatrist Andrzej Lobaczewski, who, after collecting several decade's worth of work studying the psychology of totalitarian regimes (in particular the USSR), published them in 2006 after a lifetime of censorship and meddling by members of the intellectual elite (including former National Security Advisor Zbigniew Brzezinski).[111]

In his book, Lobaczewski described a *"hysteroidal cycle"* whereby the privileged classes transmit maladaptive attitudes and behaviors over the course of multiple generations, the final result of which is a phenomenon he termed *"macrosocial dysfunction"*. Put succinctly, the dysfunctions of the few (the privileged classes) become the dysfunctions of the many (everyone else). These hysteroidal cycles consist of alternating durations of 'happy times' and 'unhappy times', where, in the former, moral and psychological knowledge pertaining to issues of psychopathology is suppressed, while the latter represents an excavation and exploration of this previously forbidden trove of knowledge. The subsequent recovery of this knowledge is then used to rectify problems created by the hoarding of this forgotten information.

Lobaczewski views social injustice as integral to the perpetuation of mass psychological dis-ease, seeing as, in his view, the upper classes necessarily exploit the lower classes in order to attain (and preserve) their wealth and good fortune.[112] Through

109   C.A. Bond, *Nemesis*, (Imperium Press, 2019).

110   Christopher Caldwell, *The Age of Entitlement: America Since the Sixties*, (Simon & Schuster, 2020).

111   Andrzej Lobaczewski, *Political Ponerology: A Science on the Nature of Evil Adjusted for Political Purposes*, (Red Pill Press, 2006).

112   The happiness and prosperity of this first phase of the cycle itself may be

conversive and hysterical reasoning, these privileged classes se-
lectively perceive information in such a way that they can more
easily justify profiting from their ill-gotten gains and marginalizing the moral, mental, and labor values of those they exploit.
Each subsequent generation suffers from a progressive "*atrophy
of natural critical faculties*" (p. 170) which ultimately culminates
in the censorship, persecution, and even genocide of those underprivileged classes, whose very existence challenges the pathological worldview of the privileged.

Control of the psychologically normal is achieved first by the
embedding of a "*pathologically hypersensitive censor*" (p. 177)
within the citizenry themselves. These are in effect, ego defenses
deployed by the upper classes who seek to preserve their own
positive self-image. It is these defects of the ego, in the form of
"*egoism, egotism, and egocentrism*" (p. 177) which is the root psychological causes of what he terms *characteropathic failings*.[113]
Moreover, not only will these privileged classes adopt pathological—and ultimately violent—attitudes toward those they rule,
but they will even develop contempt and antagonism toward
competing nations that adhere to a healthier and more psychologically integrated approach in their governance. (We may easily look at the present day United States and see a manifestation
of what Lobaczewski describes; the American upper classes regularly castigate their constituents for their moral failings, their
lack of sophistication, etc., all the while decrying other nations
which, however imperfectly they may be achieved, work far more
diligently to protect and provide for their people. Countries such
as Hungary, Poland, Russia, Iran, and China come to mind immediately).

In Lobaczewski's ponerological model, a society is comprised
of two essential psychological types: the characteropathic and
the normal. Characteropaths are those individuals who suffer
some biological condition (such as brain trauma) or genetic predisposition (for example, a personality disorder) and are thus
given to a psychological disposition of evil. Whether they are the

predicated on the suppression and persecution of some minority group, or the
under classes more broadly.
113   Modern researchers of psychopathology would characterize this phenomenon as a personality disorder.

progenitors of such evil or are merely the lackeys who happily execute the evil will of others is of little consequence. We may also call these types *maladapts*. The 'normals' are greater in number than the maladapts, and have an innate moral character in addition to a well-adapted psychological profile, but are often incapable of recognizing (or even properly resisting) this psychology of evil due to their naïve condition.

Any institution can find itself infiltrated by maladapts who then work to bend that institution to their will, which in turn signals a fertile ground for other maladapts and *pathocrats* to gain entry (pathocrats being defined as any political actor given to a psychology of evil). It is the nature of the characteropath to exploit structural weaknesses in an organization so that he may overtake it, turning it to his own diabolical purposes. Should he fail it would be his death; if the characteropath cannot ascend to the role of pathocrat, he would either wash out of society due to his own weakness and lack of social utility or be driven out by those members of polite society who have become wise to his game. We may say then that subversion and domination are among the defining traits of the characteropath. They are a biological type who cannot thrive under normal conditions—they must destroy what is good and healthy in order to live. Fortunately for us, Lobaczewski argues that,

> the pathocracy's dominance will weaken imperceptibly but steadily, finally leading to a situation wherein the society of normal people reaches for power. This is a nightmare vision to the psychopaths. That the biological, psychological, moral, and economic destruction of the majority of normal people becomes, for the pathocrat, a biological necessity. (p. 142)

The essential civilizational struggle, in Lobaczewski's view, lies between "the normal people" and the pathocrats; it is a conflict which has occurred in every civilization for as long as human societies have existed and will persist for as long as our species draws breath.

As I have noted already, Lobaczewski looks to the sciences of biology and genetics to find the origin of the characteropath. It is of interest to note that Lobaczewski was among the last class of psychiatrists in his homeland to be trained in these disciplines before the Soviets censored them and restricted the discipline to the study of Pavlovian concepts.[114] While the science of psycho-pathology has progressed a great deal since Lobaczewski's time as a student (and there still remains a great deal of disagreement over the proper diagnostic criteria for many of these conditions), I will reproduce his findings as he described them so that the reader may appreciate them in their full and unadulterated con-text. Primarily, Lobaczewski connects the biological dimension of the characteropath's psychopathology to a condition of "*schiz-oidia*". The schizoid is recognized by an acute hypersensitivity and characteristic distrustfulness; they are inattentive to the emotions of others, quickly adopt extreme positions, and retali-ate harshly (and immediately) for perceived slights against them. Typically eccentric, they are prone to projecting *("superimpos-ing"* in Lobaczewski's words) *"erroneous, pejorative interpreta-tions of other people's intentions"* (p. 123). In simpler terms, they are quick to malign others without sufficient reason for doing so. They are drawn to moral causes, although they *"actually in-flict damage upon themselves and others"* (p. 123). Owing to their impoverished worldview, they are overly pessimistic and misan-thropic as regards human nature. Schizoids have a *"dull pallor of emotion"* and *"consider themselves intellectually superior to ordi-nary people"* (p. 124).

However, we should not limit our concern to these dysfunc-tional individuals alone. Exposure to those who exhibit dys-functional personalities can twist the minds of a normal person, capturing them in the vortex of their mental illness, not unlike a starship caught in the tractor beam of some intergalactic war-monger. Proximity to characteropaths, then, is as great a risk to the average person as their mere existence is. The pathocrat is a natural parasite who can only thrive in an environment that is explicitly hostile to the needs and demands of the average per-son. As such, characteropaths frantically work to pervert the or-ganizations they join by manipulating and distorting language (to use Lobaczewski's phrase, by employing the method known as "*spellbinding*") to provide cover for their true intentions. The

114 Here we see a clear bit of historical proof for Lobaczewski's argument, as the very same phenomenon is present in modern universities.

characteropath sets himself up as an integral member of the institution, enshrining himself as a necessary priestly type who may then provide the ideological weight for the yet-to-be-adopted belief system. Where these individuals are unable to directly influence and redirect the energies of a given organization, they will form alliances with more charismatic types who may themselves be less pathological, or simply possess an earthier charm and personal magnetism that allows them to capture the imagination of a people, even without any kind of intellectual or ideological acumen to support their campaign.

Often, these pathocrats can attract less dysfunctional types (Lobaczewski calls them "*skirtoids*"), who dutifully execute their dictates and assist in maintaining the new moral infrastructure. These skirtoids

> are vital, egotistical, and thick-skinned individuals who make good soldiers because of their endurance and psychological resistance. In peacetime, however, they are incapable of understanding life's subtler matters or rearing children prudently. They are happy in primitive surroundings; a comfortable environment easily causes hysterization within them. They are rigidly conservative in all areas and supportive of governments that rule with a heavy hand. (p. 136)

These psychopaths (pathocrats), often being physically incapable of enacting the methods they propagate through oral and written sophistry, are heavily reliant on these skirtoids and a third type, which he calls "*jackals*". These individuals are "*hired as professional and mercenary killers by various groups and who so quickly and easily take up arms as a means of political struggle; no human feelings interfere with their nefarious plans.*" (p. 136). But Lobaczewski stops at the point of categorizing these types as fitting within either the skirtoidal or psychopathic dimensions of psychopathology, but rather suggests that "*we should assume this type to be a product of a cross between lesser taints of various deviations.*" (p. 136). Furthermore, he states

> mate-selection psychology produces pairings which bilaterally represent various anomalies. Carriers of two or even three lesser deviational factors should thus be more

frequent. A jackal could then be imagined as the carrier of schizoidal traits in combination with some other psychopathy, e.g. essential psychopathy or skirtoidism. (p. 136)

It is critical for these pathocratic spellbinders to nudge the normal majority away from what Lobaczewski calls its *"congenital instinctive infrastructure"* (p. 60). He repeatedly emphasizes the necessity for the *"common sense"* (p. 188) of the normal majority to prevail for a society to maintain its moral center and to thrive intellectually, creatively, economically, and spiritually. To separate the majority from their common sense, the spellbinder employs the use of doubletalk as his chief strategy for nudging people away from their natural instincts.

As a brief aside, it is interesting to note that Cass Sunstein, a legal scholar and administrator of the Office of Information and Regulatory Affairs from 2009 until 2012 wrote about the necessity for influencing popular decision making—specifically in the areas of finance, health, schooling, marriage, and environmentalism—in a book titled, coincidentally enough, *Nudge*.[115] Sunstein has long been held in suspicion by the American right for his positions on gun control and free speech. In particular, Sunstein argued in a 2008 paper (co-authored by Adrian Vermeule) titled *Conspiracy Theories*, that:

> Some conspiracy theories create serious risks. They do not merely undermine democratic debate; in extreme cases, they create or fuel violence. If government can dispel such theories, it should do so. One problem is that its efforts might be counterproductive, because efforts to rebut conspiracy theories also legitimate them. We have suggested, however, that government can minimize this effect by rebutting more rather than fewer theories, by enlisting independent groups to supply rebuttals, and by cognitive infiltration designed to break up the crippled epistemology of conspiracy minded groups and informationally isolated social networks.[116] (p. 29)

115   Richard H. Thaler & Cass Sunstein, *Nudge: Improving Decisions About Health, Wealth, and Happiness,* (Penguin Books: 2009).
116   Cass R. Sunstein & Adrian Vermule, "Conspiracy Theories", *Harvard Public Law Working Paper,* No.8-03, January 15th, 2018.

Sunstein and Vermule home in on conspiracies related to terrorism, in particular the attacks which occurred on September 11th, 2001. They discuss other conspiracies (e.g. MKUltra, Watergate, Operation Northwoods, etc.) and begrudgingly admit that conspiracy minded individuals have, in fact, been vindicated in their skepticism of the official narrative (p. 5). Nevertheless, Sunstein has a long standing preoccupation with the control of information flow and human behavior, and may very well serve as a prime example of Lobaczewski's pathocratic spellbinder, who seeks to nudge people away from their deeply evolved instincts toward attitudes that favor the governing classes.

With that behind us, we may now return to the central argument. The process of ponerization (the overcoding of a society's ethical structure from moral to immoral) necessitates a dual semantic layer, wherein the outer layer is used rhetorically against the target while the inner layer reinforces membership among those psychopaths embedded within the power structure. In effect, these differing meanings serve to re-stratify the classes of a ponerogenic culture. The spellbinders (and their collaborators) immediately recognize its hermeneutic meaning; it is only after prolonged exposure (and great labor on the part of the masses) that the targets of this ponerogenic speech are ever availed of its true meaning. To put this in our current context, we may look at certain phrases (e.g. "*diversity is our strength*") and understand how the meaning differs depending on who utters it; diversity may be a strength for the spellbinder, but as Robert Putnam[117] argued it proves to be a problem for those outside of the spellbinding class.

It should be noted that the use of such language does not just overcode cognition; in its final phase cognition is suspended entirely. The thinking, therefore, is done elsewhere—offshored to the pathocratic class, who now think for the entire society. In this way, there is a close relation between Lobaczewski's concept of spellbinding and Robert Jay Lifton's notion of the "*thought-terminating cliché*". Because the true meaning of such paralogical statements is withheld from the larger population, no meaningful engagement can be had (either intrapersonally nor

---

117   Robert D. Putnam, *Bowling Alone: The Collapse and Revival of American Community,* (Touchstone Books, by Simon & Schuster, 2001).

interpersonally) about the concept or its application, and so it is flatly accepted without resistance. Examples of such paralogical statements, or thought-terminating clichés if you prefer, would include *"support our troops"*; *"believe women"*; *"meat is murder"*; *"silence is violence"*; *"for national security"*; and so on. The person echoing these statements does not think beyond the slogan, which impairs the person on the other end of the utterance's ability to meaningfully dialogue with the sloganeer. Depending on the psychological profile of the receiver, they may simply accept this utterance passively, thus willfully joining the sloganeer's cult, or they may partition their own consciousness out of apathy or confusion—an act which has the effect of self-annihilation, and in the end, submission to the authority of the cliché.

I have made this point already, but it bears elaboration: innately these spellbinders are people who cannot function in a healthy society, and moreover, feel wronged by it. As part of their paranoid ideations, they perceive themselves as marginalized and persecuted (although in a certain sense they are correct; given their predilection for manipulation and harm, the natural response is one of ostracism). The narcissism and self-absorption of the psychopath leads him to create a kind of hero myth that justifies his own actions (if not to himself, then to those he seeks dominion over). By necessity, the characteropath casts himself as a savior—as one who has graciously taken up the causes of liberation and nobility. This approach proves advantageous for him if he operates within a society where actual injustice is present and easily identifiable (which is usually the case). Lobaczewski points out that these types construct ideological unions which are predicated upon 1) the exaltation of a wronged other, 2) the radical redressing of that wrong, and 3) the higher values of the characteropathic individuals who have usurped the organization.

Individual psychological failings (be they psychopaths, or abnormal and deficient in some other way) are then moralized into a revolutionary credo that gives them just cause for retribution, thus providing sufficient motivation to deny any self-examination. Were this technique not so repugnant, one could admire its ingenuity; the moral wickedness of their conduct (which, once stripped of its romanticism and paramoralisms, would surely be apparent to any outsider) is neatly excused and then expelled.

Such a practice is especially important for counteracting the functional conscience in those with a more typical psychological profile. The fact that true injustice *does* exist, and that this new ideology *claims to resist it* means that inductees into this new culture will be more easily swayed into rationalizing the spellbinder's doubletalk, and never question its truer esoteric meaning.

For the skeptical reader, we can dispense with the fanciful terminology and simply look to the very real circumstances we observe in our current situation. Take the language of victimization and its myriad expressions—racism, sexism, xenophobia, transphobia, homophobia, islamophobia, ableism, to name a few. Let us begin with the use of the term "racism": initially, the word was used to describe an irrational and seething hatred of other races. Those noble of heart and sensitive to the plight of, say, African Americans, knew in their souls that they did not harbor animosity toward Blacks and therefore willingly acclimated to the changing cultural and political dialectics. But as per the hermeneutic tradition of the spellbinder, the term came to take on a new meaning—that of power and privilege. The eternal revolt against racial discrimination required a new meaning for a new time, against a new generation of foes. Now, to be racist no longer means being an unsophisticated bigot, full of hatred; instead, it means to enjoy the privilege of cultural, historical, and political continuity. To be a racist in 21st century America is to hold power, unearned power, over the dispossessed other. In one sense, that power is one of an unbroken continuity of being—but in a more immediate and political sense it is about institutional hegemony. Whites, being privileged, now find themselves swimming in a racist undercurrent, where every action, every errant glance, each thoughtless utterance is actually a demonstration of sinister, unjustifiable power and racial superiority that must be deconstructed (and then disassembled). As the usage of this term and the ability to effect political and cultural change based on the desire to annihilate racism grows, more Americans find themselves scratching their heads at the new power this term wields. "*How is that racist? That doesn't make sense. I don't hate Blacks or Hispanics.*" And likely they don't. Only one no longer has to hate non-Whites in order to be racist, one merely has to *exist* in order to be racist. The jargon of pathocratic psychopathy has thus emerged from its cocoon different, changed, and now more powerful than when it first appeared.

Sexism worked in this way too; the willful discrimination and marginalization of women meant something far different a few decades ago. Whereas any social role that was denied to women was understood to be sexist, now any circumstance which affects women *differently* is evidence of sexual discrimination and oppression. With such an elastic definition, instances of racism and sexism now explode with regularity. Similarly with homophobia, islamophobia, transphobia, xenophobia, and the like, the spellbinding hermeneutics of prejudice grant more power to the characteropath and further oppress the normal and the psychologically fit. Of particular insidiousness is the use of the suffix 'phobia'; the use of a clearly understood medical and psychiatric terminology, 'phobia' has been grafted to a sociopolitical system of linguistics that overcodes an entire range of cognitions and affects, reducing them to a singular phenomenon: fear. The application of this faux-medical term paints anyone who demonstrates anything other than unflinching support (and submission) towards an underprivileged group as fearful, despotic, and mentally ill.

A new meaning for millennia old biological and evolutionary normalcies was created to psychologically wound average people who are not nearly as Machiavellian and sinister as those spellbinders responsible for creating this new moral-linguistic landscape. A whole range of emotional responses (e.g. disgust, confusion, ambivalence, reticence, self-preservation, etc.) are no longer legitimated for anyone outside of the spellbinding class, and especially for those unwilling to subjugate themselves to it. It is difficult to overstate the effect this has on the mind—by constantly changing the moral language and rules of social engagement, consciousness is split, and new sub-personalities are created which enter into a constant state of conflict. Not only do these terms create a new moral, linguistic, and affective landscape, but they also radically redraw the sociopolitical structure, creating new castes of privileged and unprivileged members, and allotting people to these new classes based on their willingness to conform to an ever-changing set of demands.

Another example would be the constantly evolving charge of anti-Semitism. Clearly it was once understood that claims of anti-Semitism were intended to characterize attitudes and conduct that were explicitly (and perhaps even implicitly) discriminatory or hostile toward Jewish people. Presently (and much like the plastic definition of racism), it is now used to designate *any* othering of Jews, be it negative or positive. And so, folded into the original meaning of these terms (hatred and fear) is any impulse toward differentiation (another "common sense" instinct as Lobaczewski would say). Interestingly, the very use of the term is curious because it creates a cleavage in the Gentile's understanding of who precisely *is* a Semite. Anti-Semitism is fundamentally about anti-Jewish sentiment, but the term Semite is a cultural, linguistic, and racial designation that encompasses a far broader grouping of peoples than simply that of the Jewish individual. Once more we see how spellbinders use language to fracture and limit the cognitive abilities of the average person.

The originators of these spells create the circumstances by which a healthy society is carved up under the new rules of engagement. But as I have already pointed out, their progeny merely inherit this system of rules and logic, often without any insight into its genesis. This phenomenon is not unlike the transmission of rituals and taboos, whereby people unthinkingly inherit these dictums but are oblivious to their intention, and so merely act on them in rote, unconscious fashion. This is how psychopathic tendencies are transmitted intergenerationally—at first as an intentional means of control, and then merely as a commonplace and thoughtless habit, not unlike how one brushes their teeth before retiring to bed. The situation becomes far worse for the inheritors of this system, as they merely acquire these attitudes through the mechanisms of conditioning and modeling. They are indoctrinated into a pathological worldview which dictates every relationship they enter, every career they take up, each choice and each breath. Children do not just inherit the material or biological traits of their parents, but also their ideological ones (particularly the farther one goes up the socioeconomic ladder, where the stakes are higher). Of course, these conditions are guaranteed to degenerate over time, as the inheritors of this system possess none of the insight, none of the self-awareness of

their forefathers, and are subsequently left with fewer psychological tools with which to manage themselves or their pathological
reactions. While they may acquire their power second-hand, it
comes with a litany of irrational and hysterical impulses which
can neither be contextualized nor dissipated. Heavy indeed is
the head that wears the crown. Naturally, psychopaths wound
themselves with their psychological contortions, ego defenses,
and general antisocial conduct. We understand very easily as
well that they wound those who are made the targets of their
pathology. But what is less well understood is how those around
them—their wives, husbands, children, nieces and nephews,
too—are victimized by their pathological and misanthropic
outlook. Their impoverished psychological worldview becomes
a mental prison that their kin rarely, if ever, escapes. Worse still,
those that do escape become permanent outcasts, as they—not
unlike cult members—have broken out of an intergenerational
cycle of psychopathy only to find little in the way of community
outside of it. However, it should be said that they often end up
worse than cult members. In many cases, these individuals lose
affiliations of race, religion, social class, and more personally,
blood relations. For these individuals it is difficult to quantify
which is worse, the spellbinding or the ostracism.

One further point before we depart from this Lobaczewskian
analysis: once spellbinders find themselves in positions of power, they entrench psychopathic attitudes and behaviors into the
culture through codification and law-making. This fact is well
understood by all. But what is less well understood, or at least less
accepted by all, is the sociological repercussion of the act. When
progressives talk about systemic racism or institutional prejudice, this is the phenomenon they are describing—a kind of cultural miasma which survives the men and women who birthed
it, thus securing a future for the attitudes and methods of control
that arose from the individuals themselves. They are preserved
not only in the legal or ethical statutes recorded by the pathocrat, but in the archetype of personhood who follows in their
wake. The characteristics of hostility, fearfulness, and the need
for control transcend the individuals themselves, the legal and
ethical infrastructure, and begin to acquire a near-metaphysi-
cal quality. In a sense they become more real than their material

origins, despite their intangible nature. We may say this is true of any institutional culture, not only the ones we hear progressives discuss so often. I speak of the *integrity* of the institution which survives and is perceptible to those with the proper frame of mind to recognize it.

Delegitimizing Identity as a Catalyst to Extremism

I began this chapter by discussing the primacy of identity and its connection to the political process. My argument emphasized the critical roles that myth, parable, and narrative play in the healthful psychological development of identity. I provided examples of how deconstructing and appropriating a people's foundational myths can disrupt both the individual and collective sense of self. Following this, I gave some examples of deleterious narratives which negatively impact a people, pushing them away from the salubrious and toward the dysgenic. Once the central pillars of the individuation process are toppled, we are all but helpless to make up the difference, particularly when they are replaced with toxic simulacra—psychological facsimiles—that are transient and wholly inferior to the real thing. We become ripe for exploitation, which is precisely what malevolent actors seek to do. Just like the stripes of a zebra confer a defensive advantage to the group, as Americans we too had collective defenses, a civilization-scale immune system which operated to shield us from would-be predators. But our defenses are now down, and we are vulnerable, we *have been vulnerable*, and are all too easy to plunder.

At this point I would like to elaborate on the finer points of identity, and further develop an analysis of the mechanisms used to delegitimize identity. It has been said so many times that it has become a boring and loathsome cliché, but it is true—we are social beings. However, when we don't know who we are, where we came from, or to whom we belong, the trauma of existential violation throws us into a state of chaos. We become desperate for answers, but moreover, desperate for belonging. If we are not able to provide those things for ourselves, to our betterment, then someone else will. And they will do so to further their own ends. It would behoove us to ignore this pathway to extremism.

It is possible to critique oneself out of existence, and this fact has as much to do with the current degraded state of sociopolitical affairs as any military, historical, or economic event of the last hundred years. Peoples have recovered from economic collapses. They have survived continual warfare. Plagues, natural disasters—all these and more—have wrought unimaginable havoc but somehow, humanity has managed to survive. But the curious anomaly of our era is the pattern of unrelenting self-criticism and deconstruction as perpetrated by academics, media personalities, and even the political class itself. We have always been an inquisitive, philosophical, and self-reflecting people, but whereas these inquiries were broadly pointed in the direction of greater clarity and understanding, they have turned toward the direct refutation of material reality and societal health. Since their inception, disciplines like philosophy, theology, and science have broached questions about the nature of man and woman, but never did they deny such categories existed. Scientists and medical researchers perfected the art of childbirth, but never did they entertain the notion of extending that biological privilege to men. Racial taxonomists (however the concept of race has been defined over time) have always sought an understanding of the characteristics that differentiated our species, but no people in the history of mankind turned inquiries such as those found in anthropology and biology into disciplines of racial self-erasure. Religion, the most centrally important and profound intellectual pursuit, having birthed all other pursuits and made civilization possible (and possibly, even, life worth living), has evolved from a system of values into one of anti-values; whereas it once beseeched us to transcend our worst impulses, it now demands that we consecrate those impoverished instincts as our highest moral pursuits. None of this is to say that these investigations (and the institutions which supported them) were always good, or noble, or that any conclusions drawn in the past were always correct. Though we are flawed and imperfectible, we can at least say that our history of intellectual thought is one that respected the contributions of the past and tried to build constructively upon them.

The United States has always been a troubled nation, one that has committed unjustifiable transgression after unjustifiable transgression. Often, in our attempts to rectify the mistakes of the past, we have only created more problems for ourselves, and consequently, for the world around us. There is no golden era which we can look upon and say, "*that was the perfect moment. At least then we had gotten everything right.*" It should be recognized, however, that this is not unique to the European peoples of North America. The choirs of civilizations long since passed do not sing in glorious harmony, rather, they bellow at us in anguished cacophonies. What *is* unique about America is the attitude we take to the past—in particular, *our* past. At the precise moment when our country found itself in a position to break from the horrors of a tortured world history, and with the resources necessary to launch head first into a future of prosperity and achievement that would make God himself blush, we took a different path. For all the destruction we wrought upon the world, we also brought beauty and order. To our detriment we have decided to highlight the former and neglect the latter. As the preeminent force on the North American continent, our forefathers surveyed the human landscape for equals and were left wanting. We now look at ourselves in much the same way generations past viewed the Amerindians, the Africans, the Aboriginals, the Orientals, and so on—as a savage and irredeemable people with no justified claim for dignity and thus, no grounds for survival. Thus began our ongoing project of self-deconstruction.

Let us begin this examination of identity by looking first at the racial component. Once again, I will draw from the work of Zach Goldberg, a researcher who has revealed much about the changing American attitudes with regards to issues of race. While there does appear to be a great deal of concordance between the average American rightist and leftist about the racial sinfulness of America's past, it is the White liberal who gleefully leads the charge in the war for racial equality. Taken from an article he published for *Tablet Magazine*,[118] the figures below indicate the startlingly isolated phenomenon of out-group bias and equality-fixation observed among White liberals. Whereas conservatives are hostile to illegal immigration and somewhere on the spectrum of skeptical-to-favorable towards legal immi-

---

118   Zach Goldberg, "America's White Saviors", *Tablet Magazine,* June 5th, 2019, https://www.tabletmag.com/sections/news/articles/americas-white-saviors.

gration (with such caveats being that legal immigration ought to be merit-based, with an emphasis on assimilation), White liberals are far more enthusiastic about the prospect of continuing the project of racial and ethnic diversification (even at the expense of their non-White political cohort, as observed in figure 1). White liberals uphold a view that sociologist Eric Kaufman calls *"asymmetrical multiculturalism"*—the idea that all racial and cultural views ought to be recognized, with a clear exception made for those pertaining to White identity. White liberals being more educated,[119] more activist oriented (figure 3), more likely to consume political media (figure 4), making up a greater proportion of internet users (figure 5), and less likely to live in diversified areas,[120] there are some interesting conclusions we may draw from these data points to better understand the breakdown of racial identity among American Whites.

On balance, do you think having an increasing number of people of many different races, ethnic groups and nationalities in the US makes this country a better place to live, a worse place to live, or does it make no difference?

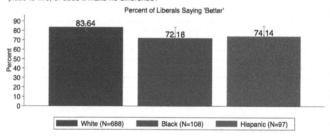

Source: American National Elections Studies 2018 Pilot Survey

119   Lydia Saad, Jeffrey M. Jones & Megan Brenan, "Understanding Shifts in Democratic Party Ideology", *Gallup*, February 19th, 2019, https://news.gallup.com/poll/246806/understanding-shifts-democratic-party-ideology.aspx.
120   Pew Research Center, "Political Polarization in the American Public", *U.S. Politics and Policy*, June 12th, 2014, https://www.people-press.org/2014/06/12/political-polarization-in-the-american-public/.

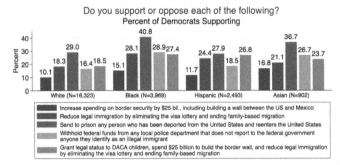

Source: 2018 Cooperative Congressional Election Study

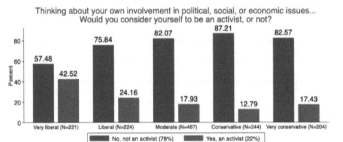

Source: Washington Post/Kaiser Family Foundation Poll: Survey on Political Rallygoing and Activism (January 24-February 22, 2018

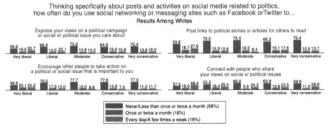

Note. N: Very liberal=221, Liberal=224, Moderate=465, Conservative=243, Very conservative=204
Source: Washington Post/Kaiser Family Foundation Poll: Survey on Political Rallygoing and Activism (January 24-February 22, 2018)

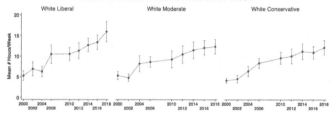

Mean Number of Internet Hours Per Week

Source: General Social Survey

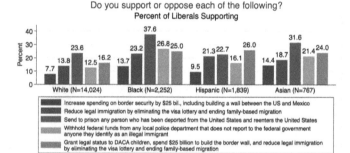

Do you support or oppose each of the following?
Percent of Liberals Supporting

Source: 2018 Cooperative Congressional Election Study

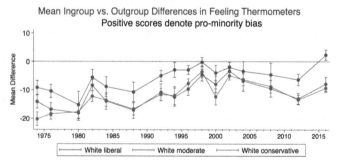

Mean Ingroup vs. Outgroup Differences in Feeling Thermometers
Positive scores denote pro-minority bias

Source: American National Election Study

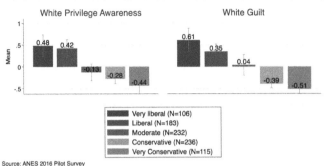

Source: ANES 2016 Pilot Survey

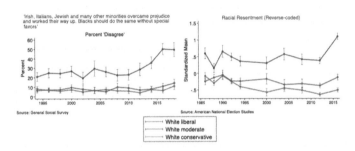

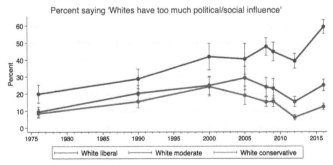

Source: Data pooled from American National Election Studies (1975, 2000, 2012, 2016); General Social Survey (1990); National Conference for Community and Justice: Intergroup Relations Survey (2000, 2005)

Are we spending too much, too little, or about the right amount on improving the conditions of blacks?

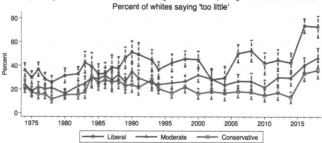

Source: General Social Survey

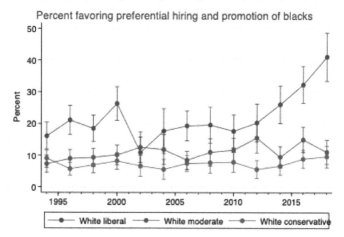

Source: General Social Survey

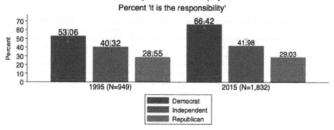

Source: Washington Post Poll: Race Relations (1995); CNN/Kaiser Family Foundation Poll: Survey of Americans on Race (2015)

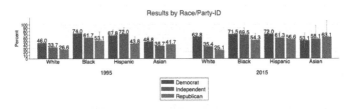

Results by Race/Party-ID

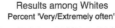

Results among Whites
Percent 'Very/Extremely often'

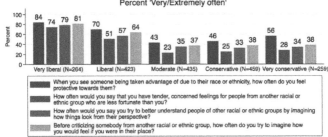

Source: ANES 2018 Pilot Survey

Mean In-Group Bias by Race/Ethnicity
Scores denote mean differences in warmth between in-group and out-group feeling thermometers (0-100 scale)

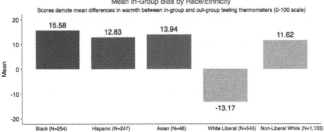

Source: ANES 2018 Pilot Survey

Mean In-Group Bias Score Among Whites
Positive/Negative scores denote pro-ingroup/outgroup biases, respectively

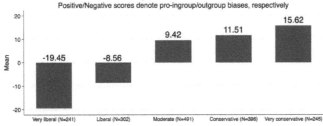

Source: ANES 2018 Pilot Survey

How serious a problem do you think racial discrimination against blacks is in this country--
a very serious problem, a somewhat serious problem, not too serious, or not at all serious?

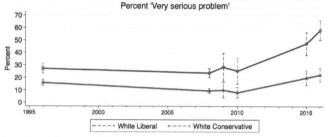

Source: Data pooled from the Roper Center for Public Opinion Research data archive

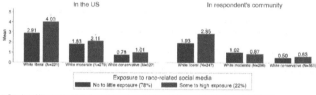

Note. Dependent variables are summed indexes of responses to questions asking whether blacks are treated less fairly than whites in the workplace, stores or restaurants, when applying for a loan or mortage, in dealing with the police, in the courts, and when voting in elections

Source: Pew Racial Attitudes Survey (February, 2016)

Please tell us your thoughts on whether people from the following groups have an advantage
or disadvantage, or neither an advantage nor disadvantage for getting ahead in the United States.
1=Large disadvantage, 2=Some disadvantage, 3=Neither advantage nor disadvantage, 4=Some advantage, 5=Large advantage

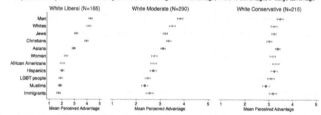

Source: Associated Press-NORC Poll, February 2018

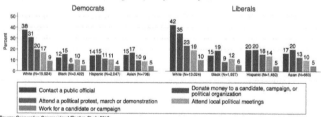

Source: Cooperative Congressional Election Study 2018

But before we do, it is important to revisit some other findings we have already discussed (and introduce a few new ones). We know from the work of Jonathan Haidt that the liberal moral foundation is rooted in Harm/Care and Fairness/Reciprocity.[121] We also know that liberals rate more highly in the Compassion dimension of Agreeableness than conservatives who rate higher in Politeness.[122] Liberals are more empathic (both cognitively in terms of perspective taking and emotionally in terms of experiential identification) than conservatives,[123] but are also prone to *concept creep* whereby the broader conceptual breadth of certain issues (abuse, bullying, prejudice, and trauma) are larger and more expansive than in conservatives, having the effect of *"problematizing harmful behaviors that were previously tolerated but might also leave people over-sensitive and emotionally fragile"*,[124] as shown by McGrath et al. Of note in this study is the finding that while empathy, liberalism, and concept breadth were all associated, sensitivity towards injustice was directed *toward others but not the self.* Empathy has shown to be negatively correlated with a preference for social hierarchy.[125] A study of collective guilt conducted in 2006 by Roccas, Klar, and Liviatan found that of the two types of group identification (in-group attachment and in-group glorification), in-group attachment was identified as being more prone to collective guilt and more closely associated with a liberal political ideology. This was validated by measuring Israeli attachment, glorification, and guilt for their treatment of Palestinians. Roccas found that Israeli glo-

---

121   Jesse Graham, Jonathan Haidt, & Brian A. Nosek, "Liberals and Conservatives Rely on Different Sets of Moral Foundations", *Journal of Personality and Social Psychology,* Vol. 96, No. 5, 2009, pp. 1029-1046.

122   Jacob B. Hirsh, Colin G. DeYoung, Xiaowen Xu, & Jordan B. Peterson, "Compassionate Liberals and Polite Conservatives: Associations of Agreeableness With Political Ideology and Moral Values", *Personality and Social Psychology Bulletin,* Vol. 36, Issue. 5, April 6th, 2010, pp. 655-664.

123   Tomkins, S.S., *Affect Imagery Consciousness,* Vol.1 (New York: Springer, 1962).

124   Melanie J. McGrath, Kathryn Randall-Dzerdz, Melissa A. Wheeler, Sean Murphy, & Nick Haslam, "Concept creepers: Individual differences in harm-related concepts and their correlates", *Personality and Individual Differences,* Vol. 147, Issue 1, September 2019, pp. 79-84.

125   Adam Waytz, Ravi Iyer, Liane Young, & Jesse Graham, "Ideological Differences in the Expanse of Empathy", *Claremont symposium on applied social psychology series. Social psychology of political polarization,* 2016, pp. 61-77.

rifiers were more likely to justify their government's actions and thus experienced less guilt.[126] Other work in the area of collective guilt has found that inducing collective guilt increases a perpetrator group members' support for reconciliatory action, fosters positive attitudes towards the victimized group and a desire to apologize for the harm perpetrated.[127] Collective shame, interestingly enough, elicits ingroup-directed anger and a desire to distance oneself from the ingroup.[128] Finally, I have noted elsewhere in this text that liberals rate more highly in both the Big Five traits Openness and Neuroticism, and trait Psychoticism (as found in Eysenck's PEN model) than conservatives.

Given the overrepresentation of left-liberals in education and media, and that liberals are on average more highly educated, consume more political content, are politically active at a higher rate than their peers, and have the personality profile that they do (high cognitive and emotional empathy, high Openness, high Neuroticism, high Psychoticism), their crisis of racial identity (that of a negative type) is quite easy to understand.[129] White left-liberals (and by extension right-liberals, though their differing temperament puts them in a unique position) are under attack by a full spectrum cultural program which exploits their

126   Roccas, Sonia, Klar, Yechiel, Liviatan, Ido, "The paradox of group-based guilt: Modes of national identification, conflict, vehemence, and reactions to the in-group's moral violations", *Journal of Personality and Social Psychology,* Vol. 91, Issue. 4, 2006, pp. 698-711.

127   Mark A. Ferguson, Nyla R. Branscombe, "The social psychology of collective guilt", *Collective emotions: Perspectives from psychology, philosophy, and sociology,* pp. 251-265, (Oxford, January 2014)

128   Dai, Juntao Doris, "#NotAllWhites: Liberal-leaning Whites Racially Disidentify in Response to Trump-Related Group-Image Threat", *ResearchWorks Archive,* 2020.

129   We should, perhaps, give the devil his due. While the consequences of left-liberal White Savior-ism have proven calamitous, it is worthwhile to acknowledge the kernel of virtue at the heart of their conduct. Left-liberals are crushed by the burden of self-awareness; as flawed as their interior self-image is, they are, to a large degree, more cognizant of themselves than right-liberals. At the least, they have some measure of narrative sophistication (perhaps owing to greater levels of education, or the observed psychometrical differences discussed so far), whereas right-liberals are entirely self-deluded and unaware of their terminal case of mistaken identity. In this regard, the hysteria of left is not unlike that of the woman whose mental state continually degrades in the face of an obstinate and unresponsive man (the right-liberal, in this case).

natural temperament in pursuit of total psychological and spir-itual dehumanization. Of course, it is only White liberals who experience this in its full glory, as non-White left-liberals of all types are more secure in their identity (not just racial, but re-ligious, ethnic, cultural, etc.) due to the American attitude of asymmetrical multiculturalism. I would like to be clear on this point, however: non-Whites in America are not impervious to this problem. The American neoliberal monoculture assimilates immigrants into the same mold of cosmopolitan and anti-spiri-tualist consumerism into which American Whites have already been subsumed. While there are some who are able to retain au-thentic features of their racial, religious, linguistic, and cultural identity, there are those who are not so lucky; over time, all will find themselves stripped of their authentic character and reter-ritorialized by neoliberal grievance-based intersectional poli-tics. Even with the demographic decline of Whites in America, political and cultural hegemony is still predominantly White (and Jewish, though not for demographic reasons), which means that the entire population continues to be held hostage by the guilt-and-resentment-based politics of White liberals. Whatev-er autonomy or individuation that non-Whites can retain for themselves is still framed within the larger dysfunction of White liberal politics.

Cthulhu's leftward drift means that despite the biological, lin-guistic, and regional differences which separate Americans from one another, the American monoculture flattens out these dif-ferences by subjecting the nation (and increasingly, the world) to the same program of education and media. Conservative or right-liberal types are certainly made distinct by their biologi-cal characteristics, but when faced with the overwhelming force of mass media, portable technology (and all its inherent repres-sive desublimations), punitive and censorious corporations, and the ever present need for social conformity, they are rendered helpless to offer any meaningful resistance against the guilt and shame based elimination of identity. The dialectic of Liberalism (neoconservative republicanism vs. neoliberal progressivism), reinforced by both State and Capital, firmly locks the American population into a frenzied battle which most are incapable of es-caping.

What then, has become of the United States' historical and mythological identity? The primary identity which now defines modern America is that of a global victimizer, one that inflicted its petty bigotry on the minority population first and then exported that same hateful ideology to the rest of the world. So it was decided during the 1960's, one of the most violent periods in the country's history. Despite instituting legislation that extended the democratic franchise to African Americans, the story that would be told for the next 56 years was of the nation's unrepentant evil. America victimized its Africans, its Indians, its women, its Jews, its homosexuals, its Muslims, and so forth. The double-barreled blast of lawfare and criminally biased education ensured that generations of Americans would never again be able to look back at their history with pride. America's religion suffered a similar though double pronged fate. Not only was Christianity delegitimized on moral grounds (as a patriarchal, oppressive, and imperialistic force), but it was also challenged on intellectual grounds by scientific rationalists. Christianity was wrong because it was a force for domination, but it was also wrong because it could not be proven true on empirical grounds. No proof for God meant that God didn't exist—and if God didn't exist, if Christ did not die and then rise from his grave, then Christianity couldn't be true. We can only repent by renouncing all the identities we have, as they are inexorably tied to one another. Whiteness is bound up in heterosexuality and its normative family values. So, too, is it bound up in its supremacist Christianity, its capitalism, its Anglocentrism, its art and architecture, its philosophy, and so on. All legitimate identities were negated by this accusation, and their continued suppression is an integral part of healing the wound of oppression, liberating the victims, and ensuring that America can never again commit such heinously evil acts ever again.

And so, one way the delegitimizing of identity may be achieved is through mythological erasure. Remove the story people tell themselves *about themselves* and replace it with a new one. Having achieved this, you must then reinforce the myth with new stories and new parables which will strengthen the self-concept that you *want* the population to have. One such example would be the idea of White privilege. Creating a myth like White privilege taps into an entire matrix of automatic and self-attacking cognitions which guarantee that, upon introducing the virus (and sufficiently amplifying it through media), over time the mind will be able to sustain it independently. To accomplish this goal, one must have complete (or near complete) institutional control. All the storytelling institutions must operate in lockstep to continually reinforce the desired narratives and create new ones when needed.

It is necessary, then, to deny the people their creative enterprises, turning them into consumers instead of creators. While not every man is an artist in the strictest sense of the word, we all have some capacity for communicating our emotional experiences to others in some unique way. Identity construction and mythic integration are themselves creative acts; if we are denied this essential psychological reality, we cease to be *individuals* but rather disintegrated *dividuals* of some other person's making. Deny man the means for self-expression on his terms and he has no choice but to speak in your language. He may even conflate the experiences presented to him with those of his own, thus alienating him from his lived experience. Without the ability to creatively construct his identity, to conceptualize his experience in terms that he uniquely understands for *himself*, contextualized by *his* community, man becomes something easily molded and controlled. Modern American identities are passively accepted by the transformed consumer classes; developed by academic spellbinders and reified by figures of cultural influence, so chosen not because they actually represent anything of significance or because they are trusted members of some community, but rather precisely because they are willing to play the role of an amplifier (or to use the language of mass marketing, *an influencer*). That is to say, their willingness to compromise themselves—to purge their consciousness and accept another in its place—is what earns them the role of high priest or priestess of the American empire. These new identities are by their very nature flimsy and disposable, and in need of constant reinforcement (or replacement); they exist in a zero-sum atmosphere, where competition with authentic and eusocial identities must be denied, for the moment that any identity with a history, with a moral and spiritual weight to it enters the fray, individuals find their allure difficult, if not impossible, to resist.

It is often the time-boundedness of our modern offerings which secures their fate. It is their mass produced and poorly constructed appeal-to-the-lowest-common-denominator quality which guarantees only a momentary possession of the collective American mind. That our modern creations are only fit for consumption—only meant to satisfy the needs of corporate stockholders—and possessing only the capacity for titillation and disruption demonstrates the fact that they can't truly move minds and spirits—only anaesthetizes them. And it is precisely when these two identities (we shall call them the classical and the modern) collide, that both the radical and the extremist are born. To the thoroughly modern person, ensconced in a 21st century mode of thought and feeling, the classical identity appears regressive, barbaric, and extreme. The inverse, naturally, is true as well. For the classically minded person, moderns are rudderless, spiritually bankrupt, cognitively facile, lazy, careless, and superficial. In the face of ever-expanding commoditization and phenomenological deterritorialization, the classical identity faces the potential for extinction. With each successive generation, both indigenous and migrant peoples inducted into the technological society find themselves robbed of their essential humanity, only to be reterritorialized with the consciousness of the 21st century man.

Pathocrats and opportunists alike, keen to this fact, can easily resolve this problem through appropriating earlier practices and modes of being to maintain their hegemonic power. Those individuals disenchanted by modernity may attempt what Terence McKenna called *"the archaic revival"*, by throwing off the shackles of the consumerist, information saturated mass culture, in favor of something with historical and cultural weight. Hungry for a mode of being that grounds them in a time and place, which provides a context and a sense of direction and alleviates the awful existential decay of the contemporary American scene, these individuals look to the distant past and even to other cultures to find existential authenticity and sustainability. Over the last few decades, we have seen this phenomenon quite clearly with the renewed interest in psychedelics, meditation and yoga, polyamory, minimalism, and similar trappings of older—and often alien—cultures. But in our commoditized and fetishized culture of opportunism, these practices (and by extension, their modern practitioners) find themselves effortlessly reintegrated back onto the narcissistic and pathological neoliberal plantation. Thus, identity overcoding and commoditization are among the first and most effective tools for psychological delegitimization.

The other technique pathocrats use to delegitimize identity is to disarm the population's common sense by attacking naturally evolved senses such as disgust. Disgust has been identified as a powerful moral intuition, most likely having evolved as a response to biological contaminants. Further investigations into this evolved response have shown that disgust is triggered by nine factors including, "*food, body products, animals, sexual behaviors, contact with death or corpses, violations of the exterior envelope of the body (including gore and deformity), poor hygiene, interpersonal contamination (contact with unsavory human beings), and certain moral offenses*".[130] It is likely that disgust is related to withdrawal, as aggression is decreased whenever the disgust response is triggered.[131] Aggression engages the approach-circuit of the brain whereas disgust seemingly engages the withdraw-circuitry, triggering an autonomic response that lowers blood pressure and heart rate, changes respiratory behavior, and decreases skin conductance.[132] We know as well that provoking the disgust response leads to changes in mate selection and attitudes toward members of the out-group; those who are highly disgust-sensitive are more likely to find members of their in-group attractive[133] and hold negative attitudes toward out-groups.[134] Research into hygiene has shown the disgust re-

130 Paul Rozin, Jonathan Haidt, & Clark R. McCauley, "Disgust", *Handbook of emotions*, pp.757-776, (The Guilford Press, 2008).

131 Richard J. Davidson, Paul Ekman, Clifford D. Saron, Joseph A. Senulis, Wallace V. Friesen, "Approach-withdrawal and cerebral asymmetry: Emotional expression and brain physiology: I", *Journal of Personaliy and Social Psychology*, Vol. 58, Issue 2, 1990, pp. 330-341.

132 The ability to conduct electricity associated with the sweat glands, which occurs more frequently/intensely during states of physiological arousal.

133 Nicholas Phelan & John E. Edlund, "How Disgust Affects Romantic Attraction: the Influence of Moods on Judgments of Attractiveness", *Evolutionary Psychological Science,* Vol. 2, September 24th, 2015, pp. 16-23

134 Carlos David Navarrete & Daniel M.T. Fessler, "Disease avoidance and ethnocentrism: the effects of disease vulnerability and disgust sensitivity on in-

sponse to strongly predict negative attitudes towards obese individuals,[135] and moreover, that obesity-related disgust overlaps with certain moral values.[136] Women are generally more disgust sensitive than men, especially regarding sexual disgust or general repulsiveness—likely a development with evolutionary implications toward sexual selectivity.[137] Studies have also found that disgust has been known to predict prejudice and discrimination;[138] using passive viewing tasks and fMRI, researchers were able to demonstrate that racial prejudice elicited disgusted facial expressions.

Clearly the disgust response is an important feature in maintaining the health of the individual as well as the collective, and so if you seek to disarm the social immune system it is necessary to diminish or impair the ability to feel disgust. It ought to be clear to us now that early education, media messaging, and strong peer pressure are deployed to nudge individuals away from their evolutionarily developed common sense and into positions and attitudes more favorable to the pathocracy. Those who do not conform to the messaging are simply forced to suppress their independent and autonomous emotions out of self-preservation. Doubt, insecurity, shame, and guilt then become powerful tools of the pathocratic class; triggering these emotions within the underclass allows the pathocracy to subjugate them more fully as normal individuals are no longer able to engage with reality directly. Instead they become trapped in a state of existential claustrophobia, unable to validate their own experience, having been denied their capacity for self-correction

tergroup attitudes", *Evolution and Human Behavior,* Vol. 27, Issue 4, July 2006, pp. 270-282.

135   Lenny R. Vartanian, Tara Trewartha, & Eric J. Vanman, "Disgust predicts prejudice and discrimination toward individuals with obesity", *Journal of Applied Social Psychology,* Vol. 46, Issue 6, June 2016, pp. 369-375.

136   Carmelo M. Vicario, Robert D. Rafal, Davide Martino, & Alessio Avenanti, "Core, social and moral disgust are bounded: A review on behavioral and neural bases of repugnance in clinical disorders", *Neuroscience & Biobehavioral Reviews,* Vol. 80, September 2017, pp. 185-200.

137   Sonja Rohrmann, Henrik Hopp, & Markus Quirin, "Gender Differences in Psychophysiological Responses to Disgust", *Journal of Psychophysiology,* Vol. 22, 2008, pp. 65-75.

138   Yunzhe Liu, Wanjun Lin, Pengfei Xu, Dandan Zhang, & Yuejia Luo, "Neural basis of disgust perception in racial prejudice", *Human Brain Mapping,* Vol. 36, Issue 12, December 2015, pp. 5275-5286.

out of fear of being attacked or ostracized. Alienation establishes itself as the primary social reality, as interpersonal relations of all forms become estranged due to the panicked need for self-preservation. Of course, the pathocracy has a wider array of devices with which to achieve its social engineering and can deploy them in any number of ways so as to assault a diverse and self-attacking underclass.

A similar phenomenon occurs with empathy, though the way it is manipulated may be even more tyrannical. Under a system of psychopolitics (we may also call this "*affective politics*"), pathocrats overcode the emotional response of the population so as to guide them into accepting everything from the ideologies of the system, to its policies, and even its desired social relations. In a proper psychosocial setting, empathy develops out of relations of trust and security, out of love and communication, all of which facilitate the individuation of the child. But when these primary social relations are subject to political antagonisms, empathy (both in its cognitive form, e.g. mentally imagining the other's circumstance, and its affective form, e.g. simulating the emotional experience of the other) is transformed from its primary role into one of co-dependency and permissiveness. Empathy is not synonymous with saccharine acceptance and lenient tolerance; rather, empathy fully allows for a complex range of emotions including anger, hatred, and the desire for vengeance. Psychologically healthy empathy may lead one to understand the actions of another, while also leading them to feel disdain or contempt for them. Affect itself has become something politicized, simultaneously denied in certain contexts while encouraged in others, always viewed in some perspectival fashion, with the end of reinforcing accepted political norms. We find that the justification for a given feeling finds itself dependent on the political status of the identities in question. Empathy may be demanded of one political subject (the protestor who fights for his freedom) but denied to the other (the law enforcement officer responsible for maintaining order, some disinterested bystander). Whom we are allowed to identify with, to find solidarity with, or even to merely *attempt* an understanding of is politicized and attempting to empathize with a delegitimized subject may jeopardize one's security within his community. Under psychopolitics, our affective range comes pre-loaded with assumptions and beliefs which bias our capacity for understanding and identification in ways that favor the dominant narratives. A White man and a Black man get into a conflict—who was justified in their actions? A woman and a man engage in a heated argument—who is correct? Who is expected to capitulate? Some imagined pre-existing history or justification may find its way into the equation which biases our evaluation in dysfunctional and antisocial ways. The science of governance in the modern age (and perhaps, in all ages) is the science of understanding the individual and then utilizing that knowledge to shape him into the kind of man the powerful need him to be. When we look at the rash of populist movements across the globe and the outbreak of anarchist violence on the streets of every industrial nation on the planet, we see the inevitable result of the governmental technique of delegitimization.

When Antisocial Extremism Becomes Violent

Long ago, the United States passed a point of no return, crossing a biological cliff whereby it could no longer maintain its trajectory of exponential growth by naturalistic means (or at least, could not or *would not* continue to democratically extend this growth), nor could justify the social and economic projects it undertook to anyone outside of the power structure. Arguments for staying the course are self-referential and tautological, centered on ideas about the market, the individual, and other more ethereal abstractions such as justice, fairness, and equality. The logic of America's method of international governance as secured by its military and economic force is the logic of self-amputation; we will deposit an arm in China, a leg in Saudi Arabia, our torso in Belgium, and we will be better for it. That is to say, the means for accruing (and exploiting) resources became the task of a multiplicity of nations, each working myopically on but a part of the economic gestalt. What we have now is a global factory, labored at by the many for the benefit of the few. No single nation, no single people group can hope for autonomy or self-sufficiency in such a system. And so, Americans, particularly those without the means or connections necessary to find an advantage in this system, necessarily discover that they are hopelessly disenfranchised and alienated in every sense of the word. Alienated from

God, from labor, from art and from love, and most significantly, from one another—above all, Americans are alienated *from
themselves*, for the social and material necessities which could
have provided them a healthy, stable, and enriched environment
in which to grow, to connect with others, to find an education,
a vocation, and inspiration, are now denied to them. The self,
which Christopher Lasch wrote so insightfully about,[139] rather
than being filled with purpose and duty, is now something like a
fully inflated helium balloon—engorged, yes, but filled with no
meaningful substance, all the while letting loose air until ultimately deflating completely.

Taking a bird's eye view of the situation, when a people pri-
oritizes values of abstraction over and above those of the social
order, the result is an inevitable unraveling of their very existence. Whether their fate is a terminal one is a question to be answered on the individual basis of each civilization. Nonetheless,
the United States, which began as a project of discrete peoples,
each with a history, a culture, a God, and a unique way of life,
gave way to all manner of fetishized abstractions which saw the
founding stock willfully unseat themselves from not only power
and influence, but relevancy, on their own continent. The logic that felled the founding stock of this nation has continued to
work its sinister black magic on every ethnic group to step foot
on the North American continent since. Its fulfillment cannot
be denied, and we seem to be rather committed to proving that
very point.

What does a child do when he finds himself unable to achieve
autonomy and denied the resources of love, labor, and discipline?
He acts out. Tumultuous feelings spill out of him in fits of chaotic rage. Americans have collectively become that traumatized
child. During the period between the mid-1950s and early 1970s,
America saw great political upheaval, including political demonstrations, riots, and assassinations. The 1990s saw much of the
same, though perhaps not as concentrated but every bit as violent
and socially destructive. Since the turn of the century, America
has not gone more than a few years at a time without domestic terror attacks, protests, race riots, or paroxysms of so-called

139 Christopher Lasch, *The Culture of Narcissism,* (W.W. Norton & Company,
1979).

lone-wolf violence. America is an extreme place, based on extreme values, governed by extreme people, and populated by an ever more extreme citizenry. What is truly remarkable, however, is that the country has not descended into the kind of street violence that is seemingly more common among our neighbors in the Global South. While Americans find their lives punctuated by violence of every kind (be it rhetorical, institutional, political, or otherwise), the prophesized eschaton has not yet arrived and does not appear to be on the horizon, regardless of how much the collective American consciousness prays for its advent. Despite the seeming crisis of legitimacy with which American neoliberal capitalism appears to be confronted, the United States has achieved a level of stability (barring some truly unforeseeable black swan event) for the time being. This stability, paradoxically, is itself a catalyst for extremist violence. With no forthcoming solution to mounting tensions and our resentments only deepening, the problem of political extremism is magnified among those individuals and communities with the deepest commitments to their ideology.

We know from various studies[140] [141] [142] [143] [144] that material deprivation and political exclusion are major drivers of violence, be it community-oriented or political. Both relative *and* absolute poverty have been identified as causal factors on the issue of violence, but so too have regime repressiveness and political marginalization played key roles in this ongoing problem. Here's an equation for political extremism that should make sense to even the most computationally challenged reader: break apart

140   Ronald C. Kramer, "Poverty, Inequality, and Youth Violence", *The ANNALS of the American Academy of Political and Social Science,* Vol. 567, Issue 1, January 1st, 2000, pp. 123-139.

141   E. Britt Patterson, "Poverty, Income, Inequality, And Community Crime Rates", *Criminology,* Vol. 29, Issue 4, November 1991, pp. 755-776.

142   Edward S. Shihadeh, & Graham C. Ousey, "Industrial Restructuring and Violence: The Link between Entry-Level Jobs, Economic Deprivation, and Black and White Homicide", *Social Forces,* Vol. 77, Issue 1, September 1998.

143   Erich Weede, "Some new evidence on correlates of political violence: income inequality, regime repressiveness, and economic development", *European Sociological Review,* Vol. 3, Issue 2, September 1987, pp. 97-108.

144   Bert Burraston, Stephen J. Watts, James C. McCutcheon, & Karli Province, "Relative Deprivation, Absolute Deprivation, and Homicide: Testing an Interaction Between Income Inequality and Disadvantage", *Homicide Studies,* Vol. 23, Issue 1, February 1st, 2019, pp. 3-19.

naturally forming communities, and then withhold the material necessities for human thriving and finally designate a political subject (or subjects) fit for condemnation. Multiply the emergent resentment, fear, and envy with wall-to-wall propaganda, and then repeat as many times as necessary. It's the political equivalent of the old *cup-and-ball* trick performed by magicians and confidence men; the pathocracy can continually move and disguise the ball to distract and antagonize the populace, all the while ensuring that they never lose control of the game—or its winnings. But this is a dangerous game, and the confidence man cannot guarantee that he will always escape the anger of those he tricks.

As the undeniable failure of this project reveals itself more profoundly (evidenced by the COVID-19 pandemic and the race riots which followed in its wake), only the most obstinately committed—and compromised—individuals dare to claim otherwise. Our dominant paradigms (conservatism, progressivism, democracy, reactionary thought), having all been defenestrated over the last half century, have left the radical and the extremist as the only viable political identities available. I don't use viable in any moral sense, but rather to speak of their vitalism, accessibility, and legitimacy in the minds of politically oriented people. Most people will not fall into either category, not actively, but all that is needed for social upheaval to occur is a dedicated and well-organized minority.

When pushed to the limit of their ability to tolerate suffering, humiliation, powerlessness, and isolation, some individuals will move beyond low-risk antisocial behavior (poisoning nascent political movements via gossip, shibboleth fetishism, and purity spiraling), and engage in the kind of self-mythologizing that turns their impotent rage into a grander act of will to power. Shootings at synagogues, churches, mosques, schools, etc., are the least likely examples of extremism, but are also the most immediate acts of retribution available to those with low agency and no imagination. Such individuals prefer the role of the martyr over that of the organizer. It should be said, however, that even acts such as these are facilitated by the power structure. The FBI has a long history of infiltrating so-called terrorist groups[145]

145   Heather Maher. "How the FBI Helps Terrorists Succeed." *The Atlantic,*

and foiling lone wolf terror plots,[146] arguing that they are keeping the country safe when a more apt description might be that
they are justifying their own existence by facilitating the very
crimes they are supposed to prevent.[147] A practice which came to
prominence in the wake of the 9/11 attacks saw many dubious, if
not outright criminal investigations and persecutions of Muslim
Americans.[148] The same strategy of facilitating violence is now
being used to entrap and frame vulnerable White Americans,[149]
just as it had been used against America's Muslim population.

Of course, state sanctioned political violence comes in many
forms. The long-practiced technique of deploying agent provocateurs (state actors who initiate or merely provoke violence at
otherwise peaceful demonstrations) is another such example,
having been used to disrupt revolutionary American sentiment
for over a century. Anti-war protests (Vietnam in the 1960s and
Iraq in the 2000s),[150] the Black Panther party,[151] and Occupy
Wall Street[152] were all derailed by state sanctioned violence. Even
today, the riots which began in Minneapolis (which have since
spread around the globe) are alleged to have begun thanks to the

February 26, 2013, www.theatlantic.com/international/archive/2013/02/how-
the-fbi-helps-terrorists-succeed/273537/.
146 David Shipler. "Terrorist Plots, Hatched by the F.B.I." *The New York Times*,
April 28, 2012, www.nytimes.com/2012/04/29/opinion/sunday/terrorist-plots-
helped-along-by-the-fbi.html.
147 Glenn Greenwald, Andrew Fishman. "Latest FBI Claim of Disrupted Terror Plot Deserves Much Scrutiny and Skepticism." *The Intercept*, January 16,
2015, www.theintercept.com/2015/01/16/latest-fbi-boast-disrupting-terror-u-s-
plot-deserves-scrutiny-skepticism/.
148 Human Rights Watch. "US: terrorism Prosecutions Often An Illusion."
Human Rights Watch, July 21, 2014, www.hrw.org/news/2014/07/21/us-terror-
ism-prosecutions-often-illusion#
149 Eric Striker. "The Base: Inside the FBI's Newest Scary Story." *National
Justice*, January 18, 2020, www.national-justice.com/base-inside-fbis-newest-
scary-story.
150 Emile Schepers. "Agent provocateurs and the manipulation of the radical left." *People's World*, September 18, 2017, www.peoplesworld.org/article/
agents-provocateurs-and-the-manipulation-of-the-radical-left/.
151 Lottie Joiner. "The truth about the party that brought 'Power to the People'." *The Undefeated*, December 20, 2016, www.theundefeated.com/features/
the-truth-about-the-party-that-brought-power-to-the-people/.
152 Todd Gitlin. "The Wonderful American World of Informers and Agent
Provocateurs." *The Nation*, June 27, 2013, www.thenation.com/article/archive/
wonderful-american-world-informers-and-agents-provocateurs/.

acts of a few agent provocateurs.[153] Whether we speak of institutional extremism used to weaken the social order ideologically from the top-down or street-level violence implemented to malign nascent political movements from the bottom-up, antisocial extremism always begins with those in power. Violent and antisocial extremism is never organic (in the sense that it emerges spontaneously, without provocation) and can never be laid at the feet of lone-wolf actors. Even in those events carried out by individuals, whether we think of Dylann Roof (who murdered nine churchgoers in Charleston, South Carolina), Nikolas Cruz (who murdered 17 people and injured 17 others at Marjory Stoneman Douglas High School in Parkland, Florida), or Stephen Paddock (who wounded 869 people and killed 59 others at a country music festival in Las Vegas), to name a few, we can always trace a causal line back to those institutions of power who—directly or indirectly—bear the responsibility for such tragic events.

Extremism transforms from a latent potential into manifest violence at precisely the moment it is necessary for the power structure to 1) distract the public from actions it does not want observed with watchful eyes, 2) deter an emergent threat to its hegemonic control, and 3) guide the population towards the attitudes and actions it has predetermined for them. There is a certain irony that the American empire, the most violent and destructive force the world has ever known, is capable of (and, for the most part, successful at) levying charges of hatred and extremism at political subjects with no real capacity for effecting change. It is a testament to its still uncontested power and ability to influence that the United States is able to pull off such an audacious and ham-fisted stunt time and time again, in full view of a population that by-and-large concedes its inherent deceitfulness.

In this first chapter I have taken a broad view of the problem of extremism. We began by identifying the most essential tool for shaping man: myth and narrative. Following that, I pointed to the false collective fictions which pervade the American consciousness and render the population vulnerable to the will of

153 Isaac Scher. "Rumors are swirling over footage showing a shadowy figure dubbed 'umbrella man' breaking windows during the Minneapolis protests." *Insider,* May 29, 2020, www.insider.com/minneapolis-protesters-social-media-users-suspicious-of-umbrella-man-2020-5.

the antisocial extremist. I then provided a *valid* definition of extremism, one that is both coherent and allows for a greater comprehension of the contemporary political scene. Our discussion went on to explain ideology itself and how a given worldview may engender antisocial and extremist views when stretched beyond its legitimate use. Using psychoanalytic theory, I described the drives behind political action and what distinguishes the radical from the extremist in terms of their differing psychological motivations. I identified the primary cause of extremism and elaborated on the techniques deployed by the pathocracy, then went on to discuss the relevant institutions of influence that promulgate antisocial extremist sentiment. All throughout this analysis, I made sure to emphasize the psychological importance of identity, and how deconstructing and delegitimizing identity are absolute necessities for the pathocracy. Lastly, I described how extremism can move from the latent to the manifest, and how state actors—and not the population itself—are the true originators of political violence. Now it is time to narrow the scope of this analysis and focus on a purely psychological investigation of extremism both leftist and rightist.

BOOK II

Investigating
the Extremist

I, in the tempest.
I, dispossessed.
Amidst the deception,
I become
Discontent made manifest.
Today, I wear the mask that you made for me
As proudly as it were my own.

Problematizing the Problem

Much groundwork was laid down in the preceding chapter. It was critical to revisit well-known concepts and take a hard look at them to see how we may properly apply them to this discussion. And while many of the positions I have staked out thus far find their origins in other, undoubtedly greater works, we could not have come to this point without laboring over them as intensely as we have. To restate my claim here once more: briefly, the extremist is a cultural creation through and through. Whatever latent genetic preconditions exist (of which there are many) must be enacted upon, enlivened by apparatuses of power—the universities, the television studios, the banks, the courts, the Church, the Congress, and so on. Whereas the regimes of the last century relied on unquestionably brutal measures of subjugation (e.g. pogroms, large scale institutionalization and incarcera-

tion, etc.), dominating public consciousness by making fear a
political device, 21st century American totalitarianism scaffolds
these tried and true methods with a more sophisticated and seductive psychological approach. Doubt, insecurity, obfuscation,
instincts of consumption and ambition are now part of the new
psychological program by which the regime secures its influence
and squelches dissent. It is no longer *as* necessary to condemn
troublesome political subjects to a life of hard labor or mental
infirmity, for today we can merely give them a college degree,
a smart phone, and perhaps even a modestly paying job within
the bureaucracy. Those who are not so lucky may be gifted any of
the debauched runners-up prizes: narcotics, pornography, their
choice of the latest gadget or garment, and a personalized myth
of victimization. Validation of the lowest psychological characteristics while satiating every perverse desire imaginable has
proven to be a most effective device for political control.

Dependency, whether to the State or to an employer, incul-
cates the same psychological relationship between the individual
and the institutions of power as one would find in a dysfunctional home; the child hates his parents, but he needs them all
the same (not just materially, but needs to love and be loved by
them). He wants to usurp them, but simultaneously fears their
absence, for he knows he would be nothing without them. One
could even say there is a particularly morbid and destitute sub-
limity to it all. He is left impotent, and thus learned helplessness
sets in. Here we see the absolute genius of 21st century American
governmentality laid bare, for any problem created by neoliberal
economic policy and its resultant extremist individualistic solipsism can be turned around and repurposed as a device of further
subjugation. Disaffected Americans may hate the corporations,
but once thrown a superficial bone of identitatpolitik, quickly
find their hatred transmogrified into love. The office of the Presidency, having been derided year after year may be rehabilitated if
the right kind of person is seated in the Oval Office. In the span of
eight years, militant overseas adventurism can be transubstanti-
ated from the sum of all evil into the highest known good. Impotence can be transformed into righteous indignation, just as the
once beloved political subject can suddenly become an accepted
object of scorn (e.g. the White woman becomes a "*Karen*"; the

observant Muslim becomes a homophobe; the Black community, previously beyond reproach, finds itself forced to confront its transphobia). By their very nature, these tactics are ephemeral and possessing a limited shelf life. And yet they can be deployed and redeployed as often as the power structure needs. They are malleable; even when they have reached the limit of their potential, a new moment can arrive which reinvigorates them and allows old wounds to be ripped open once more. After all, they are but a few of the governmental techniques available to the regime—a regime that is well studied in the art of control.

And while Americans broadly agree about the sickly, corrupt, and malevolent nature of American power, the degree to which that evil is obfuscated *and at the same time* made semi-visible, *an apparition*, creates a fog of confusion and helplessness which suppresses any available method of resistance (for example, direct political action, total withdrawal, and so on). Bipolarities of denial-affirmation, of suppression-permission, and of critique-adulation throttle the American mind, leaving it as fatigued and delirious as a punch-drunk pugilist in the middle of the Araneta Coliseum. Out of these circumstances, we find the birth of the American extremist. There are only two options that the would-be extremist encounters, and thus the question which confronts him is this: will he become a mercenary—or better still, a missionary—for the Church of American Extremism, or will he do it pro bono? Only the truly impoverished (or the truly deranged, though the two may not be mutually exclusive) choose the latter. Curiously, as we ascend the sociopolitical ladder, we do find that the two converge rather effortlessly.

The violence of extremism is not by definition immanent, just as the extremist is not by his very nature a marginalized lunatic. As I have demonstrated in the previous chapter, a wider conception of this notion allows us to fully appreciate political evil in all its hideous glory. Is the school shooter *necessarily* worse than the lawyer of intellectual property who stymies the artist's ability to create revolutionary works of beauty? What about the anti-Semite who destroys a Temple with a homemade bomb? Is he unequivocally more dastardly than the hedge fund manager who bankrupted millions? Or the writer for *The New York Times* who leads the nation down a rabbit hole of partisan madness? It is only the immediacy of the former and the hidden, distal nature of the latter which could ever convince us otherwise. It is only the perceived legitimacy of the latter—its supposed respectability and high-status—which tricks us. The violence of the first is a violence of social disintegration, one that is directed at a blameless other, and thus easily facilitates both blanket condemnation and the denial of all attempts at dispassionate investigation and empathy. The violence of the second, however, goes wholly unnoticed, owing to the tacit approval which it receives from the system.

I would like to revisit the first line of the preceding paragraph: "*The violence of extremism is not by definition imminent, just as the extremist is not by his very nature a marginalized lunatic.*" Partisan analyses demonstrate the unassailability of this fact, for the jingoistic xenophobe prays that every act of violence committed by a Middle-Easterner or South Asian can be linked to Islam in precisely the same way bourgeois neoliberals desperately seek to connect all instances of White violence to a global cabal of neo-Nazi fascism.[1] This speaks not only to the obsequiously perspectival nature of extremism, but also to the ideophilic capture of the mind (at its core, conspiratorial in the worst possible way) that leads to such inferences. As a heuristic, such thinking is not flawed in and of itself, but it is owing to the absolute fetishization of the American mind—owing to the permissibility of certain maligned political objects or others—that the process goes horribly awry. We may address this phenomenon in another way by saying it perfectly demonstrates what mythologist and artist Mark Brahmin calls *the caducean*,[2] a reference to Hermes' staff which depicts two snakes facing one another. In Brahmin's view, this symbolically represents a false opposition intended to pit two forces against each other, both of whom represent a particular (and in theory, opposing) worldview, but whose conflict can only achieve a stalemate (or rather, a further attainment of

1 That people can, in particular circumstances, transcend the narrow discourse of extremism (e.g. conceptualizing it outside the norm of individual conduct, attributing it to things other than poor mental health, etc.), exposes the lack of genuine belief in the commonly understood definition of the term.
2 Mark Brahmin, "The Caducean Phenomenon", *The Apollonian Transmission*, May 3, 2019, http://theapolloniantransmission.com/2019/05/03/the-caducean-phenomenon/.

the status quo). Trapping each side in a controlled dialectic enables the true center of power to continue unhindered; Hermes,
the Grecian deity of theft and trickery, laughs at our frustrated
antagonism and continues along his merry way.

Extremism, itself a matter of perception (where the "proper"
perception is legitimated by power), puts us in the unenviable
position of having to justify some acts of violence while condemning others.[3] The Zionist approves acts like the bombing
of the King David Hotel in Jerusalem while denying the demographic replacement of the Palestinians; the Black separatist
nods approvingly at the assault of some hapless White bystander
perpetrated by his racial brother while decrying the legitimate
exercise of force used by the police against his ethnic cohorts;
the White nationalist laments the murder and rape of his women
while cheering the egregious excesses of American militarism
suffered by the poor and downtrodden of the world. Rather than
using a moral framework to determine the just usage of aggression, ideophilic political frameworks of oppression and intersectionality dominate, forcing paralogical contortions which
can only increase with time, revealing their inherent contradictions. Such inconsistencies are smoothed over through a series
of *cognitive eliminations* (favored political subjects are treated as
individuals worthy of compassion, while the demoralized and
marginalized bear collective responsibility, and ultimately prove
deserving of contempt) and biases of availability and representativeness (themselves facilitated by mass media, which distort the
true probability of certain events, e.g. interracial crime, acts of
political violence, etc.)

Owing to these factors, it is necessary, then, to problematize
the problem of extremism—or to put it more simply, to challenge
the assumptions and conclusions drawn by those who seek to
resolve the issue of extremism. Rather than viewing extremism
and antisocial tendencies as belonging to a single category (adherents of right-wing politics) or meta-category ("the West"),

3 This poses a deeper question: what place does violence hold in a society directed by techno-informational totalitarianism? The question of extremism
challenges us to consider the true legitimacy of aggression in human action, just
as much as it challenges us to reconsider the moral superiority of Western liberal civilization. 21st century man's partitioned consciousness invariably leads
him to faulty presumptions, strained logic, and a great deal of emotional duress.

we must broaden our perception so that we may view the problem holistically, and thus identify the systemic factors at work. I accomplished this in the preceding chapter by looking at the role American institutions (and their preferred ideologies) play in reproducing antisocial and extremist sentiment. Here, I will work my way down the socioeconomic ladder and examine the political subject itself to elucidate the problem of extremism. Beginning with the mass ideology which horizontally obfuscates the reality of political evil, we will conclude this chapter by examining the true character of antisocial extremism on both the left *and* the right.

The Folly of Centrism

Whether we call them "*moderates*", "*independents*", "*the middle class*", or "*centrists*" (for simplicity's sake I shall use "centrist" and "centrism" henceforth), psychologically we find that we are in fact discussing the same phenomenon. That phenomenon, of course, which defines the political and spiritual character of the centrist is inertia. Though he is in motion, he moves only to stay in place, to maintain his current paradigmatic stance. Ultimately, he is a static figure, anxious not to lose his prosperity while also desperate to improve his social standing at all costs (a tragic illusion by which he is hopelessly ensnared). Something of an ahistorical political subject, possessing all manner of material and social wealth that few before him enjoyed, the centrist belongs more to the realm of the Imaginary than the Real. Understanding this in a Lacanian sense, the centrist, eager to differentiate himself, and thus strongly egocentric (even narcissistic), is preoccupied with notions of control and coherence which are maintained by certain ego defenses. His ego defenses operate to preserve these images of the self and to stave off confrontations with the Real (the dimension which—at least initially—exists beyond language, beyond our ability to symbolically integrate experience into our cognitive schemas). Such traumatic confrontations would expose the depth of his narcissistic middle-class delusions, namely those of independence and freedom, of choice and significance, and of just and sane institutions concerned only with merit and the truth.

As a result, he is especially vulnerable to the psychological manipulations of the pathocracy, constantly being nudged from one direction to the next like a pawn across the chessboard. The centrist, therefore, is the ideal American: irrationally rational, dispassionate and spiritually bereft, dependent on the wisdom of experts, and wholly captured both by the political myth of democracy and the psychological lies of fairness, hard work, equality, and objectivity. The fact of his psychological entrapment, being restrained by the Skinnerian incentives pulling at his nervous system and denied the vital social relations of intimacy and belongingness, renders him spiritually incapacitated and unable to reflect on his circumstance, much less to understand it. It is the centrist for whom the hedonic treadmill rolls.

So, in addition to the arborescent (or hierarchal, vertical) controls which establish and reinforce true antisocial extremism, centrism is the rhizomatic (or de-centralized, horizontal) social force that enables the pathocracy's paradigm of false extremism. Psychologically speaking, centrism is the energy within the American electorate which obfuscates the relationship between the politically banal and the taboo. Because the center seeks the approval of the high (and ultimately, desires a seat alongside them at the table) they accept the symbolism and word-craft of the pathocracy, and thus cannot be considered trustworthy observers of the political scene. They lust for the lifestyle of the high, and in their madness, become subservient to those members of the privileged class. To the degree that they can discern true problems from the political volleyballs of misdirection, centrists will readily accept prefabricated solutions which only serve the interests of the pathocratic class (e.g. solving the problem of school shootings by arming the teachers and disarming the populace, slowing climate change by taxing the rich and promoting lifestyle minimalism,[4] reversing low birth-rates by importing migrants, etc.) The centrist scoffs at or even ignores emergent conflicts. His disengaged and cynical self-interest precludes identification and engagement with the other. When he is forced to acknowledge it, his preferred solution is to merely placate antagonisms. Time and again, he cedes territory because of his habit of narcissistic ignorance and apathy.

4 While legitimate concepts, in practice they are both euphemisms for imposing further penalties on the average person.

Just as the left-liberal and right-liberal ideophiles (of both the high and the low) confuse our understanding with their tragically skewed perceptions, the centrist, in his petty rationalism and naïve skepticism, mistakes structural problems for individual ones. This shortsighted view itself is a result of his own atomization, which he then projects onto the world. The world around him ceases to be a network of interconnected spheres of influence and partnership, but rather a product of individual labor. Where he is able to see community, sociopolitical failings can further be explained by his other preferred fetishes—the irrational overvaluing of data and technique. Institutional collapse is never the result of immorality; rather it is caused by insufficient information and lack of sophistication. There are no conspiracies, there is no malevolence, all that is needed are a few cosmetic changes and everything will be *hunky dory*. People don't perpetrate acts of evil, they simply *make mistakes*. We must, therefore, identify the psychological deficits at play here, namely the centrist's narcissism and his reliance on denial as an ego defense. Furthermore, the center is characterized by its unconsciousness, and the concomitant fantasies, distortions, passive aggressions, and repressions which therefore follow.

Centrists are the chattering class. Conflict-averse by nature, they prefer dialogue to action, unity to separation, reaction to anticipation, and so on. Problems are not to be solved, merely delayed. For him, constructive action is "radical" and "not pragmatic", and therefore dismissed out of hand (considering that the implementation of such resolutions would threaten his place in the system and his goal of one day joining the ranks of the powerful). Similarly, spasmodic ruptures of extremist sentiment and violence are rationalized away and quickly forgotten, for if they were to linger, the centrist would be forced to confront the inherent failure and immorality of the system he wishes to perpetuate. Beneath the surface the centrist may recognize that he belongs to a constructed class whose purpose is to be parasitized and whose vital energies and desires are steered, redirected, to the benefit of the pathocracy. Nonetheless, he continues along his path. Identification with the overclass means that he, too, must accept the denial of his will, for this is what his master desires as well. Truisms such as "*hearing out both sides*" and "*rational dis-*

course", techniques of control which prolong suffering and allow for uninterrupted pillaging, predominate among the center until all parties are fatigued by discussion and the worst of all possible resolutions is finally selected. The center, then, is little more than a vehicle for the continuation of the system and its principles, a biomass of human capital which can be replaced or discarded as one would any other material construct. A true political center could exist, one that would more fully represent the healthful attitudes and constructs of the whole rather than simply reflecting the twisted habits and beliefs of the pathocracy, but such a radical transformation continues to be denied by the high (and with the implicit consent of the middle), because to permit a reordering of this magnitude would mean an end to their centuries-long looting of the labor classes. It should be said, then, that the center's political engagement is not meaningful or constructive, but performative; it is a means with no concrete end, no ultimate goal or direction to which it points, but rather a superficial identity or distraction. Perhaps more accurately we could say it is a form of entertainment or role play, utterly theatrical in nature—a theatricality which has seemingly overtaken *actual* theater, art, and entertainment. Whereas the bread and circuses of yesteryear were an effective strategy for assuaging tensions over the political process, political engagement itself is now the distraction; it is the technique of governmentality by which further disengagement from true political participation is secured.

Let us return to this sentiment: centrism is the denial of political will, but it is also the graveyard of critical thought. We often hear this common refrain when definitive answers are provided for hot button political issues: *"...well it's more complex than that"*. Should you press the centrist and emphatically stand your ground, he will respond by saying, *"...that sounds extreme"*, or better still, *"...don't be so closed-minded"*. Thought-terminating clichés such as these serve not only as deferrals to the wisdom of preferred experts, but deferrals to the *process* of expertise. They are a demand for the eternal investigation and the endless review of data, as if—at some point, after sufficient evidence has been gathered—there could finally be an answer. Of course, no amount of proof could ever suffice because the point of the entire operation is to forestall any solution to the problem. Only *non-answers* can be provided, *non-resolutions* which do nothing to challenge the basic assumptions or structural methods of the pathocracy. The investigative or scientific processes of the pathocracy are no different from the courtroom trial, in which, having arrived upon a decision before the hearing begins, the only remaining task then is to gather facts which justify the predetermined finding. Proofs are reverse engineered in such a way that the original desire, the a priori, is validated. Experts, then, are not superordinately accomplished at some technique or method, but rather at providing pleasure; they are the perfect whore of the bureaucrat. Expertise is increasingly determined less by one's objective accomplishments, and more by one's willingness to conform and subjugate themselves to the power structure. We may, then, say that the true definition of an expert, or at least the expert of the pathocracy, is "*one who is in good standing with the existing social structure*". He is not motivated by the pursuit of knowledge or creativity, nor is he excited by innovation. Quite the opposite, he requires his supposed domain to remain static and unchanging so that he is never moved from atop his perch (after all, he is not practiced in his craft—only in the appearance of being practiced). What motivates the pathological expert is merely the *impression* of skill, and the respectability that comes with it. Having earned the respect he so badly desires comes *power*, which naturally is his true aim. Unbeknownst to the centrist, his reliance on "expertise" places him in a paradox. The centrist's paradox here is that, through the link provided by the pathological expert, he is now connected to the extremist in the great chain of being. He may follow the laws, pay his taxes, honor his parents, and never cheat on his wife, but (as is the case with true extremists—left-and right-extremists of the high and the low), he relies upon and condones the false power of these validation merchants.

In short, centrism is an unsophisticated and controlled form of third way politics which captures political energy, suspends analytic thought and keeps these individuals firmly on the plantation. The yearning to break out of preordained political dialectics and toward a synthesis exists but is manipulated to prevent the electorate from thinking outside of the existing system's parameters. One may claim to be a moderate or independent, but rarely do their actions suggest true moderation or independence. Truthfully, it is a psychological safety net which aids the centrist's desire to never examine root causes too closely and, above all, to never meaningfully break from the mores of the pathocracy. Theirs is a psychology of maternalism; effects are never truly derived from their just causes, just as blame is never assigned, merely distributed. Negotiations and resolutions are never achieved, only flat and disappointing compromises.

And yet, we should not condemn the center for its shortcomings. A great responsibility has been placed upon their shoulders, but it is a responsibility that they cannot possibly uphold, for they have been denied the means by which to meet it. In a more just society, the duty of solving difficult problems would be undertaken by the more privileged classes (and they would undertake this duty honestly). The failures of the center are not their own, in fact; they are the failures of the high. Centrists are, on one hand, the scapegoated class, while on the other, the exalted class; they are simultaneously made to be the victims for crimes perpetrated by psychopathic elites while also being heavily courted because of the consent they confer upon the overclass. When they are not serving as the scapegoat, they are gaslit into believing that those among the low are at fault for the injustices committed by the pathocracy. When the overclass wants to inculcate the center with guilt so it may better manipulate them, it whispers,

> *"You are greedy, you demand too much! We must take from you today so there will be more tomorrow. How shallow and provincial you are. Your selfish bigotry hurts the poor and the underserved. Why are you so evil? You must be punished so others may thrive."*

And when the pathocrat wants to turn the glare of the center away from himself and his evil deeds he tells them,

> *"It is because of the poor that your income shrinks every year. If you support cuts to welfare spending, you will finally be made whole! The immigrant is the reason your sons and daughters are unemployed. Fix your hatred upon them!"*

The center merely responds to incentives and is always scrambling to make the best of their declining fortunes. With each corrupted step forward the pathocratic class takes, the center can only furiously backpedal until they eventually find themselves with their backs against the wall and a freshly sharpened blade inching ever closer to their exposed throats. Tragically, the center finds itself fighting a two-front war, always working to further itself while simultaneously fending off the advances of the lower and upper classes. This is the argument put forth by Bertrand de Jouvenel and expanded upon by thinkers in the neo-absolutist and neo-reactionary communities: the center is predated against by a coalition of the have-mores *and* the have-nots. With this understanding firmly in grasp, my hope is that the reader may rethink the psychological and political pressures with which the center is confronted. Furthermore, the factors which buttress the false conception of political extremism should be made clearer by examining the unique relationship between the forces of the center (or middle) and the high. From this point we may now, finally, begin our investigation into the phenomenon of the extremist in earnest.

The Misandrist Left and the Misogynist Right

There is a spiritual character (orbited by a particular set of psychological clusters) that animates the behaviors and beliefs of the antisocial extremist, though the exact formation is mirrored by its inverse when we consider the two types. In both cases, however, we see a psychology of collaborative opposites. By this I mean a single psychological characteristic expresses itself as an impoverished duality; clearly it is dysfunctional, nonetheless it provides a gestalt of the individual as a semi-coherent whole. I say semi-coherent because the parts don't quite align with one another in any clear geometric way, and are themselves unstable and volatile, easily disrupted by the strain of changing circumstances and other stimuli which might expose the naked incongruities within. All the same, they are "functional" in the same way that a broken chair held together by glue or duct tape is "functional"; sub-optimal, yes, but because the extremist is given to niche-seeking[5] these inadequacies are less likely to be challenged directly. It has been said that there are only two kinds of people—those who adapt to their surroundings and those who adapt their surroundings to themselves. Should such an observation prove true, we might say then that the extremist belongs to the latter type.

When examining the antisocial extremist of the left-variation (AEL, henceforth), we see an over-identification with the other and an under-identification with the self. From here we can say, then, that AELs possess a psychology of self-condemning and other-exalting. AELs embody the zero-sum mindset, whereby only one party can truly thrive, and so they engage in pathological acts of self-undermining, self-denial, and self-incrimination, so as to ensure that the deserving-other receives what he is so rightfully owed. This process of identification has a religious character; the AEL takes the position of sacrificial object while the other becomes the worshipped object. All capacity for mystical living is transferred on to this worshipped object.[6] It is important to understand the relationship between objectification and extremism: objectification is a psychological process of dehumanization and desacralization. Even in his worship, the AEL does not praise the other as a subject, capable of higher psychological and spiritual acts, but as a petrified idol. Even though his self-flagellating deference signifies a belief in the vitalism of the other, on a deeper level this act betrays an unconscious belief in the utter static deadness of human life. In some sense, the worldview of the extremist is one of a lifeworld without subjects, a social space lacking any authentic human or spiritual character. Though the AEL is a worshipful figure, his prayers are distinctly perverse in their desire for negation and destruction. Moving along, we also find an over-valuing of situations (e.g. woman is sexually harassed because of "*institutional male violence*") and

5 A way of expressing the genetic desire of the individual to match with his environment, though here I am speaking of 'types' in a broader sense than that which is merely heritable.
6 In the case of the AEL, the object of worship is always an oppressed figure, and it is through their oppression that they acquire their spiritual character. We likely have Herbert Marcuse to thank for this, as his work placed the oppressed minority as the figure of global salvation, and to whom the capitalist project would finally capitulate.

contexts juxtaposed by an under-valuing of the individual's internal disposition (woman is sexually harassed because she is irresponsible and vain, etc.) Of course, this attitude is inverted when the AEL is confronted by his socially approved object-of-scorn. His is an attitude of peaceful violence (*"I hurt my enemy because I love what is good and he is anything but"*). Lastly, we may say that the spiritual character of the AEL is distinctly feminine.

Antisocial extremism of the rightist variation (which I will refer to from here on out as AER) is the inverse of these exact psychological phenomena. Preempting accusations of horseshoe-ism[7] (a useful but flawed theory which ultimately fails to tell us anything about the innate psychological characteristics of the extremist), I find it more instructive to think of the two as variations on a theme. *The one is the shadow of the other.* Modern usages of Horseshoe theory fail precisely because of their superficial and highly perspectival application. Depending on who you read, the far-left and the far-right may be united—however significantly or not—by their anti-Semitism,[8] or their hatred for Muslims,[9] or (admittedly, with some reservations) their anti-liberalism,[10] or their authoritarianism, and so on. The inability for Americans to reflect on their a priori liberal foundations, to understand just how morally bankrupt their institutions are, or to grasp how the system perpetuates the very problems they wish to solve, deeply frustrates their capacity for understanding the psychological genesis of antisocial extremism. Extremism is not first and foremost about tactics or behaviors, but the essential psychosocial dysfunction which drives the antisocial tendency of the individual. Most attempts at moving away from Horseshoe theory that I have observed are governed by motivated reasoning (for instance, pointing out left-wing authoritarianism obscures

7 Jean-Pierre Faye, *Le Siecle des ideologies* (Pocket, 2002), 12-22.
8 Tzvi Fleischer, "The Political Horseshoe again", *Australia/Israel & Jewish Affairs Council,* posted in November of 2006, http://www.aijac.org.au/review/2006/31-11/scribb31-11.htm.
9 Maajid Nawaz, "The Left's Witch Hunt Against Muslims", *The Daily Beast,* published on December 14th, 2015, https://www.thedailybeast.com/the-lefts-witch-hunt-against-muslims?ref=scroll.
10 Simon Choat, "Horseshoe theory is nonsense – the far right and far left have little in common", *The Conversation,* published on May 12th, 2017, https://www.thedailybeast.com/the-lefts-witch-hunt-against-muslims?ref=scroll.

the true authoritarian threat on the right),[11] and are not based in genuine philosophical or scientific inquiry. Advocates of Horseshoe theory (and, paradoxically, its critics as well) fail because they do not treat political attitudes as emergent biopsychosocial phenomenon (e.g. differing hormonal profiles,[12] educational attainment,[13] attachment styles, etc.), but rather as moral failings. The extremist is an archetype, or perhaps more specifically, a biotype, given form by the political ecosystem around him. That raw biological material which separates the constitutionally progressive type from the conservative type, both finding themselves distorted by philosophical Americanism and its concomitant spectacle of media and politics, and ultimately impoverished by deteriorated social relations radiating outward across the ecosystem beginning at the family unit, join together to produce the phenomenon of extremism—whether we speak of the mass murderer or the Hollywood scriptwriter. And it is not about any position they hold on social issues, or an attitude toward democracy or free speech which defines their extremism, but rather the desire to dominate and control others, to impose anarchic chaos, to use any social means available to them for the purpose of psychologically—even physically, if possible—harming their perceived opponents.

Now to return to the matter at hand: AERs over-identify with and exalt the self, and place an inordinate importance on dispositionism (e.g. the Black is *bad* because he has lower average IQ) as opposed to situationism (the Black fails because of "*structural inadequacies*" which condemn him to a life of impoverishment, for example). The AER places himself as the subject to be worshipped, though, with none of the responsibilities or dignities which follow from a true religious practice. As is the case with the AEL, the AER makes himself into an object and not a subject

11   Noah Berlatsky, "Let's Put An End To Horseshoe Theory Once And For All", *Pacific Standard,* published on Feburary 9th, 2018, https://psmag.com/social-justice/an-end-to-horseshoe-theory.
12   Chris Mooney, "Your Hormones Tell You How to Vote", *Mother Jones,* published on June 14th, 2013, https://www.motherjones.com/politics/2013/06/how-hormones-influence-our-political-opinions/.
13   Adam Harris, "America is Divided by Education", *The Atlantic,* published on November 7th, 2018, https://www.theatlantic.com/education/archive/2018/11/education-gap-explains-american-politics/575113/.

through his willful self-reduction and self-marginalization. So defined by the opinions and characterizations of others, he takes it upon himself to prove that he is *worse* than others imagine him to be. In effect, he seeks to *become* the villain he is portrayed as in a spectacular pursuit of infamy-tinged jouissance. His is an attitude of violent peacefulness ("*I hurt my enemy so I may be at peace*"). Spiritually his character is masculine.

Let us focus on these two salient points—the feminine misandrist character of the AEL and the masculine misogynist character of the AER. Both are born of an oedipal rupture which disrupts the healthful integration of the *anima* (the feminine aspect) and the *animus* (the male aspect). In the traditional Jungian reading of these archetypes, it is the man who must integrate his anima in order to fully develop his masculinity while the woman must integrate her animus to achieve the fullest state of her femininity. However, we can plainly see that a psychologically holistic understanding of maleness and femaleness as such are missing in man and woman alike, resulting from the disintegration of the family structure and the deconstruction of these concepts in favor of impotent androgyny. Only the most psychologically vulnerable among the population and those predisposed to such a self-concept embrace androgyny; for the rest, what remains are caricatures of the masculine and feminine essence. The man predisposed to his masculine essence becomes a debased and unthinkingly callous brute, while less-secure men adopt the persona of the hysterical and narcissistic woman. The truly feminine woman turns toward egotism and licentiousness, while her insecure counterpart similarly mimics the obsessive and neurotic aggression of the lower man. The result of this process creates an individual who is wholly antagonistic towards his desired object, while simultaneously enmeshed with and dependent upon it. The man-hating AEL and woman-hating AER are united in their frustrated desire for the other; each hates their respective sex object for perceived (and real) slights experienced early on in childhood (which are only reinforced throughout their lives by the absence of a therapeutic or restorative relationship which could provide what the primary relationships did not), though their hatred is little more than a kind of psychological sclerodrama—a hardened outer shell concealing the trauma within.

Absentee fatherhood—whether real or symbolic (the latter occurring when he may be physically present but morally and spiritually disengaged)—is the seed which sprouts the fruit of misandrist and antisocial left extremism. Ruthless paternalism (the archetype of the "*Tyrant*", a shadow form of the "*King*"), itself a kind of absence (an absence of fatherly love), also plays a significant role in the development of pathological leftism. Of course, the tyrannical king is not marked simply by an absence of benevolence, charity, or love, but also by the presence of oppressive conformity to dogmatic order and the inhumanely cruel punishments which deter variances from that order. He is erratic, uncompromising, and unjust; especially during early development, the unpredictable schedule of punishment leaves the child in a perpetual state of terror as they are never sure what rule they have violated or in what manner they have failed to conform to the father's demands. In this way, the child is in a similar position to the pre-modern man who experiences disease, famine, and death as the punishments of a volatile and uncommunicative God. Owing to his failures as an authority figure, the tyrannical father often has the effect of poisoning notions of authority and conformity, which are not in their essence, immoral values. The absentee father (the archetype of the "*Weakling*", another pathological expression of the king) leaves both a real and symbolic developmental void in the life of the child; this vacancy may leave an opening for the tyrannical substitute which only further impresses upon the mind of the young the absolute superfluity—if not the outright evil—of man. Of course, if the primary experience with male authority is one of brutality (the father is present *and* cruelly dominating), this understandably brings us to the same point, minus a few convoluted and socially dysfunctional steps. Whether the child perceives woman as a long-suffering victim of tyrannical masculinity (her oppression thus serving as justification for her ascendance to the top of the hierarchy), or as a kind of omnipotent superheroine capable of redressing the failure of man, the extent to which the child develops into an adult with political ideas or ambitions is also the extent to which he seeks to help seat her upon the throne. The present-yet-absent father, who is there in the flesh but otherwise mentally and spiritually captured by some other force (e.g. infidelity, resentment, a fixation on some practice which he finds less challenging than his domestic responsibilities), leaves a powerful imprint on the child's mind—one of impotence, lack of regard, and callousness—that indelibly convinces him of the necessity for man's erasure. The fervor of the AEL's antagonism toward male authority is in equal proportion to the harshness of his paternal rejection.

We should understand, of course, that the biological diversity found among men thus produces qualitatively different types of antagonism toward male authority. The first type, being constitutively weaker, over-identifies with the maternal figure and therefore adopts her habits, affective style, and psychological mannerisms. Often the product of a single-mother household, he is an emasculated man who served as the displaced object upon which his mother could safely release her hostility without fear of retaliation. It is at least as likely that he comes from a household with a domesticated and effeminate father figure, ruled by a dominating mother (the archetype of the "*Possessive Mother*") where similar mechanisms of control and humiliation find themselves in effect. In the former, over-identification is achieved through the absence of a paternal figure, while the latter occurs through the child's need to follow in the footsteps of the strong horse. The oscillating bipolar nature of woman's affective style is then internalized by the child; he will adopt her disposition of fear, irrationality, and hostility as well as her tactics of shaming, humiliation, and degradation. He will also derive his concept of moral goodness from her, too; through his over-identification with the feminine, he will place a premium on the supposedly superior qualities of kindness, compassion, deference, timidity, and meekness. His is a will to submit, to placate, and to appease. The second type, constitutive of the stronger male form, also seeks to abolish male authority. The difference lies in the fact that while the AEL of the first variation desires an end to paternalism as an expression of his own weakness, the second uses misandrism to situate himself atop the male hierarchy. He seeks to become the kind of man necessary for justice to persevere (the kind he never knew in his formative years). Whether he is a true believer is of little consequence (after all, ideology is second to biology; furthermore, it is subordinate to one's spiritual or ar-

THE MISANDRIST LEFT
AND THE MISOGYNIST RIGHT

chetypal character)—eventually his natural will to power asserts itself. If he is to any extent self-aware, then he will pay lip service to his supposed misandrist belief system and suffer no cognitive dissonance for it.

Most female misandrism is a form of sexual signaling, intended to attract the most domineering and charismatic male figure. Among those women who have fully accepted the doctrine of Americanism (e.g. narcissistic self-interest, careerism and social dominance, etc.), their hostility toward men and male authority still lacks an intellectual or philosophical character. Rather it is an expression of pure will to power. The kind of extremism seen in men is exceedingly rare among women.[14] It is only the politically engaged woman who, for reasons of sexual orientation (militant homosexuality), or racial competition (belonging to an out-group) that their misandrist character takes on a more serious and antagonistic quality. This is not to ignore the role which sexual violence plays in female misandrism. Some number of women (having been victimized) will engage in repetition compulsion; their natural physical inferiority and innate political disengagement renders their misandric ideophilia energetically inert. Only a subset of women (again, owing to a biological difference such as hormonal and neurological structures more

14 Interestingly, a recent study demonstrated that women exhibit stronger partisan identities and have experienced more intense "affective polarization" than men. Ondercin and Lizotte attributed this to women's greater propensity for partisanship, the strength of their attitudes toward abortion, and the stronger effect partisanship has on women as opposed to men. While this could easily be the subject of its own investigation, we must resign ourselves to highlighting a few obvious causal factors: the stronger collectivist attitude found in women when compared to men, the weaponization of identity and womanhood as a political subject, and that political issues for women roundly prove to be "women's issues" (explicitly, such as abortion, or implicitly, in the case of immigration, where the immigrant occupies the psychological space that a child would normally inhabit). This has yet to result in the kind of political violence with which the establishment typically concerns itself, e.g., lone wolf terror, although women are regular participants in leftist collective demonstration (and destruction) and have been for over half a century. A crudely limited (but not wholly inaccurate) analysis might place female extremist identity along the Madonna-Whore dichotomy; the further left a woman goes, the greater the likelihood that she embraces libertine impulsivity, while the further right she goes, the more she embraces confinement. Ondercin, Heather Louise, & Mary Kate Lizotte. "You've Lost That Loving Feeling: How Gender Shapes Affective Polarization", *SAGE Journals*, November 18, 2020.

commonly seen in men) will transform this energy into manifest political action.

Owing to their essentially feminine and misandrist character, AEL's expressed values are of peacefulness, universal human dignity, and the importance of free and open dialogue. For the AEL, weakness is strength and obsequiousness is respect. It is better to ask for permission than apologize for preemptive action. Appeasement is superior to confrontation and acquiescence is akin to godliness. This is true when they are interacting with members of their political in-group, as well as when signaling through the media and communication industries. But when the ideological rubber meets the biological road—that is to say, when confronted with the out-group—everything changes. As recent history has demonstrated quite nicely, their value system can easily be adjusted to permit the use of strategies whereby conquest is won (strategies which might otherwise be considered ideological poison due to their overt connection to domineering and brute masculinity, i.e. right-wing values). Such incongruence, as I have already highlighted, is not problematic for those less ideological members who are by their nature more psychopathic.

For both man and woman, misandrist sentiment is a yearning for the return of the king, the return of a symbolically meaningful paternal figure. Despite their beliefs, AELs hold an ideal of a heroic Man-God capable of rescuing them, of righteously defeating their enemies, and ultimately healing their traumatic past. This is a basic sociological fact, given the nature of male-female relations but also the nature of Western neoliberal capitalist hierarchies. The gesture is utterly symbolic and not structural. This is also a basic psychological fact, as unconsciously these individuals do not seek revolutionary change. Rather they seek restoration, wholeness, and ultimately a return to a kind of idyllic, pre-oedipal state of existence. Beneath the resentment and the trauma masquerading as political activity is a desire for relief from a world without true men.

Turning our attention once more to the AER, we must analyze his relationship with the maternal figure, for it symbolically presages his attitude toward the other more broadly. According to Jung, woman as understood through the archetype of "*The Great Mother*" is defined by "*...her cherishing and nourishing*

goodness, her orgiastic emotionality, and her Styigan depths."[15]
The Great Mother is the giver of life and a source of abundance. In her full expression, she is the highest form of woman's maternal capacity. However, we are concerned with the shadow of the mother ("*The Devouring Mother*") as it appears in its *possessive* and *distant* incarnations, and how the archetype of the mother intersects with that of the "*Lover*" and its degraded shadow manifestations (appearing as the *seductive* type and the *frigid* type).

It is the rupture with the mother, compounded by certain genetic latencies or predispositions, reinforced by a culture of unceasing humiliation and alienation affecting the individual in a peculiar manner, which births the AER. But it is that first transgression, the most significant one of any individual's life, which opens the door to a lifetime of psychological dysfunction. The maternal figure, unable to reckon with her duty as a mother, beset by her own personal failures (such as narcissism, a history of trauma, marital discord, etc.), objectifies her child and imposes upon him conditions and demands which he is utterly incapable of meeting. By her nature, the devouring mother consumes the life energy of her child, subjecting him (or her) to the kind of psychological torture which only a mother is capable of imposing. Oscillating between feelings of intense neediness, jealousy, and on the other hand, distance and apathy, the devouring mother demands her child alternately fill the roles of father and son—of lover—on a moment's notice. Her own distorted imago[16] of man prohibits her from conceptualizing the differing roles man may play in her life and how she ought to relate to each of them. As such, her child is disciplined for the failure of some other man, from some other time, without any understanding of why he is made to pay the price for the transgressions of another.

The details of her life which lead to the ruptured attachment with her child will vary in each circumstance but are not especially meaningful to this analysis. It is enough to suggest that she is the inheritor of an intergenerational succession of barbarism and misfortune. She herself may suffer some disorder of affect or

15   Harold G. Coward, *Jung and Eastern Thought* (State University of the New York Press, 1985), 153.
16   A Jungian term, the imago is a mental image formed out of relation to the unconscious. Often (but not always) puerile and idealized, it is a false image developed early in one's life history and persists well past the point of justification.

cognition which only saturates her relationships with more disorientation and trauma. Captured by the repetition compulsion,
she reenacts patterns of discipline and control (with certain innovations unique to her personhood) which find their expression
in her relationship with her loved ones. And so, caught between
incoherent and often contradictory demands of compliance and
compassion, of playing the role of scapegoat but simultaneously
tasked with absolving the guilt of the mother, and of providing
the love and reassurance of an intimate peer despite the inherent
inappropriateness of such a solicitation, the AER views woman
as something to be contained (brutally, if necessary). This first
failure of identification, of integrating the first other into a symbolic order, lends itself to subsequent failures where all others
(Blacks, Jews, Muslims, immigrants, etc.) are denatured and
dehumanized—they all become objects to be controlled, contained, and in the most pathological of cases, exterminated. We
may describe this as a kind of psychic vampirism, for it takes
one already infected with the disease to procure new victims and
spread the contagion. In much the same way, the dehumanizing objectification which precedes these unending and irrational
series of demands is imposed from the outside and ultimately
reproduced ad infinitum by the victim.

In his pathological resentment, the AER applauds female suffering as he desires for her to experience the same humiliation
and degradation to which he was subjected. From a psychoanalytic perspective, the AER predominantly experiences feelings
of joy by way of schadenfreude; witnessing the setbacks and mis-
fortunes of the despised other reinforces his own moral certitude
("*she got what she deserved*"). Taken as a global feature of the
AER, I am correct in saying that his character is authentically sa-
domasochistic and derives its psychic energy from the death drive
(as has been noted in the preceding chapter, *Thanatos* as a psychology of pure destruction and not creation-through-destruc-
tion). Governed by cruelty (having internalized the dominant
status of woman through his relation to the devouring mother,
thus leading to his masochism), the AER maintains an ideal-ego
as that of the strong horse, of the higher man, which informs the
sadistic aspect of his identity. However, he is rarely in a position
to act out this self-perception and so engages in his delusion at

a distance, through voyeurism and spectatorship, which affirms his ideal-ego while never challenging it. Paradoxical (or collaborative opposition between) denial and affirmation are central to his psychology; his self-denial, itself a result of objectification at the hands of the maternal figure, and the affirmation achieved through his impotent ideal-ego, forces him into a position of experiencing pleasure at a distance, as a secondary characteristic or by-product of brutality and humiliation. The stifling of his will, concomitant to the denial of the healthful sophistication of the id, provides the genesis for his joyful spectatorship. Owing to his stunted development, the AER is too incompetent to move from ideal-ego (the lower, static, and self-serving mechanism) to ego-ideal (the higher, kinetic and aspirational mechanism) and thus can never become the übermensch that he represents himself as. This is precisely why he valorizes the impotent violence of his more driven counterparts: they become the symbol of his will realized.

Insofar as woman is the target of his delusion, the AER's sadomasochism has elements of both sexuality and self-preservation. The desire to harm (or see them harmed) is a secondary manifestation of his persistent self-victimization (masochism). Reducing woman to an object of punishment and self-gratification facilitates the emergence of a network of ideophilic clusters (justifications for rape, infidelity, violent oppression, etc.) which orbit the traumatic kernel at the heart of his dysfunction. He can only relate to women through the lens of aggression and frustration, and thus needs a fetishized system of thought which preserves the truth of his victimhood. The trauma of his break from the maternal serves, then, as the justification for his desire *to* traumatize; the affective energy directed at the first other (woman) is then transferred to a symbolic network of disdained others (ethnic, religious, and sexual minorities) which sees him shift from a psychology of sadomasochism to one of pure sadism. These secondary targets are infused with a similar affective charge—horror, envy, lust, and the desire to conquer.

The misogynistic character of the AER is complicated by the fact that woman is, and always has been, a problem for man to solve. Her love is not easily won nor is her compliance secured with any guarantee. His repeated failures to solve this problem only inculcate feelings of resentment and hatred, of the futility of life, and of a persistent self-loathing. In response to his suffering, he can only retreat deeper into pathological fantasies of violence and revenge, which further distance him from himself and ultimately, his desired object. At one point he was a victim, however he never matures from this position and over time draws greater power and ideophilic certainty by perpetuating his sense of victimhood. From this position he can only see the other (e.g. Woman, the Homosexual, etc.) as an omnipotent and overwhelming oppressor. So, too, can he only perceive the world as a place of denial and thus unworthy of his effort. He is demoralized, and the most high-functioning of these types will spread their demoralization. In effect, they become apostles of self-defeating misery, and in their misguided sense of having been "awakened" feel the need to share their "wisdom" with the masses of idiots and saps who have not yet been introduced to the One True Gospel Of Masculinity. Rarely, though troubling all the same, will some AER's transform their impotence into a statement of violence and attempt to punish some individual or group who represents the fetishized oppression which dominates him. Ultimately, even this act (though undoubtedly requiring *some* measure of courage or will) is itself impotent, for nothing about the supposed oppression is changed. In fact, these chaotic and degraded acts of will only serve to instigate the system to implement truer and longer lasting policies of oppression.

The differing attitudes toward the desired object as held by the AEL and the AER (on the one hand, a position of destruction while on the other, a position of domination) further validate historical attitudes toward man and woman. If man cannot rule, he must be disposed of. If woman cannot comply, then she must be subjugated. Even under a supposedly compassionate and enlightened system of progressive neoliberalism, these beliefs are more or less accepted as true (with the aid of certain justifications). Only some men are fit to be kings, and if they are unwilling to bend the knee to a mercantile and intersectional system of abstractions then they are to be cleansed from that system. So too with woman; should she challenge the naked contradictions of Americanism then she must be subjected to ever crueler methods of repression and degradation. As troubling as antisocial extremism of the rightist form is (which is to say, deeply troubling), it remains a marginalized and reactionary force that only finds its fullest expression in relatively minute and aleatory spasms of violence, often times indirectly (or directly) facilitated by the State. The lone autist from Toronto who drives his car into a group of pedestrians,[17] or the disturbed son of a Hollywood director that shoots, stabs, and rams his way into public consciousness,[18] shake us from our stupor and strain the limits of our conventional thinking. But whether it is Dylann Roof, Ted Kaczynski, or some other tragic and deranged figure, these horrifying and mesmerizing acts of violence only point us back to the neoliberal system itself and the traumatizing psychological effects that its inhuman program has wrought upon us. It speaks to the power of neoliberal myth-making that we view the random and spasmodic paroxysms of violence committed by supposed "rightist terrorists" as belonging to a well-funded, internationally coordinated, State sanctioned body of moustache-twirling ne'er-do-wells committed to anti-Woman, anti-Black, anti-Jew, anti-Queer, and anti-Muslim violence and the perpetuation of a global White supremacist hegemony, rather than viewing the international neoliberal system itself (through the influence of its multi-national corporations, NGO's, and monopoly on mass media and communication systems) as responsible for all visible and invisible dysfunctions of the world.

Unveiling the Extremist, Part I: Identifying the Pathology of the AEL

The work of the analyst is not unlike that of the sculptor: in both cases the subject starts as an undifferentiated mass, lacking in refinement and specificity. Still there is an image, a direction at the outset, that both strive to locate and bring to life. Ever so slowly, striking gently and methodically, the subject begins to

17   Dan Bilefsky and Ian Austen, "Toronto Van Attack Suspect Expressed Anger at Women", *The New York Times*, April 14th, 2018, https://www.nytimes.com/2018/04/24/world/canada/toronto-van-rampage.html.
18   Adam Nagourney, Michael Cieply, Alan Feuer and Ian Lovett, "Before Brief, Deadly Spree, Trouble Since Age 8", *The New York Times,* June 1st, 2014 https://www.nytimes.com/2014/06/02/us/elliot-rodger-killings-in-california-followed-years-of-withdrawal.html.

reveal itself for all to see. After careful examination, we have finally arrived at that point where our subject—the extremist—is revealed in all his terrible glory. Let us begin the great unveiling by examining the antisocial extremism of the left-liberal.

The success of the extremist left lies in their complete adoption of the Schmittian ethic; from the rank-and-file antisocial leftist to their upper-class compatriots in the professional managerial classes, AELs have internalized an attitude of absolute enmity toward their political opposition. The antisocial left is less defined by an allegiance to their in-group (despite couching their political activity with the rhetoric of "*protecting our communities*"), as they are conjoined by a mutual hatred for "fascism" (a loose signifier which points at wholly different—and often diametrically opposed—philosophical and political systems). As has been succinctly illustrated elsewhere by others,[19] the American left has evolved into a coalition of otherwise alienated and incompatible groups for the purpose of creating a diverse polity capable of confronting—and defeating—heritage America across all political battlefields. At one point in history, roughly 60 years ago, the left-wing genuinely represented the interests of the average American. But during that intervening period, it shifted from a functional democratic organism into a political Frankenstein, grafting the appendages of other inert political subjects onto itself and, in the process, abandoning any pretense of engaging in eusocial political action. For the antisocial and extremist left-wing, there is no humanity to be found among their political opponents, and to merely hint at the existence of such a dignity is tantamount to treason. The opposition, of course—which is broadly (though not exclusively) White, religious, and heterosexual—are thoroughly dehumanized to purge the leftist Leviathan's mind of any self-reflective capacity which may weaken political action. Absolute certainty, a central and necessary feature of mass psychology, allows the mob to enact an unmitigated will to power. Conviction is their psychological axiom, and thus petty cognitions such as doubt and insecurity must be ruthlessly excavated and disposed of in order to maintain group solidarity.

19   Steve Sailer, "The KKKrazy Glue That Holds the Obama Coalition Together", *Taki's Magazine,* March 13th, 2013 https://www.takimag.com/article/the_kkkrazy_glue_that_holds_the_obama_coalition_together_steve_sailer/.

It is important to note the ever expanding definition of political blood libels such as "White supremacist", "racist", "sexist", "islamophobe", "homophobe", and "anti-Semite", have been permitted to expand so dramatically as to contain more intellectual bloat than muscle. Owing to the plasticity of their definitions, it is now possible to have Jewish anti-Semites, Gay homophobes, Asian and Hispanic White supremacists, and Female misogynists—a fact which betrays the fundamental inability for AELs to tolerate ambiguity, nuance, or complexity. One need not espouse the arguments of White supremacy or misogyny to be labeled as such, one must merely show reticence to engage in the ritualistic witch-burning of their more fanatically extremist liberal cohort. Their quintessentially Manichean worldview imagines differing ideologies as a disease which operates like an intellectual form of miasma; in their view, exposure to verboten philosophies slowly contaminates the mind of otherwise reasonable people until they inevitably reach their final genocidal form. Interestingly, the American left, having successfully claimed ownership of science, rational thought, independence, and culture, have demonstrably shown themselves to have not accepted these as philosophical or aesthetic axioms, but rather as self-aggrandizing ego defenses in accordance with Adler's theory of organ inferiority. Theirs is not a belief in enlightenment humanism or transcendence but rather an expression of performative superiority, a self-styled delusion of membership to the priestly class. By adorning themselves with the trappings of the intelligentsia, AELs give the appearance of credibility and moral superiority where in fact none exist.

The AEL's will to include serves multiple purposes. The rhetoric of inclusivity provides a rallying cry around which otherwise opposed groups may unify and draw strength, at which point they may be strategically deployed as demographic foot soldiers on the warpath toward political conquest. Its flexible and amorphous definition allows for coalition building along lines of selfish and egotism-based self-interest which does not necessitate comprehensibility to those individuals outside of the cult of progressive inclusivity. Effectively, inclusivists can amass a barbarian horde of the genetically and socially disenfranchised, the alienated and the resentful, with whom they may storm the institutional gates of the workplace, the university, the courthouse, and the ballot box (to name a few). Such institutions are then flipped to provide cover for the more perverse and unethical practices of the pathocracy. Inherent to the rhetoric of inclusivity is the idea that these groups consist of people who have been denied their rightful place as important and influential members of American society. Fundamental to their worldview is the narrative of victimhood, thus allowing them to tap into a powerful reserve of emotional energy that resists depletion.

(These psychic energies, of course, would have no constructive place to go without the assistance of a sympathetic over-class, determined to nurture them and shepherd them along the path to political and cultural victory. Narrative-minded geniuses in the disciplines of law, philosophy, political theory, cinema, and music gave form to the affective content, helping to solidify it from its noxious and gassy state into something durable, pristine and noble. To twist, ever so slightly, an insight provided by Guy Debord,[20] the minority underclasses escaped from their marginal status, fleeing the brink of cultural and possibly even existential erasure to a utopian panacea of positive institutional and media representation—a strategy which empowered them while psychologically disarming and demoralizing their adversaries. Though they, much like the rest of us, could not have foreseen the trap they had thoughtlessly marched toward.)

This is not wholly untrue, and this modestly sized kernel of legitimacy provided all the moral persuasive power necessary to advance their cause. On a moral (and even legal) level, the treatment of the Native Americans by European colonists was abhorrent. As was the enslavement and marginalization of the African Americans a crime which could not be accepted. By America's own legal and philosophical logic, the second-class status of women and homosexuals, too, was unjustifiable. All that was necessary to bring us to this present moment in time was to simply keep extending this logic to newer causes, regardless of how much they strained the limits of rationality.

In addition to unifying disparate social groups and creating

20 Guy Debord, *The Society of the Spectacle* (Paris: Editions Buchet-Chastel, 1967), 117, "As Gabel puts it in describing a quite different level of pathology, 'the abnormal need for representation here makes up for a torturing feeling of being on the edge of existence.'"

a network of political subjects large enough to turn institutions away from their intended purpose, the rhetoric of inclusivity served also to fracture the opposition. By taking advantage of the naïveté and the complacency of the majority population, using the intergenerational changes within the majority (their renegotiated attitude toward themselves and the world they inherited) for their own ends, and exploiting the bourgeois disposition toward apathy and disengagement, the pathocratic tyranny of the margins was able to undermine solidarity and unity between father and son, grandmother and granddaughter, husband and wife, and so on. Their loyalties now divided, being neither fully against the revolution nor in total support of it—that deadening middle ground led to a spiritual and communal atrophy which has yet to be healed. So, on the one hand, the revolutionaries grew more tightly knit while their opponents fell apart at the seams; distracted by their own naïve sympathies, collective guilt, and consumerist and careerist fetishes, heritage Americans gradually became defenseless against the creeping transformation of their way of life.

Dehumanization and Enmity

Returning once more to the ideas of dehumanization and enmity, we see that these cognitive states are pivotal to the extreme leftist's psychology, and perhaps so even for their more healthfully adapted and less politically radical brethren. To oppose something in its entirety, rejecting the fullness of its essence necessitates a radical antipathy toward doubt. In the case of the extremist, their opposition moves beyond the realm of values and ideas and into an unempathetic—bordering on genocidal—desire to deny and erase the other from his own consciousness. The further along he is in his antipathy, the closer the extremist comes to pursuing the removal of the other's being entirely. In his quest to alienate himself from his political antipode, the AEL's own judgment and powers of observation slowly atrophy like an unused muscle, rendering him too psychologically infirm to meaningfully rise to the challenge set before him. His hysterical opposition, first an opposition toward himself (and because he is primarily at war with himself, he can thus never truly confront his enemy), prohibits him from rational or pragmatic courses of action and thus leaves him with only the powers of escalation at his fingertips.

Owing to the endless war against "fascism" and all its permutations, rightism has been so thoroughly abstracted and deconstructed as to exist almost purely in a theoretical or virtual realm; the multidirectional attack on rightism (facilitated by academia,[21] [22] [23] [24] [25] the media, culture at large, etc.) has forced it to bury itself, causing its adherents to necessarily seek refuge below social and cultural ground. Having self-protectively burrowed so deep, leftist antagonists often never genuinely experience a conscious interaction with the right, thus furthering the empathy divide and securing future antagonisms. Furthermore, the combination of media caricaturing and lampooning, aided by mainstream institutional right-wing operatives (who only embody the rightist ethos in a degraded form, an expression of the caducean phenomenon) serves to reinforce the sense of alienation and otherness while also denying genuine representation to those individuals and groups who themselves are authentically and temperamentally rightist.

From the standpoint of the AEL, rightists are not just confused, misguided, ideologically opposed, or even morally wrong, they are ontologically and existentially *flawed*—an accidental birth to be corrected by any means necessary. Not only is their existence a hindrance and roadblock to the achievement of an ideal leftist State or territory (whatever form they might take),

21   Christopher Ingraham, "The dramatic shift among college professors that's hurting students' education", *The Washington Post*, January 11th, 2016, https://www.washingtonpost.com/news/wonk/wp/2016/01/11/the-dramatic-shift-among-college-professors-thats-hurting-students-education/.

22   Mitchell Langbert, "Homogenous: The Political Affiliations of Elite Liberal Arts College Faculty", *National Association of Scholars*, Summer 2018, https://www.nas.org/academic-questions/31/2/homogenous_the_political_affiliations_of_elite_liberal_arts_college_faculty.

23   Damon Linker, "Where are all the conservative university professors?", *The Week*, November, 4th, 2015, https://theweek.com/articles/586794/where-are-all-conservative-university-professors.

24   Eric Bennett, "Dear Humanities Profs: We Are The Problem", *The Chronicle of Higher Education*, April 13th, 2018, https://www.chronicle.com/article/Dear-Humanities-Profs-We-Are/243100.

25   Scott Jaschik, "Professors and Politics: What the Research Says", *Inside Higher Ed*, February 27, 2017, https://www.chronicle.com/article/Dear-Humanities-Profs-We-Are/243100.

but it is a threat to their very safety. We know this to be true because they tell us so; often we have heard a visibly distressed leftist shriek something like, *"your words are violence!"* or, *"I feel physically threatened!"*

On the one hand, such statements express a deeply neurotic and paranoid mindset, simultaneously low in frustration tolerance and high in threat sensitivity. However, it is also true insofar as AELs (and by extension left-liberals, though to a far less dysfunctional extent) correctly identify that civilization is a zero-sum game. Not all ideas or aesthetics can reign supreme; eventually, someone will arrive, supported by a community with shared values and experiences and he will take command. His rule will occur at the expense of all other potential rulers. Or at least, that is the game we are currently playing: a game by, of, and for the contemporary pathocratic class, for whom notions of civility and integrity are dangerous fantasies of the childish, the naïve, and the unfit. Pathocracy says, *"The heathen has no right to participate in our society, and furthermore, he has no right to life itself."* Psychologically speaking, the pathocrat—that is, the psychopath—is the biotype or the archetype through which totalitarianism emerges.

Absolute enmity is an understandable psychological phenomenon, but by no means is it a necessary one. Magnanimous acts of contrition can erase the deepest of sins and ameliorate the bitterest of grievances. They are proof of the highest form of psychological and spiritual attainment. Only those individuals with truly religious convictions are capable of a forgiveness of this magnitude. Tragically, however, any man is capable of birthing civilization-destabilizing enmity. In a circumstance such as ours, the truth about enmity can be found in its utterly *contrived* character. Bloated and artificially supported, the seething hatred which defines our age is not unlike the habit of the small child who constantly picks at a healing wound. We would be wise to greet such an observation warmly, as it means that with sufficient motivation and the most righteous of personnel, our hostility is one that can be put to rest. Thus, we are best served to understand the psychogenesis of such tremendous hostility; simply put, it is psychologically rooted in paranoiac and histrionic neurosis. As Freud remarked in *Totem and Taboo*, the neurotic

is a theological person by nature,[26] one who finds his religious
sentiment inappropriately displaced. Clearly, we can see that the
leftist of today is manifestly religious in his political worldview.
He worships, he seeks salvation, and he even performs acts of
self-flagellation. While AELs may be secular in the traditional
sense, a proper psychological analysis indicates to us that no
man is truly irreligious. Rather, he adopts a God that is more
befitting his level of development and social feeling. Often his
God (or gods) end up belonging to the lower type and serve to
flatten rather than elevate their consciousness. The AEL's God
grants permission to act in peculiar (often self-and-socially destructive) ways instead of demanding conduct worthy of aspira-
tion and affirmation. Around this figure, some value system will
form—however vague and self-serving it may be—because consciousness itself is hierarchal and totalizing. The demand to hate,
to dehumanize, and to destroy are delivered to the AEL directly
from God himself.

Approaching the AEL
from the Object Relations School

With that brief detour behind us we can return, once more, to
the analysis proper. What I have been discussing throughout
this investigation but until this moment have not yet made explicit is the phenomenon known within psychoanalytic circles as
'*splitting*'. Initially conceived by Hungarian psychoanalyst San-
dor Ferenczi, the concept was developed more fully by Ronald
Fairbairn and the British school of Object Relations. Fairbairn
and his colleagues discovered that when an infant is unable to
combine the fulfilling aspects of the parent with the unresponsive aspects and collapse them into the same individual, the two
become disassociated, leading to a conceptualization of the good
and the bad as separate and discrete entities. This culminates in
an individual who views those they are in relation to (beginning
first with the mother and father) as the absolute personification
of virtue or vice based on whether they feel gratified or frustrated
by them. In extreme cases, the object of this relation may rapidly
oscillate between pure good and pure evil, but they never rep-

26 Sigmund Freud, *Totem and Taboo* (Beacon Press, 1913), 92.

resent a harmonic embodiment of the two values. To nest this psychological insight within a political framing, the fulfillment proffered by a leftist political operative or worldview is imbued with a quality of the good and the benevolent, while the unresponsiveness and frustration offered by rightist operatives and worldviews necessarily denotes the hideous and the profane. The dichotomy of leftist permissiveness and rightist constrictiveness further emphasizes this tendency. These critical psychological deficiencies which emerge so early in infancy and toddlerhood thus mold the individual's neurophysiology in such a way that later on, agents of the educational and politico-media-complex are able to (intentionally or unintentionally, often a combination of the two) exploit them at will.

One's self-concept emerges partly through the negotiated relations between themselves and their nurturing environment, and partly through the mastery of their nascent psychomotor abilities. Pertaining to the former, the volatility in the individual's appraisal of others (all good or all bad) is a reflection of his own volatility as he experiences radical ambivalence in his own self-concept *("I am capable/incapable, lovable/unlovable, good/bad"*, etc.) Assuming a dysfunctional family unit, the "good" parent is invariably the one who capitulates to the demands of the child, while the "bad" parent is the one who frustrates and withholds. A secondary form of splitting may occur where the child internalizes a self-concept of "badness" to preserve a positive relation with the "good" parents who are, in fact, chronic abusers. Both cases find a social environment of dependence and enmeshment, as the child becomes psychologically fused to the parental object(s) in one way or another. These problems of dependence and enmeshment persist throughout the child's life, not only complicating the possibility of healthful intimate relations with others, but distorting their capacity for accurate information processing. Questions of truth and falsehood become far more difficult to navigate, as the child's originary scene was innately—and tragically—one of deception, misdirection, and obfuscation. At the heart of these conflicts are feelings of love and aggression: the fundamental inability to rectify feelings of love and aggression toward the relational object results in the necessity to divide the two so as to never confuse the desires within a single entity. At first this takes the form of designating one parent as angelic and the other as satanic, but as the child develops further attachments, the same processes play out with siblings, peers, and other authorities throughout his life. Healthful psychological development is achieved through a process of individuation whereby the child's emergent sense of autonomy and capacity for initiative allows him to overcome his want of the other. Invariably the other (mother, father) will fail in some way to meet the needs of the child; these failures, when properly integrated into the child's developing schemas, are understood not as a turning away—or worse, a will to destroy—but as a function of individuality and its inherent separateness, which can be resolved by the child's emerging sense of self-sufficiency. However, it is attempts (intentional or habitual) on the part of the parents to stifle this emergent autonomy which disturb the individuation process and thus fracture the child's self-concept.

Putting these discoveries again into their relevant context—what troubles the AEL most is when the subject of his derision *fails* to be easily categorized in some garish or cartoonish way as "pure evil", "stupid", "ugly", "incompetent" or "lacking social graces". If a "fascist" (or simply a rightist of any type) is intelligent, good-looking, well-educated or in some other manner possess higher social status, this creates a situation of extreme tension and cognitive dissonance, thus straining the limits of the AEL's capacity for splitting. The sheer power of the real penetrates his consciousness, assaults and denigrates his map of the world, thereby inflicting yet more unmanageable suffering.

> *"How could this person think this way? He seems so normal!"*

> *"But he is so educated and well-spoken! How is this even possible?"*

Commonly we will hear such desperate and exasperated lines of questioning from these individuals as they struggle to accommodate their existing schemas with this new information. The more ideophilic AEL (or simply the less mentally adroit) will simply respond by saying, *"that's what makes them so dangerous."* In other words, psychological tension is resolved through an intensifying of the original feeling. In cognitive terms, accommodation requires the modulation of an existing schema to adapt oneself to the changing circumstances of the world around one. Owing to either a poverty of critical faculties or an overinvestment in the progressive liberal paradigm, the only available options are some form of denial or dismissal of the revelation, or a reinforcement of the existing schemas.

It is worthwhile to examine this sentiment further. "*'X' person is even more evil and sinister precisely because he is so obviously gifted.*" The threat here is twofold in that this person will be more successful in pursuing their stated political ends due to genetic and material advantages, but also because the fact of their existence threatens the AEL's mental equilibrium (which is at all times dangerously teetering on the verge of total collapse).

In the Kleinian sense we can say that AELs are trapped in what is known as "*the paranoid-schizoid position*". The paranoid-schizoid position (being the first stage of the psychological development of the child), requires a healthy nurturing environment if the child is to progress to the depressive position (the final stage of development), develop an ego, and individuate from the mother. For Klein, splitting (the schizoid half of the equation) is the necessary process by which the child can withstand feelings of hostility and destruction until the ego develops, thus allowing him to tolerate ambivalence. Until that happens, the unindividuated child fears persecution (the paranoid half), and fears being destroyed by the mother (itself a projection of *Thanatos*, the death pulsation).

To once again transpose this to our immediate concerns, if we assume that a childhood experience fraught with anguish and hostility serves as the bedrock upon which later traumas, manipulations, and distortions can shape the individual's worldview, then the AEL's feeling of persecution originates in a subjectively experienced sense of hostility from the mother—partly true, but at the same time an outwardly projected death instinct—and is further complicated by the emergent and still unindividuated sense of guilt that arises from such a wish. After all, it is the feeling of guilt generated by the child's own aggression which drives him toward individuality, toward recognizing the separateness between himself and the mother, and thus toward an integration of love and aggression. As such, rightists then become a kind of

Big Other; unknowable, distant, and comprised entirely of the AEL's paranoid projections, the Other is bound up in the subject's phantasy—a phantasy wherein the subject seeks the destruction of the Other. Lacking the ego necessary to individuate and eventually tolerate ambiguity and ambivalence, the AEL is forever mired in projections and self-persecutory phantasies of destruction.

Vertical Splitting and National Socialism

Hostilities toward a nationalist expression of socialism (or a socialist nationalism, if you prefer) are themselves a representation of splitting made manifest, as we have the "good" politic (socialism) and the "bad" politic (nationalism), and never the twain shall meet—just as there can be no merging of the "goodness" and "badness" of the parent. Here we see a vertical split,[27] as described by Heinz Kohut. The vertical split divides psychic material that is available to the conscious, separating incompatible desires through an act of mutually disavowed denial. Each desire is made distinct by its aesthetic, moral, and teleological differences; on the one side we have a more mature desire rooted in the real, while on the other we have a desire of pure pleasure principle. Unlike the horizontal split, distinguished by its defense of repression which blocks the expression of the infantile and fantastical material, the vertical split allows for the transgressive or infantile phantasy to become actionable (as in the case of addictions, paraphilias, and the like).

Nationalism and socialism are mutually incompatible not for any practical reason, and certainly not because of any intrinsic theoretical or philosophical conundrum which the combination of the two may pose. Instead, they are mutually incompatible because it is *sinful* and *psychologically insufferable* to do so. Which is not to say that a synthesis of the two is necessarily correct or advantageous (though one may very well be able to make that argument), but more significantly that it is *morally taboo* to attempt it.

Once again, we are confronted by the theological nature of

27 Arnold Goldberg, *The Problem of Perversion: The View From Self Psychology* (Yale University Press, 1995).

the neurotic AEL. Standing in flagrant contrast to his identity as a scientific and open-minded thinker, there are, in fact, no-go zones in his mind, lest thinking about these ideas in any way that does not result in a swift moral condemnation cause some unknown and unpredictable calamity to befall him and his fellow man. It is not unlike the habits of an obsessive-compulsive, who, being so preoccupied by the thought of death and destruction (often an unacceptable personal wish to bring them about), works himself into a state of delirium by crafting an unending and ever more elaborate set of rituals strict adherence to which will prevent the fulfillment of his secret death wish. AELs are often recognized by the extremely ornate and irritatingly bourgeois construction of social and political worldviews which must anticipate and prevent the (apparently) necessary violence that would emerge were their hated enemies to gain control of the political machine. Once more we can look to Klein's theory of the egoless paranoid-schizoid position and see how guilt, stemming from an outwardly projected death wish, manifests itself in ambivalent phantasies of persecutory destruction and honorable heroism.

Vertical splitting, being necessary to avoid confrontation with the taboo of Nazism (because the synthesis of nationalism and socialism by any group of people, at any point in history, irrespective of how distally implemented the synthesis may have come about, is always reducible to the menace of the Third Reich), represents a violent slamming shut of the mental door of intellectual development. Not merely a slamming shut of the door, but also a barring of it from both sides. The taboo against Nazism itself has been elevated above all other taboos previously held by rational societies, including the taboo against incest, pedophilia, bestiality, and even necrophilia. It is the apotheosis—the taboo to end all taboos—the final line in the sand, against which all Western governments have elected to frantically lock hands and draw together. In that sense, the ideophilic psychology in favor of such cravenly immoral and unjustifiable political positions (like free and open borders, unfettered migration, etc.) can be understood as a kind of manifestation, or the political realization, of a collective ego defense. In effect, these policies serve to rebalance the psychological equilibrium and dispel feelings of guilt generated by the assumption of collective responsibility for past transgressions, thereby reaffirming the self-concept of the nation and its people. Traditionally, defense mechanisms are practiced internally or even interpersonally. But one could argue that the superorganism of the State, itself a kind of entity, "acts out" these defense mechanisms in the form of implementing certain policies so as to avoid ever broaching the psychologically threatening possibility of a socialist nationalism.

The Left-Liberal's Type 1 Problem

I would like to elaborate further on this notion of the *reductio ad Hitlerum*. As I have argued throughout this work, the essential feature of the spellbinder's protocol is to impair the average person's natural ability for sound judgment and pattern detection. When presented with accurate information, uncomplicated by abstract obfuscation or motivated reasoning, the average person is rather competent at analysis and decision making (insofar as their judgment is not dependent on technically specific knowledge). While they may lack the sophistication afforded to some by exceptional cognitive ability and high caliber education and mentorship, invariably they will be able to come to remarkably accurate albeit crude conclusions with regards to the parameters of their social environment, and even the nature of political hierarchies and their given motivations. The psychopath's overdetermined sense of ability and importance instills in them a hatred of others, whom he views as necessarily lower in value and less competent than himself. In short, people are stupid, lazy, incapable of self-governance and unfit for even the most menial and undemanding of tasks. Not only must they be led, but they must be taught how—and what—to think. Spellbinding is thus the introduction of an alien consciousness, a false consciousness, into the minds of those the spellbinder seeks to control. After all, the ultimate and perhaps most necessary form of control is that of the human mind. Psychopaths are the true caste of totalitarians, and totalitarianism is the logical system of governance for these types. Freedom, choice, and will are all threats to not only a totalitarian government, but in fact, to totalitarians themselves. And so, the typical person must have choices preselected for them, their cognitive map must be provided for them, and a clear demarcation between acceptable thoughts—and acceptable people—must be determined and enforced by the pathocratic totalitarian class.

For decades, researchers in the disciplines of psychology and political science have attempted to identify the exact kind of person who is rule-following and authority-conforming, but in truth, these are necessary cognitive features of all but the most extraordinary and atypical of humans. In the final analysis, for just about everyone you will ever meet, the question is not "*will I subordinate myself to another?*" but "*to whom will I subordinate myself?*" It is a question of righteous and legitimate authority, for no one truly rejects the exceptional in toto. With the identification and acceptance of a given authority comes the expectation that it will fulfill its critical functions. The most critical function of authority is its role as shepherd; authority is tasked with proper guidance and the defense of the people against those who would do them harm. But the attitude authority holds toward itself, its own self-concept, and its very techniques of governance, have changed. Authority no longer secures groups of people or large, delineated territories, but objects and resources. Figures of power have turned inward and become nihilistic, disinterested, and antisocial. Modern authorities correctly identify those they are supposed to protect as being those most dangerous to their own security and power. This is because they are, in large part, illegitimate. And so, in order to maintain their power, they must obfuscate the cognitive maps of those beneath them and distort their ability to meaningfully analyze the information provided to them. Power must distort the friend–enemy distinction so that the lower classes cannot meaningfully organize against them. Thus, we have the problem of the left-liberal's chronic type 1 error.

Though I have specified this as a problem of left-liberalism, in truth it is a problem for liberalism and its adherents writ large (extremist and moderate, antisocial and eusocial, leftist and rightist alike). However, the problem of the false positive, of the hypersensitivity to particular symbols and signifiers, and of the overeager desire to elasticize political categories, is birthed by the hegemonic control over culture of which left-liberals are the primary beneficiaries. As such, this necessitates a more stringent focus on their particular error, for we cannot merely decapitate the Lernaean Hydra, we must thrust our burning sword directly into its neck and put it to rest once and for all.

Left-liberalism—with its emphasis on peaceful demonstration, non-discrimination, compassion, and kindness—finds a curious asymmetry when juxtaposed with its other personal and political axiom of punching Nazis and dispossessing rightists. Naturally this dichotomy belies its axiomatic humanism and indicates to us the all-or-nothing truth of the political. A contradiction such as this would not necessarily be so civically damaging if we were able to judiciously discriminate against politically and culturally damaging types—in other words, adopt a dictum of morally justifiable discrimination and non-violent ostracism (and endorse the use of violence when positively necessary). It is simply a matter of correctly identifying who ought to be the target of that prejudice, which further elucidates for us the problem of the left-liberal's type 1 error. For the statistically ignorant, the type 1 error, or the problem of the false positive, occurs when a researcher incorrectly identifies the presence of a condition. Put another way, type 1 errors occur when one fails to reject an incorrect hypothesis. These errors deal with a single condition ("*is Ted a Nazi?*") and liberals all too regularly fail to recognize the absence of the condition ("*yes, of course Ted is a Nazi. He watches Ben Shapiro videos!*").[28] The taboo against rightist politics is so strong that the most tepid and lukewarm political positions a temperamentally right-wing person could take (e.g. centrist, right-of-center, conservative, etc.) carry the moral weight equivalent to that of a genocidal maniac.

The self-evident technical accuracy and moral superiority of the left-liberal's arguments confer upon his believers a self-assuredness bordering on arrogance; it is simply not possible for him to imagine alternatives to his stated positions. Unless, of course, when he imagines that the opposite of his worldview is tantamount to pure evil (which is no different than saying he lacks true imagination). In many cases it is only necessary that

28 To borrow a phrase from Lacan, even if Ted were in fact a Nazi, the leftist's fear would still be pathological. The preoccupation is itself the dysfunction. The pleasure, (or jouissance, to more fully embrace the Lacanian train of thought), in fearing the Nazi, in identifying and persecuting him, is of a distinctly neurotic and thus phobic type.

he be confronted by *modest* deviations from his positions in order to earn the ignoble status of evil right-wing fascist Nazi. However, this psychology is aided by two key factors, which are considerably more necessary to the creation and maintenance of current affairs than the simple attitudes and habits of a given political subject: a) the dominance of this worldview, and b) its omnipresent and omnipotent representation in virtually all forms of publicly consumed media. The continual reinforcement of these values and sentiments bombards individual consciousness, demanding subjugation from all but the most disinclined members of the population (who will simply buckle under the pressure of around-the-clock marginalization and propaganda). In particular, the alternatives made available through establishment channels are themselves couched within the same framework that the left-liberal operates within, providing him a deliberately weak counterpoint which is made the target of derision and mockery by approved establishment representatives. The left-liberal is reassured of his position, while the right-liberal is held within frame, never permitted to truly consider antagonistic modes of thought and action. When push comes to shove, both left and right liberal representations will converge, thus achieving a kind of Hegelian synthesis and securing further hegemonic control of all available political options.

Media domination by politically motivated operatives results in large scale distortions which prevent the populace from developing accurate concepts or assessing the true probability of a given event. Certain traits or characteristics are attributed to a given individual or group just as certain types of events are reported while others are not. Control over perception (and thus, over action) relies, then, on the willful misrepresentation of a subject's identity and his propensity to behave in some fashion. Because we live in a complex world and are limited by time and energy, we often rely on heuristics rather than algorithms to help us navigate our environment. Algorithms are formulaic modes of cognition which are situation-specific, and if applied properly, will always provide us with the correct answer. We use algorithms in circumstances of certainty, where parameters are clearly established and we have a clear understanding of the nature of the problem. Put another way, in situations of maximum informational availability (e.g. an address and route to your friend's house, a mathematical formula, etc.), algorithms will prevail. When we lack a clear understanding of the problem, are confronted with either *too much* or *not enough* information to make a decision, or do not have enough time to implement an algorithmic approach (as algorithms, though efficient, can be time consuming), we rely on heuristics. Ambiguity, uncertainty, and expediency are the calling cards of heuristic cognitions.

Why is this relevant? Because the information provided to us *and how often it is provided to us* can distort the way we perceive sociopolitical events and conflicts. Consider the representativeness heuristic, wherein we judge the probability of an event based on prior knowledge and experience. Another way to explain this strategy might be to say that we judge a given situation based on how similar it is to an already existing prototype. Recall our friend Ted. Now, imagine you are in the unenviable position of having to decide at first glance whether Ted is a Nazi. Suppose you know that Ted is over six feet tall, likes to lift weights, watches Jordan Peterson lectures, has blue eyes, and is pro-life. The representativeness heuristic would indicate to you that yes, in fact, Ted is a Nazi. Why? Because the prototype of any given concept ("the thing most like itself") is determined by powerful figures in media (specifically the artistic media) and education, individuals who are themselves heavily biased in how they represent a given image or idea. Ideophilic academics expand our semantic network by continually elaborating new characteristics of Nazism, connecting it to increasingly implausible features which are then reinforced through the visual media of television, cinema, and the various social media networks.

The representativeness heuristic tells you how to identify a Nazi, but the availability heuristic tells you how much you should be concerned about the threat of Nazism. Again, we can look to the influence of media (in this case, the journalistic media) and education for our understanding of why this is true. By highlighting the alleged frequency of Nazi violence, we become vulnerable to the misperception that there is a looming threat of Nazism which endangers us all. The availability heuristic basically indicates to us that the more easily we can recall something, or the easier it comes to mind, the truer or more significant it is.

When journalists and reporters highlight instances of violence (while neglecting others), they bias the way we judge the likelihood and importance of a given event. We can understand, then, why the type 1 problem is so common among liberals; the informational network we depend upon skews the collective schema, bloats our shared semantic network, and leads us to a wide range of socially damaging misperceptions.

We need not assume malevolence or stupidity when attempting to understand the commonplace cognitive errors made by left-liberals, though doing so may offer us psychological comfort and a sense of intellectual and moral superiority. When no alternatives are available, we are not limited by the human imagination, but by a social reality made manifest by hegemonic top-down authority. We have all heard the old saying, "*it is easier to imagine the end of the world than to imagine the end of capitalism*". If our friends at the top do not want to conceive of an alternative (or simply hide its existence), then we are at a supreme disadvantage to do so ourselves. Naturally, those few people who are temperamentally capable of such thought, already marginalized by virtue of their atypical neurological condition, are further marginalized by the internally reinforcing strength of the social dynamic and political power. Vision, i.e. creative foresight, is a rare gift typical of the artist and the inordinately intelligent. The farther away from the norm such individuals find themselves, the more difficult a time they will have integrating into the social order and finding a positive reception among their peers. And if they are truly dissident in their visionary ability, those problems are only magnified. That such individuals look at a given image, situation, or person, and see something *other* than what hegemony wants them to, alienates them from the larger culture. By alienating people who think differently, the problem of the type 1 error only grows, as there are fewer and fewer people capable of offering a counter-interpretation.

Leftism and Ego Deficiency

A key psychological failure of the AEL lies within the deficit of his ego functioning, particularly his failure to differentiate between internal and external phenomena. Students of the Ego psychology school know this by its proper name, "*reality testing*".

In short, reality testing is the process of evaluating and aligning the objective and the real with the subject's experience of it. It is my contention that AELs in particular struggle (and often outright fail) to correctly map their subjective experience to that of their material reality. Cognitive inflexibility and a lackluster capacity for accommodation, therefore, are central features of their psychology.

The AEL manifestly presents as a psychologically underdeveloped individual, though part of his condition of being infantilized is itself a result of culturally deployed methods of control. Resistance to change and authority, the desire to passively accept personal failings and not move beyond them (often reframed as virtues or immutable psychological truths, so as to maintain syntonicity[29] and coherence), infatuations or obsessions with the habits and interests of a child—all of these characteristics point to a stunted narcissism which locks the AEL into a regressive stage of development. To a large degree the psychology of the AEL is especially oriented toward preserving what Melanie Klein called the *"phantasy"* whenever they find themselves drawn into confrontation with specific instances of reality. Defined somewhat differently between Klein, Freud, and Lacan, here we take the meaning to be that of a mirage, a pleasant or self-serving mirage of the real, created by the subject and used as his means for interacting with the world and those within it. Understood properly, it is a mediating force or psychological bubble by which the subject engages with the social reality. AELs operate very much under the thrall of their own phantasy to such a degree that they are unable to interact with the real in any meaningful way. In fact, confrontations with the real often produce intense and uncontrollable hysterical responses. The phantasy is a utopia, a feature of the pre-egoic and unindividuated phase of development that serves as the chief psychological mechanism for negotiating between the subject's desire and the external world of phenomenon.

Further evidence that confirms the weak ego functioning of the AEL can be found in his tendency for extremely poor impulse control and affect regulation, evidenced by his extreme risk taking, emotional outbursts, and inability to self-soothe

---

29 As in, "egosyntonic"; the condition of being in alignment with one's ego

once triggered into a state of hyperarousal. Prone to outbursts not unlike that of the emotionally disregulated child, AELs (and even their more milquetoast left-liberal compatriots) quite literally ball up their firsts, stomp their feet, shriek at the top of their lungs, and wallow in the complete immersion of rage and despondency. One may easily conjure images of election night in 2016, when left-liberals around the country collectively melted down sensing that the season of their discontent was only just beginning. Penetrating the phantasy too deeply provokes exactly these types of intense hysterical reactions.

In light of these facts, we can clearly see that AELs, particularly on the lower functioning end—the anti-fascist street soldier, the online Nazi hunter, and to a lesser degree (though present all the same) the activist journalist—possess a poorly developed ego and an unrestrained id. To the degree that leftist politics are a manifestation of the refutation of authority and a refutation of oppressive and arbitrary moral dictates, we see a psychology of pure pleasure principle. In particular, their political activism itself is a pleasure pursuit; they derive tremendous satisfaction by routing out "Nazis" and "fascists", though the credibility of such claims are so flimsy as to be regarded wholly as a function of phantasy and projection. Were these individuals not granted social and political license to enact their sociopolitical revenge fantasies, one could easily dismiss these people entirely. In fact, that has largely been the response of the average rightist: "*would you believe what these wackjob lunatics are up to?*" is the extent of analysis from the average, well-to-do right-wing American. Such an attitude betrays a deep and fundamental misunderstanding of the sociopolitical climate, for it is the higher functioning AELs—the media personality, the pop singer, the college professor, the corporate executive, and the human resource manager—who provide hierarchal legitimacy to the ranting and raving of these lower, more poorly psychologically adapted members of society. Similarly id driven, for that is in essence the foundation of the permissive and cavalier brand of cultural and political liberalism that has taken root since the mid-twentieth century, these individuals—the Brahmins of American society—only give lip service to the moral dictates of the cultural superego. Having found (or simply been handed) positions of respectability, the high-caste extremists adopt the veil of civility and honor in order to manage their day-to-day affairs but are quick to dismiss them in situations of personal or political gain. They are not *immoral* or even *amoral* people, they merely operate under a different rule of engagement; theirs is the positive morality of a zealot, fueled by a sense of purpose that drives their will toward conquest. It is the overwhelmingly White and bourgeois liberals who suffer the pangs of a negative morality most harshly, a superego-induced conscience restrained by a more traditional morality infused with the eccentricities of a neoliberal and intersectional order.

The activist and street protestor are the children while the professor and the journalist are the parents. As the priestly class, these individuals provide the moral and intellectual armaments (in classic Jouvenelian fashion), which their rabble-rousing allies in the underclass can then take into combat. Not only do these Machiavellian parents provide, but they also protect; when their children run afoul of the law or are otherwise exposed for their misdeeds, they are quickly rescued and able to resume their fiendish plotting relatively unobstructed. This tactic has proven to be an unabashed success: as per Christopher Caldwell's historical investigations, Americans have been operating under (and arguing over) two different constitutional ontologies—the foundational American documents of the late eighteenth century, and the legislative coups of the mid-twentieth century. Unfortunately for heritage Americans, they failed to recognize just how serious the revolutionaries were about winning that argument. AELs in the upper and lower classes fought in the courtrooms, the classrooms, and on the streets—and won—while the rest of the country blinked and went back to work. Just like the undisciplined child, having never been subjected to any form of parental reprobation, continues about his antisocial ways, AELs secured legitimization of their political skullduggery through the simultaneous phenomena of the fanaticism of their allies and the apathy of their enemies.

In a more traditional sense, the superego represents the internalization of moral laws, as represented first by the family, later by the educational system, and then finally by the larger cultural and political systems governing a society. The problem of course for American society is, whose morals? Whose dictates? On one hand, the superego of the leftist—in particular, White and hetero-sexual leftists—is a superego of shame and misbegottenness, ow-ing to a revolutionary and liberation-oriented ontology that has relentlessly castigated them for over half a century. As such, they are compelled to act in the characteristically ethnomasochistic manner which we have so richly observed thanks to the promul-gation of mass media and internet communications. Freud con-ceptualized the superego as serving a critical civilizational role: subordination of the id to the superego is not just good for you as an individual, it is good for the whole of society. When we check our sexual and violent impulses, our communities thrive. Of course, we return to the question of *for whom is it good?* Increas-ingly, old-stock leftists in the lower and middle classes no lon-ger *have* a community of their own, and so the subordination of their id (which is, in truth, a subversion of their superego) results in actions which serve the New America that Caldwell described in his book. The superego of the transracial, transreligious left-wing leviathan, however, operates under an entirely different set of moral dictates. Unlike the largely post-Christian Whites, the AEL leviathan is thoroughly Nietzschean and finds no action too unscrupulous, so long as it advances the pursuit of power. AELs of the ascendant New America possess a superego which enables the id, while leftists of the Old America suffer under the kind of repressive self-destruction that Sigmund Freud could only have dreamed of. On the other hand, we have upper-class Whites who (all too happy to engage in self-aggrandizing class antagonism) oscillate between public demonstrations of guilt and demands for the extraction of indulgences from their racial cohorts in the lower classes. Here, too, we see the deficit in ego functioning, though manifested in a peculiar way. Repulsed by the crude and nativist tendencies of "The Bad Whites", they find a paramoral justification for their revulsion, one which provides a longer-term preservation of their status in a rapidly changing sociopolitical climate.

Narcissism and the Rejection of the Ego Ideal

A central notion found within the leftist theory of the self in-cludes a rejection of the ego ideal, a fact which we can easily observe in permissive mantras such as *"you're perfect the way you are.*" Ableism, the body positivity movement, the anti-HIV stigma movement, mental-illness-as-essentialism, and hostility to any mantra of self-improvement, are now unassailable truths and function as important strategies for the reproduction of left-ist values. Physical fitness, beautification, development of tech-nologies that treat or reverse congenital disorders—these are all viewed as necessary markers of right-wing sympathy or steps on the slippery slope toward fascist ideology. For the left, though AELs have always led the charge on this, the ego ideal must be abolished because it implicitly recognizes that an objective, hi-erarchal standard *does* exist or at least can be found somewhere in the world. Any measurement is therefore a kind of oppression and conforming to a norm outside of one's own solipsistic pref-erence is its own violence. This is the narcissism of the AEL, who seeks to be accepted as they are, in a kind of anally expulsive way. According to Freud, the second stage of psychosexual de-velopment—the anal stage—represents the child's first step into adulthood. He must assume an autonomous responsibility for himself, and more importantly, he must conform to the norm of the toilet, as per the royal decree of his parents. Rejection of authority, of standards, of the will or expectation to conform to a mode of being that is outside of one's self are fundamentally indicative of an anal fixation, an expulsive personality that seeks the abolition of all limits. Curiously, it is interesting to note the myriad of ways in which contemporary American society is it-self anally fixated, from the introduction of anilingus into the American sexual vernacular, the emergent popularity of gluteal implants, the incorporation of best practices for anal sex into sexual education courses around the country, and the general loosening (or releasing) of standards and expectations both in the workplace and in the educational system. Freud observed that defecation was man's first creative act; undoubtedly it is an act of creation, albeit one of low effort. The goal of the AEL is to capture all of us within that pre-oedipal fixation, relegating being itself to the status of the absolute bottom common denom-inator. Like their psychological compatriots to their right, AELs prefer the soothing comfort of the ideal-ego, though here it takes on the quality of exaltation rather than phantasy. They are not deluded as to who they truly are, rather they delude themselves in its significance and universal appeal.

The fatal conceit of the leftist theory of self is in its reflexive unwillingness to examine the id: the pleasure principle is the AEL's psychological God, and they will under no circumstance commit deicide. Proper psychological maturity necessitates the cultivation of an ego ideal according to which the individual works to rein the pleasure principle into a matrix of axioms, values, and norms which allows him to situate himself within the broader psychosocial ecosystem to which he belongs. Understanding this, we can see that the psychology present both in the lower functioning and higher priestly leftists is primarily concerned with lowering American prestige. College campuses are a breeding ground for this type of psychology, as merely being psychologically adroit enough to tolerate discussions of triggering intellectual topics is itself a kind of fascism—a hostility to those people who have been grafted to the leftist ecology (e.g. women, homosexuals, illegal immigrants, religious minorities, non-Whites, the physically handicapped, the mentally ill and otherwise cognitively impaired, etc.) To the AEL, the ego ideal is psychological fascism, an oppressive consciousness of disappointing objectivity which terrorizes as it divides. That they take such a position speaks volumes about their fragility, a fact of which they seem all too aware. Approaching this with a more generous spirit, we might say that their insight into their own weakness provides an entirely understandable albeit mistaken basis for their rejection. Were it to be confined to the domain of the intrapersonal, we would find it unobjectionable. However, it has been given a political character and increasingly finds undue influence within the broader American culture, to the detriment of all.

The presence of an ideal exacerbates feelings of inferiority; when we identify an ideal, we are necessarily introducing difference—and in particular, distance—between ourselves and that ego ideal. Often the ego ideal is the internalization of some external object: initially it may take the form of a maternal or paternal relational object, but as the child develops more (and more complex) object relations, any number of valued community members may present opportunities for ego measurement. For AELs, ameliorating the anxiety of inferiority is achieved not through identifying the source of that anxiety and embodying the characteristics of the ego ideal, but through the elimination of the ideal altogether. Alternatively, and this phenomenon can be observed in the leftist's penchant for fetishizing alien cultures, a state of total subservience and even slavishness is taken on by the individual, often gratefully. An attitude of worship and greatness-by-proximity are adopted both to allay the anxiety, and as a means for situating the individual in a social context. *"It is better to be at the bottom than to not be in it at all."* These types are willful slaves who derive pleasure not by manifesting their will through striving and achieving, but by nullifying the will and reifying the greatness and *obvious* superiority of the desired object. In a multicultural and multiracial setting such as America, distance and difference in ego ideals also trigger other taboo anxieties, particularly racial and class anxieties. Feelings of inferiority are initially generated or implanted in youth, often as the result of harsh familial or communal experiences that lack empathy. Whether it is due to legitimate organ inferiority (or the *"first inferiority"*, the Adlerian notion of the individual's perceived lack), the extremely dehumanizing and condescending transferences of the parent, or excessive and humiliating comparisons to siblings and peers, the sense of inferiority often finds its origins in the home. It may arise out of overly harsh condemnations for failing to meet expectations, or simply result from unjust attacks for totally normal and developmentally appropriate failures of the child. In any case, this early destabilization creates easily stimulated neurobiological patterns of fear and self-loathing which can be further compounded and triggered throughout the lifespan. The *"second inferiority"*, as Adler termed it, manifests in adulthood when the individual fails to achieve in the ways one would typically expect of a fully grown adult. Or to use Adler's own language, they fail to reach a *"fictional final goal"*, i.e. they never realize their life's hidden mission. The inferiority of the second leads to a recall of the original inferiority; the fictional goal is developed as an antidote to the first feeling of inferiority, and so the failure to achieve this goal reinforces the foundational sense of weakness and futility. Whether the original feeling was real and then reified, or merely the imaginary result of a game of comparisons, the individual remains trapped within the confines of an ever-realizable prophecy of self-fulfillment. Experiences such as these are fuel for the neurotic's fire—providing them with a lifetime supply of torment from which they may never achieve respite.

Here we find a level of rage which burns with a revolutionary intensity: "*I may be nothing, but there is still something I can do about it*". That "something" of course, is the erosion of the social order. The AEL, particularly of the lower variety, never successfully compensates for this feeling of inferiority, but rather resigns himself to it entirely. His identity is inexorably defined by the inability to perform any meaningful social role or fulfill any intimate social relation, and his attempts at overcoming that inferiority find their realization through faux-revolutionary violence. However, when we look up the social ladder, we find the AELs who graduate to the level of superiority complex. Succeeding in the realization of their fictional final goal, (though in today's bioleninist world, it is less of a *succession* and more of a *selection*), they now wield their *obvious* social and vocational achievements like a broadsword, ready to be unsheathed at a moment's notice. In classical Adlerian theory, this, too, may not be about the lording of success over the peasantry, but rather an ego defense to mask the deep wound of inferiority from which they never recovered. This of course is only one possibility. More commonly, however, we see these feelings of superiority manifesting largely in people who feel that "*their time has come*", perceiving systemic oppression as the only rational explanation for why their *obvious* greatness (and that of their peoples) was not recognized sooner. In this case, their original feeling finds its resolution through a psychology of retribution which is directed at those who had suppressed them for so long. Ethnic, gender, and sexual narcissism of all kinds are observed in those people who have found themselves elevated to positions of privilege over the last sixty years, as a result of cultural changes brought about by the civil rights constitution Caldwell wrote of.

Unveiling the Extremist, Part II: Identifying the Pathology of the AER

The antisocial extremist of the right is given to—in particular,

and in direct contrast to the AEL—grandiosity and megalomania deriving in part not from an overdeveloped ego (as opposed
to the underdeveloped ego of the leftist) but an ego and superego
that nonetheless overpowers the id. It may be said that the AER
possesses an overdeveloped ego insofar as it is the psychically
dominant force between the two (ego and id), but it is not well
developed, nor does it function within its optimal parameters.
We can apply an Adlerian analysis here as well by understanding
the strong psychological need to overcome feelings of inferiority
(though the genesis of his inferior sentiment finds its roots in a
multiplicity of areas as opposed to the psychosingularity of the
AEL). Both the superego and the ego ideal are stronger mental
forces in the mind of the AER; to paraphrase Freud, the attitude
of "*thou shalt*" strongly influences the attitude and behavior of
these types (whereas it might be said that the AEL subscribes
to a morality of "*thou shalt not*"). And while the ego ideal figures more strongly in the AER's development, we must recognize its stunted and calcified nature; it is not the representation
of an authentic ideal, but rather a rigid and ideophilic notion,
having entered into a state of rigor mortis due to overidentification with and the need for the ideal to conform to certain prefig-
ured notions within the self (rather than the other way around).
What results, then, is a flaccid and disintegrated individual who
responds not to truth or virtue, but to the strong man and to
demonstrations of the will regardless of their intent or consequence. Loyalty and honor are, therefore, not in his nature—his
allegiances shift as quickly and as often as does his emotional
state. Having provided a succinct overview of his condition, let
us dig into the specifics beginning with the AER's impoverished
ego ideal.

Right Extremism and the Degraded Ego Ideal

To a large degree, the rightist is understood by his martial character. The archetype of the soldier, the conqueror, and the king
figure prominently in right-wing psychology. It is a natural consequence of his appreciation for hierarchy and order. This sentiment has only gotten stronger as American culture has moved
farther away from a method of authority that is both identifiable
and responsible for itself. As authority degenerates, loses its spir-

itual character, and cedes any notion of morality or justifiability, power becomes its own end rather than a means. AERs, being reactionary[30] and not contemplative, impotently flail at and bemoan the state of affairs until, at last, capitulating to it. Thus, the AER adopts a nihilistic will to power, merely seeking to ape the habits and conduct of the other rather than to radically alter or overthrow it. As such, the AER deals only with the surface level, with appearances and immediacies, and when seeking for an icon to internalize and emulate, looks for those historical and cultural figures who give the impression of strength. Or—he reduces multidimensional and holistic persons into a flat, two-dimensional caricature, bled dry of all idiosyncrasies and atypicalities. He, like the version of the hero he tarnishes to fit inside his tiny mind, becomes a cartoon. A figure ultimately worth no more than absolute ridicule.

The ego ideal, rather than being a challenging and aspirational psychological force, is, in the hands of the AER, not unlike the dollar store superhero costume hastily plucked off the rack by an overeager child, desperate to wear it for Halloween. It is a psychological affectation, or a political fashion, designed to make the individual feel closer to their chosen icon without undergoing a fully transformative process, one that would take them far beyond their petty resentments and grandiose visions. This fact betrays the inherent fragility of the extremist and his obvious unworthiness, as he cannot tolerate the intensely scrutinizing self-skepticism of reflective thought. In his delusion he happens upon a permissiveness of his own—a permissiveness of personal weakness and vice, of low moral character, of sub-average effort, and thus permits all the same conduct in those he fraternizes with. Extremist ecologies are feedback loops of banality and perversion, weakly sustained by shared antipathies and mass scale folie à deux, until they finally collapse under the weight of their preordained decrepitude.

Some progress will be made in the pursuit of their icon, seeing as from the outset these individuals are beset by family strife, economic depression, drug addiction, violence, and all the expected psychological torment which follows in the wake of such

---

30   Defined here as a character of passivity, of responding *to* and not acting *over and above*, and lacking in proactivity.

catastrophes. But their metamorphosis is only partial, hindered
by the biological and social limitations imposed upon them from
the very beginning.[31] The AER's innate tendency for egotism,
grandiose self-applause, and moral distancing from those less
extreme and psychopathically uncompromising than himself,
ensure that he will never reach his fullest potential. To say it another way, *the untermensch mistakes himself for the übermensch.*
It is precisely because he has never retrained his naïve instincts,
never reconsidered his life's ethos, but has instead constructed
atop his rickety foundation a self-incriminating moral artifice
which compromises his very existence. Having moved beyond
his immediate and obvious habit for self-destruction (e.g. drug
abuse, irresponsible sexual relations, volatile work habits, and
so on), he deludes himself as to the depth of his willpower. The
effort should not go unrecognized; however, it is often merely a
prelude to an even harsher fall. Having never explored the factors which put him in the first hole, he can only innovate upon
that strategy by finding bigger and deeper holes in which to land
face first.

Id and Asceticism

At the heart of the AER's repression of the id are paralogistic
connections between pleasure and sloth, spontaneity and frivol-
ity, and self-expression and degeneracy. As one *naturally* gives
way to the other, the AER cultivates a prohibitively paramoralistic view of such behaviors and retreats from them into self-aggrandizing asceticism. Of course, he does not adopt a blanket
view toward *all* pleasure, spontaneity, and expression, but rather
towards those which are most emblematic of the people he hates.
In fact, he valorizes his preferred vices, regarding them as necessities for political and spiritual salvation. The AER's paramoralisms are essential to who he is, as essential as his physical body,
and are thus not easily expelled, much less examined. Behaviors
such as these are integral to his habit of reactionary differenti-

---

31 These limitations, often being entirely out of his control, are real, and yet he
fails to come to terms with them. It is possible to—and in fact, many do—come
to terms with one's own lot in life. Alas, the AER is often a victim of his own
megalomania.

ation, not arrived at through organic principles but rather by a process of constructing himself as the moral antipode of all that is wicked (a delusion or phantasy which he is unwilling to rupture).

Another way of understanding this process may be achieved through Donald Winnicott's concept of the true and false self. The true self being defined by its authentic and organic (or essentialist) nature, affording spontaneity and creativity while offering the individual a reprieve from (or a defense against) despair and nihilism. The false self, however, is a pure simulacrum which traps the individual within a faulty conception of the humane. It is bound by a closed set of abstraction (reifying or concretizing some ideal notion or category of man), simulating a once real person or group but in a degraded, self-serving, and ideophilic manner. The false self is a persona, a mask, an obfuscating deception which gives the individual the sense of reality but denies it to him all the same. The AER is best understood as embodying the false self, disconnected from the real by individual and collective trauma. In this regard, little separates him from his antagonist, both having retreated into solipsism and narcissism. An important element which *does* distinguish them is their respective attitudes toward the pleasure principle.

A commonly understood truism of Freudian theory: superego and id exist in a state of tension, as the pleasure principle requires subordination to some ideal or system of values lest it become a force of pure destruction. While this may not be taken as a universal truth, there is something to the notion that the farther to the right one moves, the greater appreciation one develops for asceticism, and thus a hostility—or at the least a skepticism— emerges toward man's innate and original instinct for quick and immediate pleasure. To the degree that traditional religious values (such as those found in Catholicism, Islam, etc.) and philosophical values (e.g. Stoicism, and so on) are called upon to resist antagonization by extreme liberal individualism, we find corroborative evidence to this claim. For the egalitarian progressive, ideologies like these are viewed as regressive and barbaric—an affront to the enlightened age we find ourselves in. As such, they regard philosophies of restraint with the same level of disgust (if not more so) as the rightist views philosophies of permission.

We need only consider the media reaction to Jordan Peterson when he first emerged as a public intellectual in the latter half of the last decade. However indelicate and ham-fisted his delivery was, Peterson's message of restraint and self-ownership was characterized by more than a few public outlets as implicitly fascistic.[32] [33] [34] [35] [36] So, too, did his defense of traditionalism draw the ire of journalists and academics alike (evidenced best by the controversy surrounding his "enforced monogamy" remarks). Other philosophies of the ideal—self-improvement and physical fitness, for example—are now viewed as "far-right gateways".[37] [38] Similarly, negative attitudes toward pornography and sex work, video gaming and other forms of visual media, promiscuity, as well as drug and alcohol consumption, all give auctoriphobic and anti-rightist establishmentarians nightmares over their latent fascist potentialities. This overwhelming and hysterical response on the part of extreme egalitarians only emboldens right-leaning individuals to push further against the grain and embrace even more extreme repudiations of the progressive zeitgeist. Aggressive renunciation of contemporary American culture is hardly problematic, as the neoliberal monoculture which enframes us is anti-human and anti-prosperity through and through, a fact which strikes the uninitiated as counter-intuitive; progressives

32 John Steffin, "Solzhenitsyn and Jordan Peterson: Fascism, white supremacy and patriarchy", *Worker's World,* December 9th, 2018, https://www.workers.org/2018/12/40081/.

33 Pankaj Mishra, "Jordan Peterson & Fascist Mysticism", *The New York Review of Books,* March 19th, 2018, https://www.nybooks.com/daily/2018/03/19/jordan-peterson-and-fascist-mysticism/.

34 Harrison Fluss, "Jordan Peterson's Bullshit", *Jacobin,* February 2018, https://jacobinmag.com/2018/02/jordan-peterson-enlightenment-nietzsche-alt-right.

35 Noah Berlatsky, "How Anti-Leftism Has Made Jordan Peterson A Mark For Fascist Propaganda", *Pacific Standard,* March 2nd, 2018, https://psmag.com/education/jordan-peterson-sliding-toward-fascism.

36 Ben Brooker, "The 14 rules For Eternal Fascism: Jordan Peterson and the far right", *Overland,* February 14th, 2019, https://overland.org.au/2019/02/the-14-rules-for-eternal-fascism-jordan-peterson-and-the-far-right/.

37 Zoe Williams, "Do you boast about fitness? Watch out – you'll unavoidably become rightwing", *The Guardian,* September 27th, 2018, https://www.theguardian.com/commentisfree/2018/sep/27/do-you-boast-about-your-fitness-watch-out-youll-unavoidably-become-rightwing.

38 Broadly Staff, "Gym Bros More Likely to be Right-Wing Assholes, Science Confirms", *Vice,* May 25th, 2017, https://www.vice.com/en_us/article/j5e3z7/gym-bros-more-likely-to-be-right-wing-assholes-science-confirms.

and capitalists alike portray themselves as the torchbearers of humanity and prosperity, and yet everywhere they achieve prominence we find degradation and poverty. What *ought* to trouble us, however, is the practice of renunciation for renunciation's sake. The AER innovates on his philosophy of intolerance in order to improve its venomosity; he seeks to refine this technology of the self so that it may reflexively and automatically alienate others. He need not expound on his worldview to threaten others, only hint at it. He so thoroughly subsumes himself in the cult of the anti-social that his mere presence does the work of alienation for him (rendering both his gaze and mouth as a kind of surplus repulsion).

To reiterate: as one turns away from liberal permissiveness, this rejection necessarily entails a reevaluating of the relationship between the id and the libido. This is good and healthy. However, an inability to negotiate this relationship, to find and appreciate one's own pleasures without being neurotically preoccupied with condemnations of the other's pleasure, is a clear indicator of psychological disease. One walks a very fine line when he decides to reintroduce shame into a culture which has expunged this social tool so thoroughly. In a society as transvaluated as America, where the technique of shame is used to protect the shameful, just as the technique of intolerance is similarly deployed to shelter the intolerant, only the fool and the madman wield such weapons with unreserved aplomb.

The mark of the AER is an inability to holster his moral pistols. So consumed by his obsession with degeneracy, the AER becomes a caricature of the 19th century gunslinger, always ready to duel—always ready to (socially) die for his cause. He will thrust himself to the absolute margin of society to demonstrate his commitment to anti-degeneracy. His fixation on degeneracy is telling (as Queen Gertrude said, "*the lady doth protest too much, methinks.*"), for it does not so much expose his objection to degeneracy, but rather its nearness to his heart. Whether he cannot forgive himself for participating in the orgiastic degradation of the American soul, or is in fact determined to clandestinely indulge his perverse revelries, his persistence belies the lustful desire inherent to his foaming-at-the-mouth hatred.

The AER's Antisocial Tendency

A representative of the British school of object relations, Donald Winnicott developed the concept of *"the antisocial tendency"* to describe the pattern of behavior demonstrated by delinquent children. Winnicott viewed delinquency as an unconscious and ultimately *hopeful* process of seeking that which is absent—a *"holding environment"*—replete with security and predictable boundaries. Hopelessness typifies the *"deprived child"* who is less given to antisocial behavior, Winnicott argued, because of the internalized belief that no action the child could produce would generate a meaningful response. The delinquent child strikes out not to materially gain from his behavior, but rather to catalyze a responsible authority to action. Or as Winnicott himself said, *"The child who steals, for example, is not looking for the object stolen but the mother over whom he or she has rights."*[39] Deprivation is thus the source and the home of this antisocial tendency, which according to Winnicott could manifest at any point in the child's development and persist throughout his life.

The antisocial tendency operates simultaneously as a boundary-testing mechanism (*"What are the rules? What will be tolerated? What will be punished?"*), as an attention-seeking behavior (*"Recognize me. Applaud me. Punish me. Whatever you do, acknowledge me."*), as a form of affirmation or agency-establishing mechanism (*"I did this. I can move others to act. I exist."*), and as a resolution-seeking behavior (*"This crisis must not continue unabated. Whatever the outcome, it must end now."*). From the object relations view, it is an unconscious striving for correction and clarity, for holism. The behavior we see from AERs of the lower form, those belonging to the underclass, is a classic demonstration of the antisocial tendency. Poorly adjusted, lacking in social integration, and with little opportunity for economic mobility, their destructive acts (whether we speak of the mass shooter, the online activist who collaborates with AELs to expose his competitors, and so on) are ultimately hopeful acts—hopeful in the sense that they will instigate a re-ordering of society. At the proximal level that might mean calling upon the estab-

---

39   Donald Winnicott, *The Collected Works of D. W. Winnicott: Volume 5, 1955-1959* (Oxford University Press, 2016), 149.

lishment to settle petty rivalries, and at the distal level it might mean committing a sacrificial act of violence that triggers racial and class conflicts. Whatever form the act takes, it is always done with the expectation (however minor) that some restorative good will come out of it.

Approaching this problem through the language of generalities is all but assured to provide some inaccuracies, neglect instance-specific productions of the antisocial tendency, and perhaps lead to other unintended mistakes, but these are to be understood as trade-offs in the process of psychologically analyzing larger trends. Family dysfunction, the loosening of attitudes toward divorce and extramarital affairs, insufficient policies for child care and the maintenance of a stable family unit, as well as the promulgation of dysgenic attitudes toward pair-bonding and mating all set the preconditions for the genesis of the antisocial tendency. The antisocial tendency is a civilizational problem and emerges as a moral failure of leadership and a strategic failure of resource allocation. Too often the mistake is made (even by those who ought to have keener insights into the dilemma) of identifying this as an individual failing, which only serves to reinforce the right-liberal's myopic and fetishistic love of personal accountability and responsibility. Individuals fail en masse once collectives begin to degenerate. The old truism, "*no man is an island*" still holds value. For instance, the dreaded school shooter is not a problem to be solved through hypotheses of his moral badness or emotional instability. More funding for mental health services will not prevent further tragedies. Or consider violence perpetrated against ethnic and religious minorities: we should not focus our attention on the "ideology of global white supremacy" that supposedly connects random, deracinated, and disaffected pale-skinned men (be they White, Jewish, Hispanic, Asian, etc.) in an orgy of violence. Browbeating an already complacent and docile population will not dam the river of despair which threatens to flood the known world. Every explanation that sidesteps troublesome inquiries into our modern way of life, with all of its technological advancement, its empowerment of the individual and its utilitarianism, its free-market fetishism and so on, and instead puts the moral responsibility on nebulous concepts and intellectual spooks only secures a future of increasing tumultuousness and horror. Rather the conversation which ought to occur (and rarely ever does) must confront the systemic failures of authority and its obvious lack of moral integrity.

Authority which feels no need to be responsible for itself, which at best holds its subjects accountable for its own failures and at worst neglects them entirely, is an antisocial construct in and of itself. It should not surprise us to find delinquency and antisocial tendencies on the rise, as generations of young men and women have matured in an environment of continual deferral and discussion, with the very notion of finality itself having been suspended. If Winnicott was correct to suggest that the antisocial tendency operates out of an unconscious desire, a hopeful optimism, then we must update his theory, for it no longer accords with our present material circumstances. Today's delinquent, the 21st century expression of the antisocial tendency, is rooted in hopeful pessimism; its hope is eschatological in nature. No authority will respond to the pain of the child, certainly not swiftly and doubtless not justly. Only the authority that emerges from the chaos of perpetual delinquency will respond and posthumously grant the holding environment—the love and justice—that was so sorely lacking. The delinquent AER, eternally a child thanks to the psychological neoteny produced by neoliberal modernity, sets himself up as the martyr, the first prophet of the yet unnamed savior—or better still—the sacrificial offering to a God not yet born. He yearns for the authority over whom he has rights, but all our living authorities have abandoned us. And so, he must create them through acts of wanton carnage.

Chauvinism and Identitarianism

Before delving further into our analysis of the AER, I must first offer a few rebuttals. The considerable degree to which theories and temperaments of the American right have been maligned complicates our ability to properly discern the functional from the dysfunctional. We are not seeing the phenomenon for what it is, because the fog of war is far too thick. Now, there in fact *are* politically and socially dangerous elements within American right-wing politics, however most people cannot accurately distinguish who or what they are thanks to a seventy-year-long campaign of obfuscation. Thus, it is necessary that I cut through the mist so that for perhaps the first time, we may all feel the sun on our faces and see the world with clear eyes.

A common criticism of American right-wing identitarianism, and in particular what is uniformly understood as the "far right" and "alt-right", is the inherent grandiosity and superiority of those who champion it. Critiques of identitarianism and Western chauvinism (related but not identical), will mock adherents of this view for their loud-mouthed boasts of the political, technological, and cultural achievements of their ancestors—the architects of Western civilization. We often hear the refrain that these individuals are animated by the successes of their predecessors, claiming for themselves the victories of their forbearers, which are wholly unearned and unjust, as these individuals have no such achievements of their own upon which they can stand. Far right extremists, in this view, are misguided in their identification with the champions of the past because they utterly fail to build in any meaningful way upon the ground laid out by those who came before them. Put more bluntly: to be born a Virginian does not make one the immediate successor to the legacy of Thomas Jefferson. This is somewhat of a plain (if not obvious) truth, however the veracity of the statement is not in question; rather, it is the intent behind the statement which concerns us.

A second and far more insidious criticism is made by similar individuals when they take the argument a step further and claim that there is in fact no such heritage to draw upon. This argument is made possible by delegitimizing the Western tradition on moral and scientific grounds. Our interlocutors will offer us the idea that on the one hand the West is illegitimate because its global hegemony was achieved by way of violence and subjugation. Morally, the *true* legacy of Western peoples is one of brutality and oppression. Then they will tell us that on the other hand there in fact *is* no Western tradition because its constituent members are all unique people groups with no actual cultural affiliation and no firm claim to ownership of their land or language. Furthermore, the men and women of the West can be scientifically reduced out of existence through the deployment of myopic games of semantics and data mining. Appeals will be made to disciplines such as genetic anthropology using wholly motivated reasoning in order to justify otherwise absurd claims.

They will tell us that, scientifically and philosophically speaking, there is no Western tradition because the "West" never truly existed. Because the "West" is merely a social construct with no true validity, it can thus be dismissed out of hand. This argument is then transferred onto the people of Western civilization using the same logic of destruction.

We can grant aspects of the first argument despite its innate contradictions, for the colonial project of the aggregated Western empires did tally up a frighteningly high body count. Worse still, despite the program of decolonialization (initiated by those very same empires), the reverberations of their initial conquests continue to haunt us. The second argument fails to stand on its own, and it is only the rapid shifting between the two (thus disorienting honest debaters) which grants it efficacy at all. Ultimately what legitimizes the meta-argument ("*you are a bad person, born from bad stock, and thus deserve to be dispossessed and even killed if necessary.*") is not its persuasive effect, but rather that other 'p' word: power. Institutional support grants arguments like these the power to change minds, and more importantly, legal and cultural institutions. At either rate, these psychological time bombs must be disarmed before we can proceed.

Such criticisms fail on each front, the first being that at the same time as indigenous peoples of the West are educated on the wrongness and foolishness of their cultural pride, those *others* (be they of racial, religious, gendered, or some other minoritarian identity) are simultaneously encouraged to draw strength from their past. *And rightly so.* The great chain of being to which we all belong necessitates that we draw strength and inspiration as inheritors of a grand historical tradition. In fact, healthful psychological development is itself predicated on the identification with, and embodiment of, the historical and archetypal heroes found within one's own lineage. The transmission of these stories engenders a sense of connection to and embeddedness within a historical, geographical, cultural, and mythological context that provides the individual with a sense of meaning and a relation both to the world at large, and to himself as an actor within the lifeworld. Without access to a tradition, man is left to his own devices. He must forge a new path without the benefits of a community, a language, a metaphysic, or a philosophy of life—without any of the things he needs to make it in this world. Man needs myth and parable as much as (if not more than) he needs food and drink. Yes, we would die after a sufficient period of starvation and dehydration. But the eternal satiation of these needs does not in and of itself lead us to thrive, much less innovate. Our stories tell us who we are, but more than that, they tell us who we can be. Just as all men and women, we must be allowed to represent ourselves *to ourselves*. And it must be done on our own terms. Without our history, without our collective fictions, we are nothing. No man is an island.

The impulse to deny someone his own history is an act of violence which erases the individual's own sense of continuity, but when enacted on a wide enough scale, all but guarantees the mass failure and nihilism of his collective. In a multicultural context such as we see in the United States, the privilege of historical and cultural continuity is weaponized to legitimate some groups of people at the expense of others in a zero-sum competition for the pursuit of political and cultural dominance. The very techniques employed against the alien-others of America have since been refined, magnified, and finally turned against those who benefitted from them in the first. To deny this basic human necessity is to manifest the kind of antisocial political extremism which this book is dedicated to analyzing (and ultimately, eradicating). In this view, only *some* people are permitted the luxury of genetic and mythic continuity; this is effectively a moral campaign masquerading as an academic one. Only "*the good people*" are deserving of a genealogical inheritance. Those good people, whose goodness is defined as a consequence of their status as historical victims (itself a politicized, and ultimately moral argument—not a factual one), are continually reinforced by the professional classes of the bourgeoisie, who in the present pathocratic era of American culture no longer see their roles as dispensers of fact or truth, but as popularizers and reinforcers of a moral paradigm that at once reifies the political paradigm of the ruling class, while affirming their status as diligent and dutiful foot soldiers of the righteous progressive moral campaign of history.

Secondly, we must understand the presumption which guides the left progressive's approach to scientific inquiry. Academics and activists, being committed to what philosopher Tyler Hamilton has termed "*operational erasure*" are a priori committed to the ontological delegitimization of their political opponents. It is taken as a fact that certain human taxonomies are by their very nature illegitimate—a fact for which providing the necessary scientific proof is but a mere formality. Are such categories as "the West", "White", "British", and so on to be understood in any significant or essential way? Do they exist, and if they do, who has license to claim them as such? The more ideophilic the antagonist, the more he will deny the existence of such categories. And should he be willing to admit such categories *do* exist, he will deny those who would identify as such the exclusive right to do so. Outright denial is not the only means necessary for effecting the political marginalization of one's opponents; elasticizing well-established categories of identification is also an effective strategy for erasure. For those untrained in recognizing a priori metaphysical commitments, the veneer of credibility afforded by the empirical process gives the impression of facticity when in fact no such thing exists. It is the hidden axiom—that unspoken belief—which guarantees that the inquiry will lead to the conclusion assumed from the very beginning. And so, we see now the failures of each argument: masquerading as historical and scientific facts, it should be obvious to all that they are, in reality, *subjective* moral and ontological claims made *objective* by the power of the institutions which disseminate them.

Having said all this, we can now return to the ideas of chauvinism and identitarianism clear eyed and open minded. I submit to you that they *are* in fact problematic, or at least when taken up by psychologically disturbed and disaffected minds, can *become* problematic. Sidestepping the pathological element for the moment, psychologically overidentifying with an abstraction (e.g. civilizational or national ideals like "The West", "America", or racial and ethnic categories such as "White", and so on) demonstrates a stifling and self-destructive impotence that can only be justified through tautological means. Not only is it impotent, but an identitarianism that is stagnant and only looks to the past without catalyzing a forward momentum is also *illegitimate* as a category of identification. It is illegitimate by virtue of signaling a decayed culture and inert spirit. Evolutionarily we could even say it is unfit to continue. Flaccid and lending itself to self-parody, right-chauvinism and right-identitarianism in particular strike me as anachronistic and misguided; to hold racial or civilizational ideals as superior during a time of obvious decline reveals oneself to be deep in the throes of self-delusion. Such individuals entirely lack the capacity for dispassionate appraisal, often mistaking the self-propagandizing tendency of races and nations for the things themselves. In essence, these types are not identifying with the real, or the thing-in-itself, but rather with pure simulacra. Many rightists (be they moderates, radicals, or extremists) base their political and social identities on fictionalized accounts of Westernness, Americanness, Whiteness, Heterosexuality, etc., both as a defense against the program of deconstruction committed by their ideological opponents, but also as a psychological defense against their own confusion and the ambiguity of the very concepts themselves. The falsity of their identification (being revealed in the rightist's inability to articulate them when assailed by a more competent debater), its quality of being out-of-time, and perhaps most importantly their inherent malleability—the creative destruction of their meaning—renders traditional rightists of every stripe unable to coherently act on their identities nor combat the deconstructionist seriously. Perhaps the more salient issue is this: if the elites themselves have disinherited these identifiers, have rendered these supposedly definitive characteristics malleable for their own ends, what social or political utility do they have for the average person? What psychological function do they serve? What communities may be forged around simulations of the real? The answer, sadly, is none. At present, they are merely false collective fictions, psycho-ontological traps deployed to imprison the naïve and further subjugate the powerless.

Denied meaningful attachment figures with which to bond, as well as strong role models to formulate himself after, the AER embraces a full-throated chauvinism and makes a God of his racial or historical type. His ego ideal is drawn not from the immediate family or community, but distant figures from the historical past, projecting onto them all manner of deprived paternalistic sentiment which were denied to him, and stealing for himself the heroic virtue which these historical myths were based on. The AER imagines he is their natural successor despite engaging in the lowest forms of cowardice and petty antagonism. Because he believes, rightly or wrongly, that adopting these identities thus places him in the role of chief antagonist to the progressive liberal project of the New America, his lack of social feeling and incapacity for creative and imaginative construction actually places him in the position of their pawn. The AER does not exist; he is a husk who gets by on the last remaining fumes of the great men who came before him. His persona is founded upon the grandiose and chauvinistic sentiment which exalts him above all others. By virtue of his race, sex, national origin, and religious sentiment, he stands above the "degenerates" and the "catamites", the "race-mixers" and the "race-traitors", despite conducting himself in far less honorable ways than his perceived antagonists. By adopting these ego-inflating ideals, he imagines himself the enemy par excellence of the establishment when in truth he is an easy (and more easily discarded) tool of the power structure. Whenever the establishment needs to reassert itself, or to justify expanding its hegemonic control, it can count on gullible malcontents to assist them in their plans. He is neither a revolutionary nor a freedom fighter, neither hero nor God. From any reasonable perspective he is hardly any different in his political worldview from the softer and less edgy targets immediately to his left. Rather, he mistakes his utter inefficiency and radical hostility for a philosophy of life—one that he believes elevates him far above the others. It is not the belief system which allows us to recognize him as an antisocial extremist, for in truth, his petty racial and religious antagonisms are of the garden variety. Instead, it is his willingness to turn feelings of impotence and inferiority into a social weapon which he wields without thought for its broader consequences. Much in the same way that we always hurt the ones closest to us, the AER takes his resentments and frustrations out on the ones he has the most direct access to—those individuals who have also been forced to the political margins.

To restate this point, overidentification with these abstractions reveals a failure to individuate oneself, condemning the individual to derive his own meaning and character from an external source that he did not create and cannot control. As I have already elaborated, this is not an indication of pathology nor should we meld this analysis into our investigation of the AER. The vast majority of people who fall into this trap are simply engaging in the only means of identification and social integration available to them and are not at risk of developing an antisocial character as a result of this process. We have observed this fact elsewhere: identities are *pre-constructed* and provided *to* the average person, which they accept passively. Having assumed this pre-arranged form, most people will seamlessly fold into the matrix.[40] Of course, the defining character of the extremist *is* his pathologically antisocial character, his condition of undersocialization which leaves him incapable of meaningfully connecting to others and unable to subordinate himself to *any* formalized set of rules, much less a healthily structured one. Thus, the AER arrives at this overidentification due to his penchant for grandiose delusion. He takes himself to be the apogee of Western man and thus the vehicle through which the Occident may be restored to its previous greatness.

Both the AEL and the AER are inordinately preoccupied with the need for power, and as such seek avenues for pursuing power. The problem for such individuals, however, is that the pursuit of power requires a high degree of agency and thus the individual must be able to marshal his will time and time again (a process which guarantees repeated failure until at last his goal is achieved). Neither the AEL nor the AER are individuals with deep psychological resources; at their core, they are anarchic people with profound inferiority complexes. They are only able to temporarily satiate this need by pursuing low-effort goals (e.g. online slacktivism, cancel culture) or by vicarious participation in the demonstrated power of others (by idly cheering the victories of the autonomous). Since the pursuit of power is frustrated by their inadequacy, they are caught in an endless feedback loop of resentment and despair which imperils those individuals and groups whom the extremist can most easily strike out against. Most will not take this route, although most do not need to. It

---

40 Or as seamlessly as can be expected (especially considering the rapidly increased dysfunction of the American matrix). Even in its degraded state, we should note that America is still capable of plugging the holes of her sea-weary ship.

only takes a handful to sabotage nascent political movements, and it only takes one to seek violent retribution against the despised other.

As the AER sinks deeper into his misanthropy, he seeks out icons of extremity for whom he may substitute himself. The more loathsome and perverse a condition the AER finds himself in, the greater the extremity of his chosen icon. When that decisive moment finally arrives where the AER decides to enact his vengeful plot, it will occur because the combined torment—induced internally and externally—finally found a language, an iconography, and an ideal through which it could be acted upon. And he will act upon it in the name of some chauvinistic or identitarian value in the clumsiest and most self-serving of ways. Contrast his actions with that of the Bolshevik, the Zionist, the American Whig, or members of any other insurgent movement which come to mind. These were highly organized and well-funded groups with strong philosophical and aesthetic foundations. Every action they undertook was part of a long-term calculation desired to produce a specific end—liberation and self-governance. Even the AEL (for everything that is repugnant about him and the world he wishes to bring about) can boast of his highly organized and teleological approach to political action. The AER is a solipsistic idealist of the highest order who does a grave disservice to his cause and his fetishized notion of identity. It is bad enough that a select few act as cravenly and egregiously as they do, but it is far worse when they are valorized for it.

Megalomania and the Power Process

It is worthwhile to home in on these phenomena, and especially at this point, having concluded the previous discussion by examining the need for power. Megalomania might as well be synonymous with—or at the least, descriptive of—the psychological type who is most given to the power process (the meaning of which should be taken at face value, as opposed to Kaczynski's notion of the power process, which had more to do with the striving for autonomy). Christopher Lasch made the point quite well that the defining psychological feature of American liberal society is narcissism. In Lasch's view, a multi-century program of market fetishism and progressivism-as-religion has gradually eroded child-parent attachments, pluralized truth, and denigrated the wisdom of experience, leaving us with a culture utterly preoccupied with a neurotic conception of "the self". All social interactions in the culture of narcissism are reduced to a series of performances and calculations, where each participant seeks to extract some value from the exchange for the purpose of maximizing their position as market actors. Our culture, being so preoccupied with the self (and with the realization of the self), has proven itself to be the most efficient producer of narcissism (rooted in rage and self-loathing; power is a means for assuaging the pain of unimportance) and megalomania (rooted in the need to dominate; power is an end in itself), and thus the perfect environment for participation in the power process.

The problem of the AER, insofar as political organization is concerned, is the old problem of *"too many chiefs, not enough Indians"*. Those AERs drawn to leadership, being inherently megalomaniacal (obsessively concerned with status and compulsively manipulative) are only hierarchically-minded in the sense that they envision themselves at the top of the hierarchy. Beyond that, they have no tolerance for the unglamorous work of coalition and infrastructure building, personnel management, and all other tedious minutiae necessary for political success. As such, megalomaniacs will inevitably derail nascent political movements (as they are incapable of collaborating with others if such effort does not satisfy their lust for power) or overtake them (if they are sufficiently charismatic and those around them are easily hypnotized by their magnetism). Power-seeking is not necessarily pathological; rather, anyone who involves themselves in the power process is not *by definition* a megalomaniac. What characterizes pathological power-seeking is its vain and irrational character[41] which defies productive collaboration and goal achievement.

We can easily identify the megalomaniacal character by his uncompromising pursuit of domination and by his habit of rallying people around him while ostracizing those who stand in his way. With regards to the latter, the narcissist engages in similar behavior, though its causes are found elsewhere. Narcissists fear

---

41   Not irrational in the sense of being illogical or self-contradicting, but rather as a way of conveying its affective or dispositional nature.

being discovered, and ruthlessly attack anyone who may expose their hidden inadequacies. Megalomaniacs fear being denied and will attempt to remove competitors who are as capable (usually more so) of ascending to the top of the hierarchy. Both types manipulate those around them to obscure their true intentions, working hard to maintain a righteous or self-justifying image that resists penetration. There may be overlap between the two psychologies, and of course, we may come across the megalomaniac who is truly narcissistic in character. However, the true difference is that the narcissist is inherently neurotic, while the megalomaniac is inherently psychopathic. Narcissists are quite insecure in themselves and suffer a great deal of existential angst. Their habit of manipulation and deception are defenses *against* their perception of inherent worthlessness. The narcissist is always reacting against internal conflicts which keep him psychologically disintegrated. Megalomaniacs are far more self-assured, and their need for domination reflects their raison d'etre. Every action the megalomaniac takes is an expression of his need to dominate. He is psychologically whole (at least in comparison to the narcissist) and experiences little in the way of self-attacking cognitions. Because of his active character, the megalomaniac's skullduggery has an extra level of power—a further teleological distance than that of the narcissist.

Given the diversity of human psychology and the fact of dysfunctional overlap, we should expect to see a great deal of pathological admixture. Individuals are best understood in a unique context, and our analysis must always be subordinated to the unique qualities of those we seek to understand. Having said that, we would be at a serious disadvantage were we to neglect the foundational psychological differences between the various archetypes of AER. The megalomaniac pursues power because he must, while the narcissist (to the extent that he is engaged in the power process at all) does so because he must ameliorate the feeling of insignificance.

Grandiosity: The Mask of Superiority

Before bringing this analysis to an end, I would like to highlight one last feature of the AER: his grandiosity. The fatal conceit of the rightist theory of self is its lack of humility. A sense of low origin and of one's inherent unworthiness flies directly in the face of the AER's Nietzschean revivalism. As is the case with many of the positions the AER adopts, his venomous opposition to humility is rooted in a rejection of certain ubiquitous American paramoralisms. He bristles at the aspects of American culture which are provincial and small, and which seek to restrict his will in a predictable and rote manner. That particularly Christian ethic of meekness chafes at him like a winter coat one size too small. Riding to the rescue, that prophet of beyond-good-and-evil beckons him to find his inner strength and cast aside the small-minded timidity of the rabble.

> "*You are a genius of spirit, cavalier and noble! Sail beyond the horizon and don't look back! When you die, songs will be written and stories will be told of your Promethean grandeur! Go and become the man that none else dare imagine possible.*"

And so, he excavates his latent genius, discovers a sense of wonder and bravery of which he scantly knew existed and sets upon the hero's journey. Only he is not the over-man—never was and never will be. He imagines himself as such, but in truth reveals himself to be a malformed Quixotic discontent for this new century—only worse; lacking even a misguided sense of romantic chivalry, the AER replaces it with a spirit of unbounded hateful vengeance and confused moral enlightenment. This is not to speak ill of hatred or vengeance (two emotions which are beautiful and necessary in their own right), but to demonstrate how libidinally possessed and weak he is.

Of course, an excess of humility is no more a virtue than its complete absence; we can forgive those who rebel against the cultural stain of weakness which stifles even the smallest demonstrations of vitality, for the poverty of America's moral courage is plain to see. Surplus humility is as much a play at superiority as the Nietzschean will to power is. The man who undermines his high-bloodedness, who would feign a roll in the mud before declaring how much he deserves his good fortune is every bit as repugnant as his antipode. But that correct psychological center, the proper identification of one's utter banality eludes the AER altogether. Like all good zealots—having been initiated into the black magic of scientific racism and esoteric Hitler worship—the AER can no longer stand among the common man, despite repeatedly invoking his name. He is beyond man, beyond the average, and beyond history itself. He belongs only to himself. He is... *homo superioris.*

The self-estimation, in the end, is merely an appearance or presentation and not a psychological fact. For the AER, his grandiose attitude is only the mask of superiority, a power projection with no substance. Grandiosity and its cousin, megalomania, find an unnerving regularity among those whose sense of self is in part a paradoxical reaction to *and incorporation of* the ongoing and intensifying project of marginalized humiliation, neglect, decayed social relations, and self-glorification. I say paradoxically, because the AER's worldview is supposedly predicated on a rejection of America and its obvious failings. One would expect that a self-styled revolutionary guerilla warrior and survivalist would strive for psychological and political coherence, but this is not true. The AER's lack of critical and reflective thinking is part and parcel of his enmeshment with the American object he supposedly detests.

In much the same way that the AEL fixates on his weakness, elevating it to the position of true self, the AER is similarly consumed by feelings of inadequacy. At one moment, he extols the virtue and superiority of his race, his sex, his religion, and when push comes to shove—even his nation—but in the next, he fetishizes the state of violence and degeneration in which he finds himself mired. Though purporting to fear and loathe the genocide he claims is being perpetrated against his kin, he cannot pull himself away from the images of violence which seem to validate this belief. Not only must he bask in their perverse glory, he must share them far and wide. This practice feeds his racial and cultural resentments, but also reinforces the victimary status which he has willingly accepted. Once more, the masochistic character of the AER is revealed; he wallows in anti-White savagery, dependent upon it to prove that he even exists. Without pain, without humiliation, can he even be certain that he is really alive? At the least, the vicarious sense of persecution stimulates him in a way that the genuine feeling of emptiness does not.

Far from being the high agency, ass-kicking übermensch that

he imagines, through this ritual the AER demonstrates his truly impotent and fairness-obsessed liberal character. It just isn't
right what is happening to his people. Someone must *do something* about it. Doesn't anyone *respect the law* anymore? Don't
these vicious cretins believe in *basic human dignity*? Thus, it is
revealed that such individuals are anything but radical in the
sense of a political worldview, but are instead highly dysfunctional and socially displaced rightists of the conservative type.
They share the same temperament as conservatives; bemoan the
loss of culture as conservatives do; signal their outrage and moral indignation as conservatives do; make appeals to conceptions
of moral universalism as conservatives do; and most significantly, they stymie actual radicals—*just as conservatives do*. AERs
may fancy themselves radicals or revolutionaries, but they come
to this conclusion precisely because they misinterpret their rage
and dysfunction as expressions of a vanguard political identity
rather than understanding them for what they truly are—evidence of trauma and abandonment.

Deprived of the social and material resources necessary for
proper psychosocial development and affectively motivated by
feelings of resentment, rage, and envy, the AER marries grandiosity with chauvinism, all the while wielding ego defenses as
both a shield against his obvious psychological deficits and as
a sword against the despised other. Like his compatriots in the
AEL, he also has a loose definition of the other; initially con-
sisting of racial, religious, and sexual antagonists, with even the
slightest and most *innocuous* of provocations it may be expanded
to include his fellow marginalized and politically aligned racial
cohorts. In truth, his tribe is not founded on race, religion, or
even nationhood—the AER finds group cohesion along neuro-
developmental lines. He is aligned in the most fragile and tenuous of ways only to those people who share his level of cognitive
dysfunction and social atrophy. Whether his damage was caused
by concussive trauma, drug addiction, a bad roll of the genetic
dice, or some deficiency occurring in the neonatal period, its origin cannot be determined from as casual and distant an analysis
as my own. What can be said conclusively, however, is that the
AER's level of political dysfunction is always and forever second-

ary to his biological and psychological dysfunction.[42]

In those areas where the individual feels insufficiently developed, lacks autonomy, and finds he is unable to cultivate a positive self-concept—that is where the mask of superiority will emerge. And with that mask, too, will emerge chauvinisms and grandiosities of every kind, replete with the necessary ego defenses (operating not unlike the white blood cells of the immune system), which work tirelessly to protect the fragile and underdeveloped self. Alfred Adler argued that superiority complexes emerge as an adaptation to the presence of intense feelings of inferiority. In the healthful individual, actual mastery is pursued in order to erase or attenuate these feelings of inferiority; a will to power is marshaled to drive this person into a repetition compulsion precisely designed to help them develop a sense of familiarity, then competency, and ultimately mastery in an area that previously triggered strong feelings of worthlessness and self-directed antagonisms. Over time, these individuals learn to make accurate self-appraisals, and do not struggle with social comparisons of status or ability. However, we are not discussing the psychologically well-adapted; in the dysfunctional types, it is only the sense of superiority that develops, and never the proof necessary to justify such a self-concept.

To us non-pathological people, the discrepancy between the AER's self-concept and his material and social realities strikes as painfully obvious. When confronted by this incongruity in our own lives, we become acutely aware of the distance and work to bring the two into alignment. But because the AER lacks psycho-

42 Upon reviewing this section, I feel it necessary to anticipate a potential criticism (or perhaps it is a lack of clarity provided in the initial writing of this work). Throughout this work I have emphasized, and in fact singularized, the role that narrative and mythological works play in the development of political extremism. I have also strongly argued for the significance of civilizational decline in the emergence of this phenomenon. That I now highlight a certain essentialist feature of the low AER does not invalidate these earlier claims, but points to an additional reality—that of a truly marginal psychological animal. Such individuals are maladapts in a very real sense; and at the nadir of a civilization's decadence and decline, these men prove themselves to be a genuine menace.
However, civilizations do not fail because of such men and so I do not see a contradiction between pointing out the essentialist nature of their unique psycho-political dysfunction and highlighting the more significant ailments which so efficiently sink the ship of high culture.

logical holism, he cannot make the necessary character adjust-
ments to bring his true self into accordance with the proof of his
existence. As such, those AERs who cannot impose or enforce
their superiority complex through brutal methods of social violence will then struggle with the feelings of inadequacy which
inevitably emerge. There are those who, lacking a truly strong
will, may feel complacent toiling in relative anonymity, or enjoy-
ing some ultimately meaningless niche of dominance. The insignificance of their chosen arena may, for a time, safeguard them
against the crushing tide of objectivity. At some point, the AER
will experience that traumatic confrontation with the real—and
the loftier his pursuit, the higher the likelihood that he does.

When a genuinely autonomous and competent individual
arrives (often better liked, naturally a higher status individual),
the façade of superiority is ruptured, and these individuals will
be forced to react. Naturally, that reaction fails or thrives on its
strategic wit; we cannot say for certain what method the AER
will employ to successfully remove this threat, though often we
find that he resorts to techniques such as subterfuge, innuendo,
and character assassination. Direct confrontation is risky, for if
the AER misjudges his opponent's strength of character, his fall
from grace will occur with humiliating suddenness. The better
situated he is, the higher up he sits on his throne, the greater a
chance that confrontation will prove successful. It is important
to note that his self-enhancing cognition exists only to ameliorate the feelings of anxiety and not to actually help him adapt
better to his environment or achieve better and more successful
outcomes. Whether he manifestly suffers from a physical infirmity (Adler's notion of "organ inferiority") or simply has internalized a sense of weakness, he *proves himself to be ineffectual*
and therefore finds destruction a far easier and more available
path to recognition than creativity.

On the one hand, the AER's illusory superiority may be an
elaborate defense, but then again it may be a genuine self-perception arising from an inculcated cultural superiority, passed
to the individual as a child through the norms, values, and educational practices of the community. Cultural supremacy may
arise out of the outstanding achievements of the people group
(descendants of a great empire may feel an inordinate sense of

pride and reflexive hostility toward out-groups), or it may be a kind of mob ego defense, developed to strengthen the in-group (religious chosenness, for example). The same narcissism found on the cultural level may exist within the family unit, similarly imbuing the child with a peculiarly overestimated sense of ability. Whatever its genesis may be, the ultimate challenge is what the individual does when these self-perceptions conflict with material reality. Better adapted individuals will either accommodate their self-concept should their perception prove flawed or reinvest in their abilities so their outcomes finally match their ambitions. The dysfunctional type will lash out, double down, and avoid reappraisal at all costs.

What is commonly called the "far-right" is comprised of two groups of people: middle and lower class Americans (who, having been abandoned by their representatives, seek refuge in a subculture which purports to resist their further marginalization), and those exceptional individuals who either by choice or by force have been thrown to the margins because of their intellectual incompatibility with the progressive neoliberal project. Often, we find that in this untermensch–übermensch dichotomy, those individuals most plagued by feelings of inadequacy and grandiose delusions react to the reality of their inferiority by cannibalizing their own subculture. Governed by a crab mentality, these tragically dysfunctional types prefer to police their subculture rather than to see it bloom. While they themselves are often not violent, their race-to-the-ideological-bottom finds them routinely encouraging and innovating more dysfunctional and antisocial rhetorical devices and "political strategies" to bring about the end of anti-Whiteness, liberal hegemony, or whatever particular antagonist they claim at the time. This creates fertile ground for the truly despondent (and often psychologically impaired) to take matters into their own hands, sometimes of their own volition, but often as a result of encouragement from federal operatives who infiltrate dissident subcultures with the expressed intent of fomenting violence.

A Brief Comment on "High" Rightism

I have alluded to the extremism of "high" rightism but have not yet elaborated upon it. Institutional conservatism (or right-liberalism) differs from its left variation in some important ways, necessitating a careful application of the term "extremist". As I have detailed throughout this work, left activists of both the high and low classes neatly fit my description of extremist due to their ideophilic possession and their dysfunctional character. It is less obvious that this is the case on the right. I have made my argument for "low" rightist extremism, but what might be said of those high-caste rightists? Available psychometric data makes it clear that political rightists have a cleaner bill of mental health, and so I cannot make any strong declaration as to their dysfunction—not in the way I have of political leftists. And yet their willingness to comply with the culture of decay *does* indicate to us at least a habit of timidity, and at most a pathological desire for conformity and acceptance. Zizek speaks of the desire for rightists to be included in the leftist dialogue;[43] what does this desire for inclusion tell us? What can be gleaned from their desire to participate in a conversation about their own destruction—a conversation where the opposing party mocks the very notion of inclusion? The dysfunction of high rightism may not, in fact, be psychological but spiritual. One important flaw of high rightism is its intolerance for disruption. High rightism seeks a continuous and smooth economic flow, uninterrupted by petty politics or other insignificant events[44]. The lack of dialogue is one such disruption; rather than confront this reality, the high rightist can only bemoan the incivility of his opponent while simultaneously capitulating to him in the desperate hope that perpetual submission will finally gain him a seat at the table.

The other critical flaw of high rightism is its pathological adherence to the ideals of individualism and market economics. I explored this thoroughly in the preceding chapter, but it bears greater elaboration. High rightists are true believers in these ideals, and the earnestness with which they argue these positions makes it all the more difficult to dissuade them. The high rightist or conservative is hardly distinguishable from the Marxist,

43 Vladimir Lenin, *Revolution at the Gates: Selected Writings of Lenin from 1917*, (Verso, 2011).
44 Once more, the conservative reaction to COVID-19 highlights this fact. Whatever we may say about the true severity of the coronavirus, rightist unseriousness derailed any possibility at eradicating the virus and preserving the market.

and the reason for this can be found in their shared exaltation of materialism and the perfectibility of man through economic logic. Their blindness to the totality of man forever disadvantages them against the decline of man and civilization. It is precisely because high rightists hold these views and because they have institutional control of rightist politics and culture that they hold the rest of the country hostage to their naïve and self-destructive economic materialism. While these individuals may not be pathological (though certainly, some in fact are), the values themselves, once put into practice, wreak havoc upon the human spirit. The school shooter may harm or even murder dozens, but how many men, women, and children die every year from causes which could otherwise be prevented? Poverty? Homelessness? Malnutrition? Lack of adequate healthcare? Drug addiction? Suicide? Conservatives and other high rightists will lament the death toll of communism—but what of the free market and financial capital? Intentional or otherwise, many are impoverished and outright erased under market logic. High rightist extremism is real, and it is deadly.

At long last, we may conclude our investigation. Having exhaustively analyzed the phenomenon of political extremism, for the first time we can approach the issue with the necessary clarity and heart. However, this text is not merely intended to be descriptive; I will conclude this work by offering what I believe to be the first steps in overcoming polarization and removing the obstacle of extremist thought from American politics. If such a thing can be done—if it is not, in fact, too late—then this work will prove essential to that goal. At the least, I have provided the closest thing to an unbiased analysis of the problem of political extremism as has been attempted by a psychologist. But before we can move from the descriptive to the prescriptive, we have one last item to discuss.[45]

45   There is one last aspect of rightist psychology that, while not fitting neatly within the context of this chapter, deserves investigation. We could not quite describe it as extremist in the same sense as I have been using the term, but it is certainly extreme in so far as it indicates a degradation of the mind and spirit. I speak of the rightist tendency to romanticize lost causes. Much has been made of the conservative impulse to glorify principled losses, but I believe the problem is more significant than a mere lack of gamesmanship. (Anti-vitalism is indeed a civilizational sin.) There is a certain uncritical veneration of both

the Antebellum South and National Socialist Germany which are troubling—not because it is necessarily immoral to do so—but because the rose-colored historical view which is taken up by conservatives and ostensible "fascists" attributes a perfectness to those eras which do not match the historical records. The pleasure derived from idealizing these eras overrides the ability of the individual to think rationally about their strengths and weaknesses, and to extract from them useful strategies and insights which could further the advance of rightist ideas and culture in the present day. It is precisely this backward-directed focus, the nostalgia-tinged romanticism, and the idealization which catalyzes the stagnation of rightist politics. In every era and within every society we may find great men and awe-inspiring acts of daring heroism, but veneration of historical greatness must not be permitted to stifle the will and vitality of those in the present moment. Were I to engage in political taxonomy, then I would name this particular breed *Nazis republicanis*—a variation of normative rightism that is indistinguishable from establishment conservatism but which fashions itself as vanguard, elitist, cutting-edge, et cetera and possesses none of the musculature or grit necessary to support the claim. Members of this species lay claim to all the vulgarity, timidity, and hubris of the high rightist, but possess nothing in the way of material or social wealth.

BOOK III

The Digital Demiurge

Cast adrift in the digital sea;
You say it's not real, but it feels that way to me.
Trading faiths by way of anonymity,
Through my fingertips thus spake the community.
Away from the watchful glow and piercing
*   techno-gaze,*
I work to appear—a singular coherency.
But thanks to the digital demiurge,
I am forever at war with my exigent
*   multiplicities.*

What Has Become of the Infobahn?

It is worth examining the influence that emergent communication and information technologies have had on distorting the public consciousness, thus leading to further polarization of opinion and greater intolerance of dissenting thought. Particularly during the first decade-and-a-half of our new century, when the novelty and excitement of alternative media was high, there was a great sense that new possibilities could emerge. Based on the commonly held beliefs of man's capacity for rational and dispassionate thought, his willingness to discard faulty positions once presented with information that disproved them, and the notion that pursuing truth was a universal value of utmost importance, it was thought that we could potentially enter a new age of enlightenment spurred on by the innovations of the digital age. While it is true that we enjoyed an informational gold rush during the early years of the internet's maturation, having now settled into its adolescence, it is clear that the opposite has actually transpired. Digital communication and media have allowed for easier and more immediate satisfaction of prior biases, as well as a greater ability to isolate oneself from networks of dissent. Far from bringing about a new era of human progress, the internet (primarily through social media and alternative news outlets within the digital sphere) has revealed the truest aspects of human nature: given the ability to choose what information to consume, we do not choose based on some principle of enlightenment and intellectual honesty, but on lower bases—those of comfort, community, and confirmation bias. Even the decision to expose oneself to an opposing view and to interact with it is (for most) rooted in attitudes of fear, loathing, and derision. Naturally, this is not the case for all individuals; some will gravitate toward dissenting voices out of an unconscious longing, while others are motivated by pure and rational reasons. Such individuals, however, are outliers.

Part of this is rooted in the overwhelming stream of data by which we are continuously assaulted. More choice-opportunities do not, in fact, lead to better choice-selections. Nor does it necessarily lead to satisfaction-of-choice.[1] Rather, this unprecedented surplus lead to cognitive collapse, rendering us unable to choose *meaningfully*. Contrary to popular opinion, we are not liberated by *more* choice and *more* freedom; rather they oppress and stifle us. Left exasperated, we either resign ourselves to apathy or select the path of least resistance. We go with what we know, with what is familiar, and with what makes navigating life simpler, not more complicated. Pursuit of truth is really the pursuit of isolation; the more we are willing to confront and overturn wrongly held beliefs, the more conflict we are likely to have when interacting with those around us. Not only does a philosophically inquisitive life jeopardize social harmony, it creates inner turmoil as well. It is an imperiled life, to be certain.

In some sense, radically overturning the cognitive applecart

---

1 Iyengar, S.S., & Lepper, M.R., "When choice is demotivating: Can one desire too much of a good thing?" *Journal of Personality and Social Psychology,* Vol. 79, Issue 6, 2000, pp. 995-1006.

does not produce evolutionary fitness. For one thing, consumption of new information does not immediately lead to comprehension of new information. To be continually inundated with strange and disheartening information is to exist in a state of continual disorientation. Just as we need time to digest large meals, we also need time to synthesize and integrate new ideas and concepts. The more significantly we are challenged by new information, the longer that process will take, as we are naturally resistant and hesitant to overturn stable and long-standing schemas. It comes at great cost to do so, not only because of the immediate strain it places on our relationships, but because of the doubt it casts on past (and prospective) decisions, like what education or line of work to pursue, lifestyle choices and consumptive habits, etc. One may easily be overwhelmed by feelings of guilt or shame, despair, and a persistent existential anxiety, thus thrusting one into a potentially irresolvable crisis. At this point in time, the information age is proving for many to also be an age of damnation. While digital technologies are swiftly moving toward ever-increasing sophistication, the biotechnology we call consciousness remains as dense and elusive as ever.

All this to say that the advent of alternative media networks (a great number of which, curiously, have become legacy networks in their own right, either through acquisition or imitation) are accelerating us *toward* extremism rather than away from it. And how could it be any other way? Technological advance is always achieved on the back of some prior philosophical assumption about the nature of man, the world, and life itself. Incorrect (or simply *incomplete*) axioms will either suspend progress altogether or limit its full actualization. Did the automobile liberate us, or has it ensnared us? Does email make communication more effortless or more onerous? There is always a question of what technological progress brings to the forefront and what it leaves behind. We might also ask ourselves which doors are opened by the decision to pursue a line of technological thought and which are firmly, hopefully not fatally, closed? Echoing Heidegger, the disposition which we hold toward the world of God and the world of Man dictates our actions in each. Without challenging our fundamental beliefs about life and all its possibilities, we constrain ourselves to a set of pre-determined actions within it.

Free will, to the extent that it truly exists, is dependent on our ability to accommodate ourselves to the truth of existence, rather than merely assimilating it in ways which uphold our naïve and self-serving delusions about it.

To bring this analysis back to its main point, it is precisely the way in which newer alternatives affirm the dominant paradigm, enframing us within its mode of thinking, that we need to concern ourselves with. The fantasy of possibility, that intoxicating dream which convinces us of the difference and uniqueness of the new, must be met with loving skepticism—a skepticism which does not seek to nihilistically deny and refute for its own sake, but to affirm on proper grounds. The optimism of the new disarms us and impairs proper judgment; be it a new medium, a new message, or a new messenger, these siren calls lure us to the bottom of the ocean all the same. The very youth of our century deludes us, enticing us into the fantasy of possibility, as if its mere existence served as a guarantor of progress achieved. Nothing is to be held as true simply because we occupy a particular moment in time. However, we should inspect this issue of the ubiquity of choice more thoroughly. It is the fact of these possibilities which also deludes us into thinking that their very availability is symbolic of their distinctiveness and opposition to the existing paradigm (whichever perspectival term we may give it, e.g. Neoliberalism, Capitalism, the Patriarchy, White supremacy, Hypermodernity, etc.) I say this not to induce pessimism, or even to suggest that all facets of American life are hopelessly tainted and perverted by the many tentacles of modern neoliberal techno-capitalism. Rather it is to say, as Heidegger did, that we must challenge ourselves to adopt the proper attitude to reveal the truth through each affordance granted us. Unconcealment, revelation, and the like are not to be found in the truth of the new's existence, but in our willingness to conceive of them properly. As for what defines a proper conception, we shall elaborate this more fully in the following chapter.

At a time where our ability to retain information shrinks but our need for stimulation grows, the only way for media and news outlets to compete with one another is to hyperbolize their stories and load them with rapid-speed hyper-arousing visual imagery to capture attention before it inevitably dissipates. There is little concern for ethics or journalistic integrity because to prioritize anything beyond the capturing of attention is to put forth a failing business model.[2] The more sensational the image or headline, the more immediately you capture attention, and thus the more successful your brand will become. Such a practice is as exploitative as it is effective. So, the feedback loop at play here is rooted in the failure of our moral and emotional development's ability to keep pace with technological expansion. Not only are we not keeping pace, we are regressing. We are Doctor Frankenstein, and the techno-informational society is our monster; the internet is not unique in this regard, only the clearest and most efficient manifestation of the same principle. Rather than being a device of forced conformity (like the television or the radio), the internet and the alternative platforms it makes available are simply a more sophisticated means for choosing ideological conformity. It is precisely the power of choice, or rather the power of illusory choice, which makes psychological manipulation and conformity more effective, for the individual believes in his choice and his ability to choose. The abundance of choice-opportunities (which give the impression of difference and distinctiveness) thus seals the individual's fate.

Simulated Communities

In a more traditional sense, communities are proximally bounded, meaning they gain their definition and coherence from the immediate factors which comprise them. For example, a community refers to a particular location, inhabited by a particular group of people, all of whom share a language, a religious or mythic tradition, a style of artistic expression, a homogeneous gene pool, and so on. They are defined by and derive meaning from their nearness, and as such, are not pure abstractions. Modern communities (particularly in the United States) are increasingly defined in a more abstracted way. The United States itself is, and always has been, a nation predicated on certain phil-

---

2 All the same, many of these emergent platforms *still* fail, partly due to over-saturation and partly as a result of incompetency. Certainly, there are other factors at play, but a further investigation of these causes is beyond the scope of this work.

osophical, political, and economic groundings which strain the limits of traditional community formation. While we can test this statement and find inherent weaknesses, the undulating procession of time shows this to be true. Here are two points of support: firstly, we now speak of communities as a composite or aggregate of some supra-schema, the membership of which is typically found along a single point of relatedness (the Italian-American community, the LGBT community, the medical community, the Jewish community, and so on). Individuals belong to such communities insofar as they share a primary feature of identity (e.g. ethnicity, sexuality, race, profession, etc.), even if they are fatally incongruent with the communal pastiche in other ways. A Black American may interact with other Black Americans, but he or she will never have a direct confrontation with the Black community itself, as it does not truly exist (the meaning of the word "community" having been turned from representing a social dynamic into representing a political idea). As such, the paradox of membership reveals itself in the way that, in practice, their belongingness further isolates them. What we find then is that, in at least one sense, an organic social dynamic has been transmogrified into a political signification which seems to indicate nothing concrete or actionable. In fact, this transformation represents only the latest iteration or attempt at the destruction of genuine communities. As a result, the constituent members are reduced to the status of an object, rather than a subject. On one hand, we loosely understand what is being pointed to by such terms, but the signifier being called upon can never become a subject of action. This is to say, they are contained within a political abstraction which impairs their agency and political significance. As the abstraction captures a larger and larger biomass, the social group experiences a greater loss of agency and significance.

Secondly, when we speak of actual *material* communities (we might call them proximal communities), we find that these, too, have lost their true coherence and purpose. Whereas at another time in our history, communities could be understood as social dynamics imposed upon us by birth and thus demanding reciprocal duty from their members, we are now able to choose the communities we wish to belong to (as well as the level of obligation to which we wish to be held). But the luxury of a "correct" choice is only afforded to a select few, typically for economic reasons. Consider the following: a family moves into a new neighborhood. Perhaps they select this particular neighborhood because it allows for an easier work commute, gives them access to quality schools, daycare, or for other related benefits. Their inclusion into this "community" offers them certain material benefits, but in what way does it enshrine them within a meaningful social order? We find enclaves of true communities around the country, but increasingly it is only the financially and politically privileged who are fortunate enough to participate in the sacral social order. Irrespective of their living arrangement, many Americans cannot lay claim to a community of their own because they are too isolated from those they live alongside. Even when they share commonalities (e.g. language, religion, etc.), many are simply too poorly socialized or too apathetic to forge relationships with those around them. More and more, we find that what most Americans *do* have are *anti-communities*.

Naturally, we have the pathocratic class to thank for this. E. Michael Jones has painstakingly detailed the strategic destruction of organic communities perpetrated by the monied classes.[3] Intraracial conflict between the hegemonic WASP class and the upstart ethnic Catholics resulted in the destruction of the latter's communities. This practice has been widespread and has found many permutations and expressions throughout American history.[4] And while we might feel inclined to attribute exclusively particularist motives to the over class (racial animus, religious intolerance, and the like) for their actions—and often those motives were significant factors—we must understand that the same dehumanizing program is to be implemented against all who are powerless against it.

One of the (unfulfilled?) promises of the internet is that it brings us closer together. In a certain sense this is true, as we can connect with others based on shared interests and experi-

3   E. Michael Jones, *The Slaughter of Cities: Urban Renewal as Ethnic Cleansing*, (St. Augustine's Press, 2002).
4   Gabrielle Bruney, "A Very Abbreviated History of the Destruction of Black Neighborhoods", *Esquire,* May 30, 2020 https://www.esquire.com/news-politics/a32719786/george-floyd-protests-riots-black-comminity-destruction-history/.

ences (what has been called *"the tribe of the mind"*). No doubt this has offered us a great deal of benefit, but the downside is worth examining as well. As actual communities disintegrate and man's social skills regress (resulting as much from increased technologization and the demands of market logic as it does the increasingly onerous rules for social engagement, i.e. political correctness), digital sociality shifts from a peripheral or supplementary activity to a primary one. Take one simple example: online courtship. The idea that digital dating would supplant the real thing was laughable only ten years ago, and now it is so commonplace that to abstain from it seems a bit queer (if not outright dysfunctional). Everyone you know is online, and everyone is sharing themselves indiscriminately for all to see. American society has fully shifted into a panoptical surveillance state, a condition achieved equally through coercion and voluntary choice. Unsurprisingly, the weight of the all-seeing-digital-eye bears down upon us with its awesome, crushing might.

The hermit was that rare, peculiar character who lived far away from society and eschewed relations with his fellow man. Now, the techno-informational society has made hermits of us all. Fully ensconced within the cyberreal, Americans (particularly the youngest ones) are increasingly at a loss as to precisely how they might navigate the precarious minefield of real-time human interaction.[5][6][7] Given the opportunity to bypass it altogether, many do.[8] Lest I be accused of limply shaking my fist in the air from the comfort of my porch, with my Tommy Bahama shirt stained by A1 steak sauce and Miller Light, let me assure you I am at least *trying* to grasp something significant here—

5 Karen Kaplan, "Americans are having less sex now than 20 years ago", *Los Angeles Times,* June 12, 2020 https://www.latimes.com/science/story/2020-06-12/americans-are-having-less-sex-now-than-they-did-20-years-ago.

6 Rhitu Chatterjee, "Americans Are a Lonely Lot, and Young People Bear the Heaviest Burden", *NPR,* May 1st, 2018 https://www.npr.org/sections/health-shots/2018/05/01/606588504/americans-are-a-lonely-lot-and-young-people-bear-the-heaviest-burden.

7 Allison Sadlier, "1 in 4 Americans feel they have no one to confide in", *New York Post,* April 30th, 2019 https://nypost.com/2019/04/30/1-in-4-americans-feel-they-have-no-one-to-confide-in/.

8 Uptin Saiidi, "Social media makes millennials less social: Study", *CNBC,* October 17th, 2015 https://www.cnbc.com/2015/10/15/social-media-making-millennials-less-social-study.html.

we're losing touch not only with each other, but with ourselves. Woe unto that man—the cyber-hermit - who abstains from social networks, who meets his lovers in the streets and has not renounced his very humanity. He resists, perhaps in an act of pure futility, his fate as the Last Man.

Speaking more seriously, we can see just how the internet has progressed from a simulation of sociality to nearly supplanting it altogether. Anything that is important happens in the digital space, and it is there where the important things are discussed. Online relationships become at least as significant *if not more* so than those occurring in the flaccid and unsatisfying meatspace. The possibility of having some repressed or undernourished part of you fully realized online makes "true" life seem quaint and oppressive by comparison. And of course, the immediacy with which online interactions provide reinforcement far outstrips the true reality's ability to compete. The intensity and immediacy of stimulation is so great that there is simply no justification to unplug oneself from it. The digital personas of those we interact with become imprinted as schemas and seem even more real than the person themselves. "*Even better than the real thing*", as Bono once sang.

The Public-Private Self

Yet again, we are confronted with a feature of digital interaction which is not unique to the medium, but is certainly intensified and democratized by it—the extent to which social networks encourage one to show not only their *public self* (persona), but their *public-private self* (the layer of the self which lies outside of the "official" or "accepted" persona, but is also out of reach of the true-private self). Once limited to the celebrity class, the seductive and invitational habit of melodramatic confessional testimony now finds itself figuring prominently among the influencer class, the influencer-wannabe class, and the average smart phone user caught within a mimetic cycle of repetition.

The public-private self is a simulacrum of the *true-private self*, a mere facsimile or imitation of authentic conduct which is more readily accepted and rewarded, all the while providing the benefit of staving off the awkward and prickly aspects of truly private intimacy. In a fit of digitally induced bipolarism, such individuals will oscillate between grandiosity and humility, earnestness and irony, but at no point can it be said that any of their posturing and jockeying is truly real—it is merely simulated, a possibility offered by the very unreality of the medium (the truth of any expressed belief or disposition is only sustainable so long as it is rewarded.) Within the public-private self, the act of sharing is guided by an instrumental rationality that carefully considers the outcome to maximize its effect. This is not to suggest that *intending* to achieve some effect is in and of itself evidence of falsity, but rather the intention to represent oneself *falsely*, or at least, inaccurately, for the purpose of satiating some coerced desire is *false*. And so, we understand that theirs are manipulated responses facilitated by a system of incentives designed to manipulate behavior and turn emotion chaotic, thus legitimizing deceptiveness and selfishness as real and socially acceptable modes of existence. Whereas the true-private self is defined by its internal consistency, its exclusivity, and its permanence, the public-private self is utterly performative in nature and depends on an informational feedback loop to guide it into action. The digital actor must be fed so that he may regurgitate what is expected from him. The system (in this case, the digital system) depends on the existence of *users* who need an outlet or medium to provide them with potential *useds*. The logic of the system is so strong, the efficacy of its techniques so unquestionable, that most anyone who seeks to profit from it can be transformed into one of these users. All disciplines and endeavors are subject to this logic, though of course we are limiting this analysis to the use of the (digital) system for both political and *parapolitical* ends.

The cycling between (or even reversal of) beliefs and moods is less jarring within digital space because they are ultimately flat, two-dimensional, and unbounded images of a person without the context provided by "real" three-dimensional experience. We know less about these people than we otherwise would because they are less accessible to us—we have no hard proof, no truly social information about them. Not only do we know *less* about them, but we cannot even be sure that we *know* what is accessible because of its completely simulated nature. The tension between staying "on-brand" and presenting a version of oneself that decontextualizes or expands one's brand blurs the line between simulation and reality. Or perhaps it is more accurate to say that this merely exposes the multiple layers of simultaneous simulation.

Digital simulation offers a greater ability for individuals to adopt highly stylized and caricatured personas; this fact is as evident in the realm of politics as in any other (perhaps more so). Of all the viable personas one might craft for himself, the religious dimension which imbues political engagement lends it a greater aspect of rigidity and intolerance which far surpasses any other identifier. More so than "true" or "actual" reality, the political persona of the digital realm is so defined by its performative nature because it is ultimately of less consequence than self-presentations crafted outside of it; in this way, the less significant the pursuit, the freer one is to lose themselves to it. By "significant", I simply mean this: the less a persona or project challenges one to grow beyond its present limit, the less it requires proof of its truthfulness, the less it demands an individual to act, and thus the less significant it is. As I just highlighted, the less consequential it is, the easier a time one has fully committing to it. It is the ultimate road to nowhere. One feels that he is progressing because of the inherently rewarding nature of the medium, but it is nonetheless illusory.

In effect, these digital networks achieve the status of a radicalizer or multiplier; exposed to content and communities which must necessarily ratchet up the intensity of their ideological commitment to sustain their own existence, individuals "return" to reality more uncompromising and less able to dialogue with those of differing worldviews. (They have been initiated. Though they cannot be certain that what they have been initiated into is true or even beneficial, the surge of moral sentiment compels them all the same.) While it is reasonable to assume this effect was constrained by the generational lag in technological competency, that is to say, those most acculturated to the internet were also most likely to exhibit this effect, we can no longer definitively say that this is true. Thanks to increasing ubiquity and ease of access, we have transcended that generational gap and now people of all ages (insofar as they are moderate-to-heavy internet users) can find themselves a niche parapolitical ideology exquisitely suited to their level of consciousness. From this point they can only engage in futile and irrelevant argumentation over disagreements they can neither fully understand nor overcome. Reality, that is, the true and physical lived experience of which we all partake, must necessarily be subordinated to the ideophilic digital niche within which each individual has embedded themselves.

Politics without Action

To elaborate further on the relationship between increased political consciousness/fealty and its concomitant stifling of political action, we should note that the latter arises as much due to the reasons provided above *as well as* by political identification's function as an ameliorating agent or anesthetic. I will once more borrow the well-worn concept introduced by Marcuse—that of desublimation. Political engagement, particularly of the digital variety, is little more than a repressive panacea which buries as it heals. For most who partake in it—the articles, the videos, and so on—it is like finding a well filled with cool water after travelling miles in the blistering heat of a bleak and oppressive desert. Yes, his consumptive habit restores him to life. But we also find, particularly among those individuals who thrust themselves deep into the heart of some digital subculture, that his vital political will is dissipated the further he sinks into his parapolitical fixation. He enjoys his politics, sans the expectation of direct action.

Let us look at a few examples. Infowars-adjacent QAnon (which sprung up alongside Trump's campaign), amassed a gargantuan following by whispering into the ears of naïve Conservatives that salvation was just around the corner. "*Fear not, for a wave of arrests lie just beyond the horizon.*" Of course, these assurances never materialized. Collapsitarians were similarly defenestrated by the belief that a racial bloodbath would ensue following the imminent deterioration of American infrastructure, so they, too, had no reason to take action against ongoing injustices. We can roll back the clock and look to the preppers, the prophets of the second civil war—among others—and find the same trend of instantaneously gratifying desublimations. Just as art became a status quo affirming commodity, so too has politics suffered a similar fate.

Over time, the collaborative tension between radicalization

and disincentivization produces a uniquely demoralizing and destabilizing effect on the psyche. Such people are (or believe themselves to be) more aware of what is going on around them, more acutely aware of the horror of the world, better able to understand and express the "who, what, and why of the world", but are ultimately unable to do anything about it (after all, *someone else* is on the job). So, we "know" more but act less. We enjoy more connections with people who think as we do but are further alienated from those people with whom we actually share our lives. We find ourselves more sensitive to the betrayals and self-betrayals of the American way of life but are lodged within increasingly precarious positions. Only the truly brave (or truly insane) take it upon themselves as a mission to solve these problems (and are increasingly penalized for their efforts). For most, though certainly not all, the only sure return on this investment is an increase in misery and despair. Only the most enlightened or the most characterologically flawed among us can survive in such an environment without wounding their souls.

As I have noted throughout this work, the social and technological circumstances of our present moment facilitate and exacerbate these conditions. Even for the highly functioning and eusocial person, online activity is an increasingly irresistible and alluring scene for social engagement (if not altogether obligatory). For all their personal strengths, they, too, fall under the misanthropic spell of the digital demiurge. Now imagine someone who is lacking in the developmentally appropriate regulatory and social capabilities: put them in a purely digital space where none of the normal checks and balances, none of the corrective social measures are available. What fate might befall them? Make no mistake—I am not a Luddite, nor am I the reincarnation of Nancy Reagan, scaring up bogeymen where none exist. A great many things distinguish us and separate us from one another, but among those qualities which unite us is the collective capacity for degradation.

Initially, these people find within the virtual realm the kinds of encouragement, reinforcement, and community they never had in a physical setting. They can share and connect, commiserate and create in wholly unencumbered ways—a partial fulfillment of the digital promise brought forth earlier. But because of the habituating and escalating nature of the nervous system's reward pathways, further satisfaction of these social desires demands more extreme conduct, more extreme positions, and as such, ever increasing antisocial tendencies. We might say "novel" instead of "extreme", but in truth the intense speed of modern gratification calls forth a psychology of greater transgression to generate further pleasure. While it took us two hundred years to go from Bach to Schoenberg and only a half century to get from Chuck Berry to Chuck D, the speed of the techno-informational society shifts the transgressive quality of novelty into extremity much more rapidly than before.

Alongside the extremity of *content*, we see the extremity of *conduct*. While these individuals often do not engage in direct political action, they will happily participate in oblique measures of parapoliticality. These would include defamation and character assassination (leading to its final form, de-personing), senseless vulgarity and bigotry, glorification and even the instigation of violence. Not for all who partake, mind you; the lunatic fringe is always on the margins, of course, but it is the system's logic which emboldens and expands the margin. More importantly, mere exposure to the logic of the techno-informational society (and its systems, such as the digital space) has a compound effect—the longer you swim in its water, the deeper it will pull you in.

Yet again, I feel it necessary to highlight the insidious (and often unremarked upon) fact in all this—the degree to which the most heinous consequences of this system are manufactured, are intentionally brought about. It is a principal technique of neoliberal governmentality to generate not only the *image* of evil, but its manifest *form* as well. The image is constructed through propaganda in the form of entertainment, journalistic reports and exposés, as well as the very speech of political actors themselves. The manifest form of evil (which is always present and available) is artificially multiplied, either through some technique of classification (expanding its definition to make it more inclusive), or through the deliberate arming and instigating of the vulnerable and the malicious. I would like to emphasize this point before we disembark: the dysfunction produced by this system (here we are still speaking of the digital system, but this is no less true outside of it), the inherent degradation which it wreaks upon those who use it, is neither a fluke nor some unintended consequence. We cannot say that its effects are wholly some passive and unobserved rule which its designers were blind to,[9] because the opposite is true. Neither can we say that the violence it generates is wholly organic either.[10] Both elements—the passive and the active, the unintentional and the intentional—ought to be recognized as the decisive cause of debasement. And both derive from a peculiar will to dominate, an instrumental reason which overshadows any mode of thinking which could derive alternate effects from the use of such technologies.

A Will to Transgress

There is something to be said for the role that political "engagement" plays in the lives of 21st century Americans. We might say, in a reversal of the original authoring of the phrase, that the political is personal; at a time when politics as a discipline, as a sphere of life, has become absolutely meaningless, political identity and political engagement has become *more* meaningful for millions of Americans. It is precisely the access to "important" political actors, and the ability to hemorrhage opinions and feelings about current events which platforms like Twitter provide, that has transformed politics from a mundane necessity of life into a therapeutic act of catharsis. To this very point, a recent study showed that individuals who show addictive habits of social media use were more likely to be motivated by certain antisocial tendencies—in particular, manipulation and cruelty.[11] While the study examined the habits of Snapchat and Facebook

9   Olivia Solon, "Ex-Facebook president Sean Parker: site made to exploit human 'vulnerability'", *The Guardian,* November 9th, 2017 https://www. theguardian.com/technology/2017/nov/09/facebook-sean-parker-vulnerabili-ty-brain-psychology.

10   Eric Striker, "Skinhead Group Members Sentenced To Decades In Prison After FBI Entrapped Them and Then Destroyed Exonerating Evidence", *National Justice,* July 23rd 2020, https://national-justice.com/current-events/skin-head-group-members-sentenced-decades-prison-after-fbi-entrapped-them-and-then.

11   Meshi D., Turel O., Henley D., "Snapchat vs. Facebook: Differences in problematic use, behavior change attempts, and trait social reward preferences", *Addictive Behaviors Reports* vol. 12, December 2020.

users, one might easily imagine how similarly addicted and mal-adapted personalities might make use of other platforms (such as Twitter) to engage in political discourse. And this tendency is not restricted to the disaffected plebeians among us, but celebrities and politicians partake of it, too.

A cursory look at President Trump's own Twitter page (when he isn't getting censored) reveals the morbid commitment of countless Americans, intent on letting him know how vile and unworthy he is (over the course of five to seven tweets, no less). Unrelenting hatred flung at public figures is nothing new, but such activities have become a national pastime for millions of Americans. No longer is such behavior reserved for public fig-ures to sow chaos amongst themselves, it is now available to any-one within digital arms' reach. Increasingly, the will to trans-gress is being directed at people with no influence whatsoever. It is quite democratic, in fact.

No doubt maladapts will flock to these platforms and conduct themselves in predictably terrible ways, but the power of imme-diacy and of connection is strong enough to turn even the most stoic and reserved of individuals into foaming-at-the-mouth lunatics if only once in a while. One of the themes of this text which is once more raising its head here is impotence; such be-havior categorically reveals the degree to which Americans have less and less control over their lives, but more to the point, lack a constructive means or healthful place to air their frustrations. A well-known psychoanalytic fact tells us this: unfulfilled wishes, unexpressed desires don't disappear, they burrow underground where they fester and rot until some moment arrives when they can finally emerge—like psychological zombies—startling us with their hideous and unrecognizable image. The digital space has become the place where our affective zombies roam, limp and malnourished. And just like a zombie, they are not quite so threatening when we can see them coming, especially if they are isolated. It is when they take us by surprise, en masse lunging at us, that we are truly in danger. We inhabit a digital graveyard, haunted not by spirits of jilted lovers or the specter of a long de-posed and depraved royalty, but by the apparitions of our own impotency, of our fear over a world that continues to move in a predictable and terrible direction—away from us and toward an increasingly privatized clique of psychopathic wannabe dignitaries.

It is the will to transgress, that pleasure of overstepping and taking for oneself what belongs to his superior, which more than any other psychological characteristic typifies this kind of behavior. The desire to violate, to penalize, and ultimately to destroy—these are the motivations which lie at the heart of such interactions. As has already been made clear earlier in this analysis, we understand this to be true of the extremist, but it is not his (or her) purview alone. More and more, the average person is invited to participate in this new social ritual—to vilify, degrade, and shame the apostate of neoliberalism. We can take this even further. It is not just a public ritual of humiliation; it is the new sacrificial act. Abstracted sacrifice, yes, as generally people lose *only* their reputations or their jobs, but it is sacrificial nonetheless. In some sense, and I do not wish to draw out this idea too far, it is the supra-abstracted nature of this sacrifice which makes it uniquely painful if not worse than *actual* sacrifice. There is no finality to it, not in the same way as being literally sacrificed to a deity, and so it is an extended agony, a pain which can be revisited and re-exploited. Neither is there any honor to it; there have been cultures (the Incans, for example) where to be selected as the sacrificial object was a noble and desirable experience. A highly ordered practice with specific parameters, many cultures regarded the ritual with a great deal of veneration and respect. In contemporary times, it is a random and chaotic event performed out of mendacious spite. One just might find it preferable to be a corpse rather than a ghost.

It is precisely because individuals exceed their mandates as citizens and go beyond the role of peer and into that of the persecutor that we might properly describe this as an act of transgression. The prevailing psychologies of our time (hopelessness and loss, moral self-righteousness, narcissism, and rage) combined with free and easy access to total strangers creates the perfect storm of opportunity for irrational (and consequence free) retaliation. The retaliatory object itself is symbolic, for it is almost never the case that the transgressor was personally slighted by them. Rather they are the image of the oppressor, and as far as the powerless are concerned, the symbol or proxy of the oppressor is just as good a target as any other.

The Digital Crowd

Throughout this chapter I have described the fact of the digital simulation supplanting the real. Let us continue further along this road. The digital space has become the scene where mobs congregate. And those mobs (or crowds) are given form by digital demagogues who can harness the latent psychic energy of their audiences and direct them toward their own ends. Crowds lack an intrinsic character, just as they lack a direct telos. What the crowd *does* possess are its primal instincts, but it does not know how to use them. As such, the mob desires to be shaped by a leader. We have grown accustomed to the language of marketing (e.g. "influencer"), corporate jargon which, tiresome as it may be, keenly understands the power of the individual to exploit his or her audience. However, it is a mutual exploitation, as the mob can exert pressure upon its leaders just as the leader can exert pressure upon his or her audience. Both push and pull each other, even if the general direction of the relationship is from the top-down. Eventually, the relationship becomes symbiotic, bi-directional, and even the strongest influencer can be broken by the will of the mob. If the mob senses weakness or hesitancy in its chosen leader, it can turn feral and unpredictable. The relationship between the influencer and the mob is like that of the horse rider and the horse; the horse is neither good nor bad, and we cannot say prima facie whether it is friend or foe, it merely has its instincts. But those instincts can prove dangerous, and so the horse must be broken to the will of the rider. If the rider cannot achieve this feat, it certainly spells his doom. The influencer will not die, but his influence will. And so, it is a careful process of analysis and cold reading. On the other hand, not *so* cold, as the nature of digital networking provides more information to the influencer than could be attained any other way.

People congregate online not only because it is easier, but because it is increasingly more onerous to do so in "real" life. The real makes demands; it is uncompromising, often unintelligible, and cannot be whisked away with the click of a button. While the digital comes with its own problems, it is a far more permissive lover.

The audience is the mob; the influencer is the mouth and mind of the mob. Naturally, the establishment is suspicious of influencers who wriggle free of their spandex-tight persona, of the comfy niche selected for (or by? or both?) him. Consider the cases of PewDiePie and Kanye West—two more or less harmless entertainers who, for much of their careers, were engaged in little serious discourse and not regarded especially highly by dignified society (this might be less true for Kanye West). Throughout their careers, both individuals have seen their stars soar on the back of supposed faux pas, saying or doing something outside of the prescribed norm which jolted their audiences out of their stupor, challenging them to elevate their consciousness, to think about the world differently. PewDiePie's alleged racist and anti-Semitic flirtations with the Alt-Right, no different from Kanye West's dalliances with chauvinism and Trumpism, created minor ruptures within the popular culture. In the end, the effects of these cultural fissures proved negligible at best (though it may be difficult to ascertain their true impact), while still demonstrating the danger which rogue influencers pose to the stability of neo-liberalism's cultural hegemony.

So not only does the influencer mold his mob, but if he is crafty, if he proves capable of sincerely challenging himself, then he can continually remold his audience as he transforms himself. The rapidity of digital communication means that an audience of thousands, tens or even hundreds of thousands, can be transformed—in part or in whole—by a series of tweets, or a short video.

Gustave Le Bon[12] wrote of the malleability of crowd consciousness, and how the mob was essentially capable of both great virtue and terrible criminality. Extremism of the kind that typifies American political discourse is only possible thanks to the work of influential demagogues, individuals of great power who wield their social capital to stir the emotions of the crowd and direct them like pieces on a chessboard. Social media has permitted the control of global crowd consciousness, in a way that has never before been achieved in human history. Corporate control of these social media platforms simultaneously allows for the cordoning off of wrongthink, which keeps the larger crowd

12   Gustav Le Bon, *The Crowd: A Study of the Popular Mind*, (1895).

docile and removed, while also permitting wrongthinkers and their ideologies to fester in isolation, thus more susceptible to self-cannibalization and irrelevance. The toxic element continues to grow in toxicity, and those who participate in these communities lose the ability to test their ideas against opposition or to organize against said opposition. Social isolation and ideological wrongthink are the strongest tools of establishmentarian extremism, allowing for continued control and expansion of power.

Lacking a sense of noblesse oblige and situated in positions of control largely through pathological and Machiavellian means, the establishment can do nothing but grow in its extremism. As the legitimacy of its moral certitude wanes and the true reasons for its oppressive expansion reveal themselves, the establishment has little recourse but to force itself upon the populace through techniques of increasing cruelty and hypocrisy. In doing so, the stewards of neoliberalism further expose their true aims as well as those who actually benefit from their machinations. At the time of this writing (mid-afternoon on Friday, July 31st 2020), the stomach-churning revelations of Jeffrey Epstein and his partner Ghislaine Maxwell's sordid affairs continue to shock the nation. Allegations made by accusers claim that the pair procured teenage girls from all over the world, engaging in round-the-clock orgies which featured other cultural icons such as former president Bill Clinton, England's Prince Andrew, and respected attorney Alan Dershowitz.[13] [14] The same accuser claimed that Maxwell trained her (and other young girls) as sex slaves in an elaborate and international trafficking scheme in which Epstein also figured prominently.[15] Epstein, who has been a prominent public

13 Ben Feuerherd, "Court doc details Maxwell's 'constant' orgies with young girls on Epstein's island", *New York Post,* July 31st 2020, https://nypost.com/2020/07/31/ghislaine-maxwell-had-continuous-sex-with-young-girls-on-epstein-island/.

14 A further wrinkle in this story involves the efforts of Dershowitz and Mike Cernovich, a prominent right-wing journalist and personality, to obtain legal documents which might exonerate the former of any potential wrongdoing. To my knowledge this remains little more than innuendo but is curious all the same.

15 Victoria Bekiempis, "Ghislaine Maxwell trained underage girls as sex slaves, document alleges", *The Guardian,* July 31st 2020, https://www.theguardian.com/us-news/2020/jul/31/ghislaine-maxwell-underage-girls-sex-jeffrey-epstein.

figure for decades (and whose associations include prominent public intellectuals like Steven Pinker, billionaire tech moguls like Bill Gates, as well as past and present U.S. presidents Bill Clinton and Donald Trump), may not be the worst of the worst, but he is the symbol of elite violence and perversion. Ghislaine Maxwell, who had been on the lam since the beginning of the Epstein debacle, was only recently apprehended in New Hampshire. In this moment, where Americans are beset by economic catastrophe and political revolution, the most powerful people in the world are being exposed for the malevolent, narcissistic, cruelly inhuman individuals that they are.

Digressions aside, the power of media—and of social media in particular—is the ability of the system to coerce consent from the populace. Whether this is achieved through virtue-signaling blackmail campaigns (such as the "*Blackout Tuesday*" campaign which followed in the wake of the George Floyd killing), or by overwhelming individual consciousness through the technique of information overload, or simply by taking advantage of the average person's desire to participate in the power process, neo-liberalism's techno-informational stranglehold proves itself the force majeure of governance.

And so, to restate a few key ideas before moving on from this discussion, the immediacy and interconnectedness of social media allows individuals to reinforce the prevailing paradigm and to punish wrongthinkers and members of the perceived out-group. Social engagement becomes at least as much about enacting vengeance and retribution upon people who have in fact done nothing wrong, but become targets for the resentment and frustration of others either because they represent in some way the wrongdoer, or simply because they are accessible. Interestingly, journalists, politicians, and worrywarts of every kind correctly identify social media networks as hotbeds of radicalization, but they of course only understand this in a very narrow way. They overlook (or are simply ignorant of) the fact that the networks themselves are mere vehicles for the transmission and enforcement of radical or extremist ideology, and that in the pockets of the internet where genuinely antisocial ideas are spread, they are in fact cultivated and maintained in part by agents of the intelligence community who seek, in a Chestertonian way (as in his novel "*The Man Who Was Thursday*"), to control and direct the energies of anti-system thought. Ideas alone are rarely dangerous; it is the assumptions one has and the way he applies the idea which grants them the potential for destruction. Social media, a medium of depersonalization and simulation par excellence, provides the conditions necessary to exacerbate social tensions and encourage the kinds of dysfunction that would not find oxygen in a live setting. However it is only the latest innovation in a long list of mechanisms of control; the extent to which the digital space allows for counter-system thinking *and* truly anti-social extremity are both damning indictments of neoliberalism itself—a point which our interlocutors are not willing to admit.

Declarations and Identity Formation

Thus far, I have taken it as a given that identity formation occurs and has described the social factors which contribute to its creation but have not yet elaborated meaningfully on the *process itself*. I would like to take a moment to discuss one such technique used to achieve this psychological fact. An interesting observation made nearly one hundred years ago by psychologist Kurt Lewin found that making public commitments "freezes" attitudes in place. In effect, there ceases to be any further evaluation of a stance taken once an individual has made a public and social commitment toward a given position. A student of social relations, groupthink, and identitarianism, Lewin's work has much to offer us in furthering our understanding of political extremism. This process, while necessary for cultivating individuality and clarifying one's belief system, when centered within a dysfunctional context can impede growth; it also impedes humility and understanding, all factors which, when taken together, create a self-reinforcing group dogma which never gets rectified. Unless there is some traumatic external event, the position takes on the significance of a theological decree which a group can rally around and use to strengthen individual identity and in-group cohesion. We easily see how, in the market of identity where individuals are desperate for a sense of belonging, one can be easily coerced or manipulated into making public declarations without careful consideration to the meaning of the declarative statement (much less the consequences of making it).

Social media platforms have allowed for an unprecedented democratization of opinion formation and expression. Attitudinal freeze (in Lewin's view, being central to groupthink), occurs not because of the inherent truth value of the declaration being made (though it may or may not be factually true, it may be "true" in the sense that it validates an intuition, suspicion, or bias) but because it reinforces some previously held belief (or desire) and fits neatly within a preexisting worldview. There is no other time in history which we can look to and find a society that had the technological capacity for random, socially powerless individuals to share their thoughts and feelings and have them reinforced by their peers, much less by total strangers. (Of course, in global neoliberal society, we are all "peers" in some sense.) So, it is not only the declaration itself but the reinforcement of the declaration which gives it stronger weight, further solidifying it in both the individual and collective consciousness. Contrary points of view, rather than simply being a form of dissent or dialogue, become *contrarianisms*, an antisocial act determined to weaken group cohesion and undermine individual and group agency.

Hundreds of years ago, what might have been an unthought thought or unformed sentiment, an inkling of an idea whispered to no one (perhaps not even to oneself) over time has been given a medium for dissemination. The ability to communicate—to mass communicate—gives one the license to think and to share. In the present day, there is no interaction, no interpersonal *trying out* of an idea, no lag or delay between the thinking of the thought and the sharing of the thought. The immediacy of digital communication helps a lie get around the world before the truth can pull up its pants, to borrow an old phrase. Or in our case, it helps a desire get around the world before one even understands what that desire *desired*. The truth value of the statement itself is to some degree of less importance, what is more significant is the functional value of that statement and the worldview it helps to engender. Feelings of persecution can quickly become codified into a definitive "factual" statement when paired with some data point or anecdote which structures the feeling. Even if the desire is true, we can delude ourselves into believing *the statement itself* is true, if only because the social proof of the community which exists around such truth statements legitimizes its truth value.

The more we say something, the truer it becomes. With each repetition, that truth moves closer to our hearts, toward our concept of our self (and thus we are less inclined to reevaluate that truth statement). And as that statement is validated by the group with which we seek to ingratiate ourselves, the less social reason there is for abandoning it, for abandoning some declaration may very well lead to abandonment by the community who once accepted us. The declaration is proof of our very existence, and to abandon it is akin to self-erasure. We may make such declarations, not even as an expression of some deeply held belief or half-hearted ponderance, but merely to be initiated into a collective.

This psychological reality leaves the door open for cults of extremism, as online political discourse and in fact social and personal commentaries of any kind are part of the game of social media. Antisocial extremists must first stake out some ideophilic territory upon which to build their community and stabilize their identity as a unique and radical entity. Having laid claim to a set of issues, they signal their importance through mimetic repetition, thus creating a lexicon for which they might be known. A common political refrain of the AER, "*there is no political solution*" is an example of this very phenomenon. The community takes this stance, and would-be inductees into the cult affirm the declaration themselves to gain entry. Upon doing so, the declarative act works to form the structure of their identity. As these individuals repeat the mantra, they move further from reasonable political discourse, thus warping their ability to dialogue rationally with others. To the extent the AER can even conceive of a rebuttal or counterexample, they will reflexively deny it on any grounds possible.

The act of defining oneself is simultaneously one of affirmation and of alienation, for with every declarative statement one makes, he both refines his self-concept while also distancing himself from others. Psychological resources are mounted to further justify the statement, reinforcing the affirmation to such a degree that these individuals are no longer able to think critically about the sentiment. In a climate such as the one online, the transgressive novelty which defines existence on social media—the need for new opinions, new content, new imagery—can push people into making ever bolder declarations without thinking reflectively about them (particularly in a milieu motivated by resentment and envy, where such statements serve to defend the ego of extremist and radical participants in online discourse). As the positions are rarely staked on strictly empirical or rational grounds, such individuals trap themselves in a hysterical state, paralyzing them from action and all but certainly guaranteeing their continued spiral into antisocial extremism.

"They don't gotta burn the books, they just remove 'em"

By this point I have all but exhausted my analysis, having dug as deeply as I can into the phenomenon so that we may discuss it with the utmost clarity. I would like to conclude this discussion by offering some potential points of exit, not only for the extremist himself but for all of us who are trapped within the claustrophobic neoliberal discourse which seeks to further restrict our thinking. Before I do that, I would like to touch upon one last aspect of the problem, one which has not been examined as thoroughly as everything else discussed thus far: censorship.

The title of this section comes from the Rage Against the Machine song, "Bulls on Parade". Here is the full lyrical excerpt:

> *Weapons, not food, not homes, not shoes*
> *Not need, just feed the war, cannibal animal*
> *I walk the corner to the rubble, that used to be a library*
> *Line up to the mind cemetery now*
> *What we don't know keeps the contracts alive and movin'*
> *They don't gotta burn the books, they just remove 'em*
> *While arms warehouses fill as quick as the cells*
> *Rally 'round the family, pocket full of shells*

Censorship is a contentious issue precisely because of the mythic character of free speech in the United States. To be clear, I am not a free speech absolutist and I do not consider censorship to be a necessary feature of totalitarian governance. A healthy society, in my view, is one that does not condone any speech or act which operates in the spirit of debasement. For example, sexual imagery which is pornographic instead of erotic; violent imagery that revels in its senselessness and purposelessness; speech which is willfully deceitful and treacherous; this is hardly a thorough or complete examination of the issue, but it will suffice for now. We learn much about the psychology of a people when we study the things they consider objectionable. Paramoralistic thinking which reflexively and unreasoningly deems certain images or ideas as "bad" leads us to the kind of censorship which *can* stifle creativity and innovation and ultimately oppress a people both spiritually and materially.

Even when we are permitted to laugh at such allegedly tyrannical acts, the subtext is always one of evil and of otherness.[16] Censorship is always something that malevolent, cruel, and fearful people do—nothing liberal about it!

But one might say that *it is in the interest* of the governing class to censor material which threatens its stability, thus rendering censorship a technique of governmentality. A minimum of censorship would suggest to us the healthfulness of the governing structure, as this indicates a relative poverty of threats to its power (as well as the vitality of those it governs). Neoliberal governance is far afield from the kind of healthful government I am speaking of, and arguably more censorious than the supposedly totalitarian regimes of the 20th century. I understand that some of my readers might balk at this statement precisely because of America's history of protected speech and its self-perception as the moral guardian of the rights of the individual, but I would invite you to re-examine this idea. Scratch beneath the surface and you will find this to be another example of the false collective fictions we discussed only a few chapters ago.

In our techno-informational society, censorship emerges as the preeminent technique of governance, as digital communication offers a veritable cornucopia of problematic discourses which might potentially destabilize the tightly controlled flow of ideas and dialogues. While we are often cautioned (perhaps

---

16 I am reminded of a scene from Spielberg's third *Indiana Jones* film. While trying to recover his father's diary (a critically important text for the film's plot containing information about the Holy Grail), Harrison Ford's titular character is confronted by Adolf Hitler in the middle of a book-burning rally in Berlin. The punch line of this scene arrives when Hitler signs the diary and promptly turns his attention to other rally-goers, allowing a panic-stricken Indiana Jones to continue his pursuit.

a stronger word would be *gaslit*) about the book-burning and blacklisting habits of illiberal governments from the preceding century, the removal of digital information by 21st century corporations hardly seems to capture the imagination in quite the same way. In truth, this evolving technique of removal is far more insidious because it is not only limited to works of political thought, but it occurs outside of the watchful eye of the public. Instantaneously and without warning, your favorite piece of music or film might evaporate from your library because the digital provider no longer can (or wants) to make it available. Your bank may elect to suspend your account, leaving you with little in the way of recourse (but a lot in the way of headaches). And in the most representative example of censorship, your life's work (or simply the work of your favorite author or commentator) may be withdrawn from the market due to refinements made in the policy of speech, conduct, or some other such contrivance.

Part of the mystification around censorship lies in the following commonly held belief: the various spheres of American influence are wholly distinct from one another, and thus operate under different systems of logic. Or to put a finer point on the issue, when the government engages in censorship it is a tyrannical overstep—but when a corporation participates in the same practice—it is simply a corrective action of the market, one which can be remedied by simply plying one's trade elsewhere. One of the great insights of Marx was to recognize that economic institutions and their leaders were not separate from the political institutions. Rather, they merely divide the labor of sovereignty across different industries of influence. Offering a variation of the Grecian theme which states that quantity has a quality of its own, economic actors can easily exercise powers traditionally limited to governmental institutions because of their accumulated wealth and influence. This same principle explains the power of celebrity: Why do people care about the political opinions of athletes and pop stars? *Because quantity has a quality of its own.* There are many paths to the throne but for each one the directions remain the same: accumulate, accumulate, accumulate.

In a society ravaged by the sickness of neoliberalism, censorship remains a technique of survival all the same; the difference here of course is that it is implemented on behalf of the disease-makers.

BOOK IV

Solving the Problem of Extremism

Woe unto the man, that crusading hero, who
Ignorant of his own darkness, sought to erase
  the evil surrounding him.
Given to self-deception, he worked to punish the liars
  in his midst.
Disdainful towards the corruption of others, but tolerant
  of the corruption within,
He desired to silence them forever.
Filled with an uncompromising, blistering vitality –
Woe unto him for he did not first, begin with himself.

Solving the Problem of Extremism

I have set up for myself the unenviable task of solving the problem of political extremism, a problem which billions of dollars and thousands of years of collective wisdom have not yet been able to remedy. Before I offer my humble suggestions, I think it would be prudent to highlight the reasons for our present lack of success. Where contemporary efforts fail (or at least one of the most significant causes for failure) is in the decidedly uncompromising and wholly ideological approach taken by the anti-extremist industry. Of course, even in communicating this fact a *second* cause for failure is immediately revealed.

Take the example of Robin DiAngelo's book, *White Fragility*:[1] DiAngelo opens her book with an anecdote of personal anguish and despair; for years she had to contend with the hostility and resistance of disinterested parties, furiously opposed to her message of anti-Whiteness and White fragility. I found it difficult to ignore the impression her story left me with—one of self-servingness. Clearly this is a very personal and emotionally charged mission for Robin; however, "personal" and "emotional" are not synonyms for "noble" and "honest".

A few things jump out at the reader as suspicious even before grappling with the ideas found within it: for one, the maliciousness of the language DiAngelo develops throughout ("*white tears*", "*white fragility*"), and for another, the curiosity of an ethnically Italian-Jewish woman championing the cause of Blackness. It seems unproductive, if one claims to be an educator motivated by a well-honed sense of the ethical, to antagonize the audience one seeks to convince. Her arguments depend on the mineable resource of human guilt, for without such a feeling they would be wholly without impact. Throughout her book, DiAngelo digs her heels in to extract as much guilt as possible. Furthermore, it seems cynical, opportunistic, self-righteous—and perhaps even a bit malicious—to announce oneself as the champion of the other and to then insinuate yourself into a conflict of which you are not directly involved.

There are a few useful insights in the book: calling attention to the primacy of race (p. 89), challenging the narcissism of American individualism (p. 11), the naïveté of color-blind ideology (p. 40), among them, but they are overshadowed by DiAngelo's heavily motivated reasoning. While she manages to fumble her way toward some useful critiques, when considering the approach she takes, the ideology she inhabits, and the very fact of the book's mainstream appeal, it is difficult to see how she accomplishes anything other than the complete obliteration of her own legitimacy as a sociologist and educator.

DiAngelo goes to great lengths to reposition racism as a systemic form of injustice and not merely a personal moral failing—as picturesque an example of the technique of spellbinding as one is likely to find. Here, DiAngelo leans into certain aspects of

---

1 Robin DiAngelo, *White Fragility* (Massachusetts: Beacon Press, 2018).

the American mythos (e.g. personal responsibility, moral erudition) with the intention of manipulating them to her advantage. Anti-racism is a personal quest, one which every White American must embark upon—*rebuke your Whiteness or else!* Discipline and control, external scrutiny and internal self-subjection, these are the calling cards of Robin DiAngelo's *White Fragility*. There lies a curious inconsistency in this point, as well, which I will return to momentarily.

By holding disenfranchised civilians of the present day morally responsible for the actions of a bygone elite, DiAngelo reveals herself to be upholding the very system she seeks to overturn. For DiAngelo, it is the average White person and the life he or she wishes to provide for themselves (and their families) that is inexorably flawed; until they deterritorialize their psychological Whiteness, they shall always be the most significant roadblock to racial equality. I am struck by the narrow-minded vindictiveness of such a position which attempts to equate the direct action of the few with the passive acceptance of the many. Once more, the counterargument which I have not yet fully explicated (the very same which you have almost certainly arrived at on your own) lies barely hidden behind DiAngelo's argument.

White Fragility is less about solving racism than it is introducing a new disciplinary technology into the American consciousness. We might even describe White fragility as a kind of disciplinary wellness program, for it so neatly fits alongside the slew of other holistic corporate initiatives designed to make better, more docile workers. Yes, they are disciplinary insofar as they are institutionalized mandates designed to further impose upon the individual a crushing level of psychological scrutiny, but they are also promoted as being "*for your benefit*". Perhaps a generation ago wellness programs were intended to remove the stress of family and work, of the hectic commute and so on, but today the worker's stress is of a different nature altogether. It is the stress of unconsciously contributing to the suffering of the other, racial or otherwise.

While more obviously pernicious, corporate anti-racism or anti-sexism programs are hardly any different from those wellness initiatives which preceded it (e.g. mindfulness, meditation, yoga retreats, and so on); all function according to a certain instrumental rationality which strips these practices of any deeper, more meaningful value, and appropriates them entirely for the purpose of improving productivity. Moreover, within this corporatized context, all accord to that Foucauldian logic of observation, normalization, and measurement, thus giving them their disciplinary power. As with corporate sponsored gym memberships, sports leagues, psychological services, and hot yoga classes, anti-racism training promises to make the workplaces of the world a safer, healthier, more productive environment for everyone. In the mind of the neoliberal, raising political consciousness has the same holistic value as any diet or fitness regimen. For better or for worse, neoliberal governmentality has proven far more effective at creating the New Man than any communist or fascist regime ever could have.

Now we arrive at the fatal conceit which undermines DiAngelo's entire project: if White supremacy is an omniscient cultural technology which secures racial inequality, and if Whites are too fragile to confront their racism, then why did DiAngelo's book get published? Why does she command speaking fees in excess of $30,000?[2] Why is her message the same one found in corporate boardrooms, high school and university classrooms, and human resources offices around the country? The answer to these questions brings us right back to the problem we posed at the beginning of this chapter. So, let us ask the more pointed question: why can't America solve the problem of extremism? At the risk of being a cynical materialist, it is simply not profitable to do so. While this is not the sole reason (I will elaborate on this more later), the financial incentive to perpetuate both 1) intersectional progressivism and 2) extremism (whether real or imagined) is real and very strong. Contrary to what obese and bespectacled thirty-something men on social media say, one does not go broke when they go woke. Rather, the price for not going woke grows steeper by the day.

So, on the one hand, America is ideologically unequipped to combat extremism; the solutions it proposes are themselves divisive, ideophilically arrested, and extremist in their own right. Just as one does not burn fat by continuing to shove greasy

2   Charles Fain Lehman, "The Wages of Woke", *Washington Free Beacon,* July 25th, 2020 https://freebeacon.com/culture/the-wages-of-woke-2/.

cheeseburgers down one's throat, governments do not eliminate political extremism by confronting them on identical moral and philosophical grounds. On the other hand, there is a strong profit motive (shared by the intelligence community, the military-industrial complex, Hollywood, higher education, and so on) to create simulacra of anti-extremism which achieve little in the way of stymieing extremism (quite the opposite in fact, they create extremists where there had previously been none). The profit extracted by anti-extremists is twofold; first they gain materially (e.g. corporate sponsorships, government contracts, crowd-funded donations, ticket and record sales, etc.), then they gain socially. As these individuals commit themselves to the popular moral campaigns of the day, their social status skyrockets, propelling them to greater heights than they might have achieved on a purely meritocratic basis. Even the most reviled members of society can see their public image reversed by taking a popular anti-extremist stance (consider the fact that former president George W. Bush is now regarded fondly, having publicly slammed incumbent Donald Trump for his alleged racism).[3]

But of course, political extremism is an effect with multiple causes. I would be remiss if I concluded my analysis here, for the issue is not solely material or economic in nature.

Power and Anti-Power

Political power always produces its own anti-power. Whether this is accomplished through its own foibles, or by errors of judgment and miscalculations, or even by deliberate machinations, power breathes life into the limp body of anti-power. As such, any given hegemonic force can no less permanently abolish the extremist or radical tendencies which it generates than it can eliminate itself. Anti-power is at once the political and cultural energy which lies outside of power (and therefore seeks to challenge and usurp it), but is at the same time a latent resource that can be harnessed by power in service of itself (thus becoming an

3   Sandra Sobieraj Westfall, "George W. Bush Breaks His Silence on the Direction of the Country Under President Trump: 'I Don't Like the Racism and Name-Calling'", *People,* February 27th, 2017 https://people.com/politics/george-w-bush-on-trump-presidency/.

auxiliary to power). We may think of radical politics as largely belonging to the former, whereas extremism resides almost entirely within the latter category. To draw this idea out even further, we can also say that while anti-power enjoys public visibility owing to its counter-cultural outlier status (whether that visibility is self-generated or manufactured by power itself), it enjoys little to none of the positive influence of power.[4]

And so, another reason why extremism continues to be the gadfly of neoliberalism is that it *is* neoliberalism. The professionally successful father may look upon his drug-addled criminal son with disdain (seeing only the lack of his own virtue), but were he to gaze beyond his ego defenses then he would surely recognize the fruit of his labor. An unhealthy society can only perpetuate greater disease; even the good that it produces comes with an early expiration date. Truly dysfunctional and anti-social extremism is the natural byproduct, or perhaps logical conclusion (not a mere afterthought) of neoliberalism. For America to eradicate violent, antisocial political extremism once and for all, it would need to suspend the very techniques it employs in service of itself. Effectively, it would need to commit geopolitical suicide. Extremism and radicalism are both the result of a particular governmental logic which seeks to outsource moral labor (just as it outsources physical labor) for its own profit. But whereas neoliberal governance offshores manual labor internationally (constraining "willing" parties to its own logic, thus reaping greater profits and eliminating potential geopolitical competitors), it offshores moral and psychological labor *domestically*—thus constraining its political subjects to a kind of technique of responsibilism, dooming them to lives of frustration and disillusionment by foisting upon them duties which are, in fact, not theirs alone. This governmental technique of responsibilism removes (or at the very least, severely cripples) domestic competitors of power by saddling them with a psychological debt which no man can ever repay[5].

---

4 "Positive influence" here may denote its desirability or mass appeal, but it can also refer to its failure to achieve political goals.

5 As an aside, I often hear people speak of "America's legitimacy crisis", "late-stage capitalism", the "crisis of neoliberalism", and so on. I believe them to be gravely mistaken in claiming such things. Because of this deferral of moral responsibility, Americanism, capitalism, neoliberalism (all different words for

To bear this out once more, just as neoliberalism gives birth to extremism (the false image of resistance), so too does it give rise to radicalism (true resistance incarnate). Whenever an individual, or an institution, or a nation errs, a competitor (or at the least, *would-be competitor*) seeks to enter the fray. In the realm of the political, anti-power is that competitor. Radical American anti-power is the political force most opposed to neoliberal hegemony, and were it provided the material resources necessary to achieve its goals, would therefore become the strongest and most effective site of resistance against the international pathocracy. But without social proof, material support, and frankly, the right collection of people, it can never progress from anti-power to power.

It should be said, however, that the pathocracy (being comprised of mere humans) is not infallible in its approach to anti-power. In the lead up to the 2016 election, the media class gave too much attention to the alt-right (possibly out of morbid curiosity, perhaps due to an attitude of low-time preference), while the political class (Hillary Clinton in particular) helped unify it with the broader American right-wing. Within a relatively short period of time, illiberal American anti-power transcended its natural limits and slowly began to change the public discourse. However this transcendence was not of its own doing and the very fact of its self-overcoming only serves to highlight my point: even when power does so seemingly in error, it is the only force capable of granting anti-power its political gravitas.

We know now that the establishment learned its lessons from the previous election cycle and has shifted in its strategy toward anti-power. By propagandizing against it, fracturing it, and ultimately using its existence as further justification for the expansion of certain political aims, anti-power is now just another technique of neoliberal governmentality to be wielded for

the same beast) only enjoys the *image, the self-representation* of moral authority. While the veracity, the credibility of this image is certainly in decline (thus revealing that it is only might which substantiates America's claim to moral superiority), the strength of the system which America has brought to bear upon the world shows no such symptoms of decay. If anything, it has demonstrated a staggering capacity for resilience in the face of an ever-escalating series of challenges.

its own benefit. And so, for a few reasons America struggles to rid itself of extremism. The first of which is that America cannot help but produce it in the first place. Despair and violence are eternal facts of human existence, but American neoliberalism generates such an astonishing surplus of tragedy that we can take it as a certainty that we will be confronted by them over and over again. Secondly, the ideological basis of contemporary radical anti-power has its roots in civilizations that are thousands of years old. Illiberalism, too, is an eternal fact of political thought and no amount of tyranny will ever remove it from the collective mind. More significant than the fact of its eternal intellectual relevance—illiberality is a biotype. Short of reengineering the human genome, you could not rid society of it even if you burned every copy of Plato's *Republic* and Hitler's *Mein Kampf.* Perhaps most significantly of all, the allure of manipulating anti-power is simply too strong to resist. At any time, for any reason at all, dissent can be weaponized as a device for setting and achieving political goals. Asking a liberal politician to not exploit unrest or manipulate dissent is like asking a crackhead to not rob his next door neighbor for drug money—it just won't ever happen. We may consider anti-power a chief principle of metapolitics, and thus incapable of being dispensed with (just as we cannot dispense with metaphysical realities—such as God—no matter how hard we try).

Why Deplatforming Doesn't Work

Putting aside the material interest in keeping political extremism alive (as well as the metapolitical aspect which all but guarantees the longevity of radical and extremist opposition toward hegemonic power), there is one final aspect to the problem which I would like to discuss before moving on to potential solutions: censorship. This may be a contentious claim, but I believe it is a demonstrable fact that censorship and deplatforming do not stop the problem of extremism. There are two main reasons for this, but before we explore them let us briefly review the academic analysis of the matter.

What censorship and deplatforming unquestioningly achieves is a disruption and diminishment of dissident communication. According to Joan Donovan, the accountability research lead of Data and Society, when a commentator gets deplatformed, *"there's an initial flashpoint, where some of their audience will move with them, but generally the falloff is pretty significant and they don't gain the same amplification power they had prior to the moment they were taken off these bigger platforms."*[6] It is true that in the short term the Streisand Effect prevails, but for most activists (and in particular the less notable ones), they struggle to maintain their influence down the line. Angelo Carusone, President and CEO of Media Matters observed that, *"I think the anecdotes are what makes a difference here—each individual, when you add them up, you get a net effect. You don't need much data behind it to point out that with Milo, he lost Twitter, and the result was he lost a lot. He lost his ability to be influential or at least to project a veneer of influence."*[7] Dr. Robyn Caplan (a Data and Society affiliate), noted *"The good that comes with deplatforming is, their main goal was to redpill or get people within mainstream communities more in line with their beliefs, so we need to get them off those platforms."*[8]

Dr. Joe Mulhall, a senior researcher at "Hope Not Hate" documented the extensive damage done to the political careers of individuals such as Milo Yiannopolous and Tommy Robinson by deplatforming efforts. The following is an excerpt taken from an article he wrote for HNH's website:

> Those who've been deplatformed on the far right have articulated how it has severely retarded their influence. Milo Yiannopoulos recently moaned:
>
> > *I lost 4 million fans in the last round of bans. [...] I spent years growing and developing and investing in my fan base and they just took it away in a flash.*
>
> He goes on to state how he and others have simply failed to build a following on platforms such as Telegram and Gab that are large enough to support them. "I can't make a ca-

6 Jason Koebler, "Deplatforming Works", *Vice,* August 10th, 2018, https://www.vice.com/en_us/article/bjbp9d/do-social-media-bans-work.

7 Jason Koebler, "Deplatforming Works", *Vice,* August 10th, 2018, https://www.vice.com/en_us/article/bjbp9d/do-social-media-bans-work.

8 Jason Koebler, "Deplatforming Works", *Vice,* August 10th, 2018, https://www.vice.com/en_us/article/bjbp9d/do-social-media-bans-work.

reer out of a handful of people like that. I can't put food on the table this way", he explained.

In March 2018 Yaxley-Lennon was permanently banned by Twitter, and then in February 2019 he was banned from Facebook, where he had more than one million followers, depriving him of his primary means of communication and organising his supporters. Another major blow came on 2 April 2019 when YouTube finally acted and placed some restrictions around his channel, which resulted in his views collapsing.

Hundreds of thousands of fewer people now see his content every month, which is a huge step forward. It may have also played into the severely reduced numbers we have seen at pro-Lennon events this year. During the summer of 2018 London was witness to demonstrations in excess of 10,000 pro-Lennon supporters, while this year numbers have struggled to reach beyond a few hundred. The reasons for this are by no means monocausal, but his and his associates' inability to spread the word about events and animate the masses beyond core supporters has clearly played a role.[9]

Other investigations into the success of online deplatforming turn up similar results: a team of researchers led by Eshwar Chandrasekharan at Georgia Institute of Technology found that censorship on Reddit resulted in a nearly 90% reduction of hate speech, and ultimately a mass exodus from the platform. "For the definition of "work" framed by our research questions, the ban worked for Reddit. It succeeded at both a user level and a community level. Through the banning of subreddits which engaged in racism and fat-shaming, Reddit was able to reduce the prevalence of such behavior on the site."[10]

Continuing right along, anti-extremist researchers at Swansea University examining the deplatforming of a group known as "Britain First" found that, *"the removal of the extremist group Britain First from Facebook in March 2018 successfully disrupt-*

9 Joe Mulhall, "Deplatforming works: Let's get on with it", *Hope Not Hate,* April 10th, 2019, https://www.hopenothate.org.uk/2019/10/04/deplatforming-works-lets-get-on-with-it/.

10 Eshwar Chandrasekharan, et al. "You Can't Stay Here: The Efficacy of Reddit's 2015 Ban Examined Through Hate Speech", *Proceedings of the ACM on Human-Computer Interaction*, Vol.1, No.2, Article 31, November 2017.

ed the group's online activity, leading them to have to start anew on Gab, a different and considerably smaller social media platform. The removal also resulted in the group having to seek new online followers from a much smaller, less diverse recruitment pool".[11] While encouraged by the success of the deplatforming, the researchers were troubled to find that, *"despite the decrease in followers on Gab, the themes found in Britain First's imagery demonstrate a move towards more extreme content in the course of their migration to Gab, likely due to the platform being less likely to censor content."* Audrey Alexander duplicated similar findings when examining the effect censorship had on English-language Islamic State sympathizers on Twitter. In his study he says that, *"although English-language IS followers struggle to maintain their hold on the platform, and fail to attract the same degrees of followership after suspension, mounting evidence suggests that supporters continue to adapt to the online environment."*.[12]

In particular, the findings of the last two researchers lead us toward a significant problem with the approach presently being taken by anti-extremists: while censorship and deplatforming does diminish instances of hate speech on those platforms which take action against them, it achieves little to nothing in affecting the digital ecosystem at large. Researchers specializing in this area are quite aware of this fact as well.[13] Summarizing an article on this very point, author Noemi Derzsy says,

> Johnson et al. show that online hate groups are organized in highly resilient clusters. The users in these clusters are not geographically localized, but are globally interconnected by 'highways' that facilitate the spread of online hate across different countries, continents and languages. When these clusters are attacked — for example, when hate groups are removed by social-media platform administrators (Fig. 1)

11 Lella Nouri, Nuria Lorenzo-Dus, and Amy-Louise Watkin, "Following the Whack-a-Mole: Britain First's Visual Strategy from Facebook to Gab", *Global Research Network on Terrorism and Technology,* Paper no. 4, July 2019.

12 Audrey Alexander, "Digital Decay? Tracing Change Over Time Among English-Language Islamic State Sympathizers on Twitter", *The Program on Extremism at George Washington University,* 2017 https://extremism.gwu.edu/sites/g/files/zaxdzs2191/f/DigitalDecayFinal_0.pdf.

13 N.F. Johnson, et al, "Hidden resilience and adaptive dynamics of the global online hate ecology", *Nature,* 573, 261-265, 2019.

— the clusters rapidly rewire and repair themselves, and strong bonds are made between clusters, formed by users shared between them, analogous to covalent chemical bonds. In some cases, two or more small clusters can even merge to form a large cluster, in a process the authors liken to the fusion of two atomic nuclei. Using their mathematical model, the authors demonstrated that banning hate content on a single platform aggravates online hate ecosystems and promotes the creation of clusters that are not detectable by platform policing (which the authors call 'dark pools'), where hate content can thrive unchecked.[14]

Richard Rogers is another such investigator into the habits of online extremists, one who also laments the present state of research, stating that "*less research has been performed about the effectiveness of the ban for the health of social media or the Internet at large.*"[15]

To his credit, Nathan Cofnas (a philosopher of biology who has regularly confronted well-known "online extremists" in an effort to debunk them) took note of these problems in July of 2019. Writing for *Quillette*,[16] Cofnas had the following to say:

Advocates of deplatforming tend to think only one step ahead: Throw people with opinions you don't like off mainstream social media and you won't see them again—out of sight, out of mind. But the deplatformers should try thinking two, maybe even three, steps ahead: What will people do after they're banned? How will their followers react? How will this be perceived by more or less neutral observers? With some forethought, it's easy to see that banning people with supposedly "bad" or "wrong" views may not be the victory that deplatformers think it is.

Banning people from social media doesn't make them change their minds. In fact, it makes them less likely to change their minds. It makes them more alienated from mainstream society, and, as noted, it drives them to cre-

14 Noemi Derzsy, "Strategies for combating online hate", *Nature,* August 21st, 2019 https://www.nature.com/articles/d41586-019-02447-1.

15 Richard Rogers, "Deplatforming: Following extreme Internet celebrities to Telegram and alternative social media", *European Journal of Communication,* Vol. 35(3), 213-229, 2020.

16 Nathan Cofnas, "Deplatforming Won't Work", *Quillette,* July 8th, 2019, https://quillette.com/2019/07/08/deplatforming-wont-work/.

ate alternative communities where the views that got them
banned are only reinforced.

We have partially examined the first reason why deplatforming
doesn't work: there is always somewhere else to go. Not only are
there other places for people who are interested in these discourses to go, but the stronger willed among them (and simply those
who have a sufficiently strong counterwill, or will to resist), will
only deepen in their resolve. Just as often as suppression truly
buries thoughts and feelings, it can have the effect of psychologically strengthening an impulse, not weakening it. In this way,
deplatforming only increases the fervor with which extremists
and radicals hold their views. Those individuals who flip and re-
nounce their hateful ways invariably reveal themselves as people
without serious conviction, as opportunists, and as people whose
beliefs and preferences were merely social and aesthetic, not moral or philosophical. The unjust persecution of true believers does
nothing to invalidate or convert them. While it may demoralize
some, it will have the effect of pushing high agency individuals
into cleverer and cleverer ways of disseminating their message.
If it has not already, censorship will cause them to form physical
networks and work toward institutional development, as well as
seeking resources outside the jurisdiction of their persecutors.
They will become, as the now common phrase goes, antifragile.
Taking this view, the aggressive policing of dissenting views actually serves as a catalyst to greater political agency. Power once
again creates its own anti-power.

The second reason why censorship and deplatforming fails to
drive the final nail into the coffin of political dissent has to do
with the kinds of people who take up the mantle of anti-extremist activist and make it their life's mission to rid the internet of
hate speech. Before I fully explore this, allow me if you will, to
share a brief anecdote. I had the good fortune to befriend certain leftists embroiled in this battle of ideas, individuals whose
identities I will refrain from divulging. In my conversations with
these people, certain themes rose to the surface repeatedly. These
were generally honest, authentic, compassionate, and truly radical individuals who sought real conversations with the other
side because they believed in things like truth, love, and respect.
Several of them had come into conflict with members of their

own side because they (correctly) perceived their fellow travelers to be self-aggrandizing and moralizing blowhards who were only involved in these activities for "the thrill of the fight", so to speak. Their supposed comrades were not truly committed to the ideals of anti-racism, anti-sexism, equality, and so on. Borrowing a page from DiAngelo's book, these faux radicals were effectively liberals who wanted to present as anti-racists but were still, in their hearts and souls, hardly different from the chauvinistic and bigoted rightists they opposed. In some cases, these intra-clique conflicts led to the painful ousting of the more genuine radicals (who would later share these stories with me in confidence). These stories solidified a conclusion which I had, from a distance, arrived upon some time ago.

Why does the technique of removal fail to achieve its ultimate goal? While there are researchers and tech moguls who take the problem of extremism seriously and study the efficacy of their strategies with painstaking scrutiny, many of these faux radicals are only concerned with collecting digital scalps and raising their profile among peers. Their identities are so closely bound up with their object of hatred that they simply do not exist without them. Without an "internet Nazi" to chase down, their lives would be hopelessly and utterly without meaning or satisfaction. And so, bereft of a traditionally operating moral compass, these individuals cultivate a persona which perfectly conforms to the value system of the existing power structure, and in doing so invert the truth of the reality before them: they are fighting the international and all-powerful scourge of the world—other people on the internet. Naturally, such people don't arrive at this juncture unassisted; they walk one step at a time (with their hands held by the media and political classes) until finally they arrive at the position of pro bono anti-fascist. Even if they hunted down the last wrongthinker on the internet, their mission would not be complete. They would need to create a new enemy to destroy or else face the bottomless pit of despair which their Nazi fetish presently obscures.

In summation, there are three reasons why political extremism persists despite all attempts to fatally suppress it:

1. Material interest

2. Metapolitical logic
3. Human psychology

And so, it would seem we can add a third item to Christopher Bullock's list of certainties: death, taxes, and political extremism. But that is not the end of this discussion, for it would appear that we have one final question left to answer.

How Do We Combat Extremism?

While I do not believe that taking up grand transformational missions are ever wasteful efforts, I must be frank and say that we can't meaningfully defeat extremism, and when we consider the current methodology for doing so, the project appears doubly flawed. Individuals and organizations who engage in salvational programs (such as the battle against extremism, racism, poverty, climate change, and so on) often find themselves denatured and reterritorialized by external forces (e.g. the logic of corporations, political operatives, etc.) who are fatally opposed to genuine change. But before such attempts are sabotaged from without, they are first betrayed from within—betrayed by compromises, by concessions, by intentions both impure and ignoble—and are often betrayed simply by good old-fashioned naïveté. There are good reasons to be skeptical of anti-extremist initiatives given the relationship between power and anti-power, the incentives in place for combating (read: maintaining) extremism, and the un-willingness of the current pathocratic class to engage in fruitful self-examination (let alone restitution).

An aspect of this unwillingness on the part of the pathocracy has a great deal to do with its vision for the future. We often hear how we live in "post" times: post-Truth, post-Christian, post-Nation, and even post-State. For a period of time during the Obama administration, it was even possible to believe we were entering into a post-Racial society. We may argue the veracity of these claims (and certainly some are truer than others), but the most significant one to me seems to be our emergent post-Human era. It would likely be correct to say that we could not arrive at this new phase without first passing through each preceding one, shedding these formerly sacred but now vestigial cultural technologies just as a rattlesnake sheds its skin. This forthcoming post-human age is inevitable, they tell us, but it is also quite necessary. (How convenient.) It will bring limitless prosperity, fulfill the promise of endless longevity, and finally resolve those petty human problems which morality, religion, and philosophy have shown themselves utterly incapable of bringing to a close. (They might even go a step further and tell us that it was these disciplines which *generated* such problems.)

Just as the old saying goes, if it sounds too good to be true—that's because it is. For all the progressive neoliberal talk of inclusivity, the pathocratic vision of the future is decidedly *non-inclusive*. One might be forgiven for yearning for the halcyon days of old where we merely disdained the poor, the disfigured, and the savage; back then, we detested and loathed others for being *insufficiently* human, *insufficiently* civil and dignified. But now, with the advent of the social sciences and generations of researchers having scientifically "proven" the intractable nature of mankind's most problematic aspects, we now loathe humanity *itself*, and thus "logically" seek to "evolve" past it. In this process of evolution, most of us will be left behind and so it will be done—for "the good of mankind". As I write this it occurs to me that I may be incorrect in saying that political extremism will never be resolved. The solution simply requires technologically liquidating man himself.

The defining characteristic of the pathocracy is its narcissistic certainty, which permits the members of its class to anoint themselves judge, jury, and executioner. And to fulfill their duty as moral arbiters requires the abolition of self-reflection, for doubt and hesitation are the mortal enemies of will. Perhaps they second-guess certain decisions, but there is no reason to believe that the pathocrat questions his priors. (Which is precisely what allows him to arrive at "solutions" like transhumanism.)

In a certain sense, the task of resolving societal conflicts ought not to fall upon the humble shoulders of the common man, particularly since he is not responsible for them. He did not birth them, he did not nurture them, and he is certainly in no social or political way capable of affecting them. However we must also acknowledge that refinements in neoliberal governmentality impose new duties upon us, not merely as a result of its own particular style of governance but also as a means of honoring and fulfilling the liberal tradition of subjectivity, autonomy, and individuality. As such, we must play the hand we have been dealt, to use a tired phrase, and discover new modes of operating within our evolving techno-informational society. Traditionally, these would not be our duties, but we do not live in a traditional epoch. We are given space, however precarious it might be, to propel our ideas, to thrust ourselves into the social scene and make a great mess of things. Perhaps it *is* our responsibility to make it a beautiful mess, a Dionysian catastrophe capable of being well-ordered by future mess-makers. If such a thing is even possible then I will offer my thoughts.

A good place to start may be found in attacking (and ultimately replacing) the pathocrat's vision for the future. Were we to create a truly inclusive societal gestalt, one that actually cherished the natural diversity of man (all the while respecting his strengths and weaknesses, never condemning him for his natural failures) and provided a style of life best fitted for every class of man, only then could we truly turn back the rising tides of despair and violence. This new vision would have to account for all the failures of present day pathocracy as well as the projected failures of the pathocratic future. By necessity, this new vision would have to provide reasons, or at the least, incentives for participating in this new societal gestalt. Within this vision would be a new methodology of relation, from self to self, self to other (and to Other), self to community, self to State, and so on. An important requirement for this vision would be its ability to psychologically shift the collective consciousness from narcissism, irony, and cynicism toward one of earnestness, faith, and duty, thus transforming the moral and psychological character of the people. Vitality, generativity, and participation would be central tenets of this new vision, offering all three to all social strata. It is critical that this new vision expels the callous transience to which modern man has grown accustomed; while it is true that change is an undeniable fact of life, our New Man must be guaranteed a measure of permanence which secures his continued investment and participation in his society. His basic dignity must not be trampled, and his sacrifices must always be noble. Perhaps most importantly, our New Man must not be constructed out of whole cloth, but rather there must be an unveiling of that which he already is. This is the character which must inform our new vision, one of unveiling and of delivering what is true out from its concealment.

At this point I feel slight embarrassment over the vague description I have provided, so I will try to get to the essential core of my message. Man must be provided an alternative to steer him away from despair, but also to disincline him from taking immediate, thoughtless, and destructive action out of sheer frustration. It is precisely this absence of another way of living, of another way of ordering existence, which drives some men into apathy and self-gratification while at the same time driving others into madness and desperate violence. The claustrophobia produced by liberalism and its derivatives is not an anxiety over physical spaces so much as it is an anxiety of metaphysical spaces which stifle man's relation to himself, his fellow man, and to God. For this we can thank our sightless visionaries who, in keeping with the narcissism of American neoliberalism, encourage the development of ever more extreme technologies of the self, rather than, say, technologies of the other which might foster a sense of inter-relatedness and duty to those around them.

Today's visionaries are individuals who have, in fact, *lost sight* of their role as shepherds and thus lead not for our sake, but for their own. Truly visionary anti-extremists—visionaries of every kind—must be willing to offer man a better deal, and not corral him into accepting the unjust one which has been foisted upon him without his consent and without consideration for its effects. We have discussed Terence McKenna's idea of the "*the archaic revival*" in an earlier section but let us revisit it (this time without the cynicism). The instinct to retrieve values, rituals, and modes of being that have been lost along the way toward our modern techno-informational society is a noble and intelligent one. Unfortunately for the many people who heard McKenna speak these words, the archaic revival meant getting naked in the desert to do drugs and host debauched orgies. A truly visionary archaic revival would not seek to revive only the cathartic and ecstatic habits of our tribal ancestors, but the values of honor, duty, beauty, and truth which could restore the soul of man to its rightful place.

With regards to the more immediate strategies for combating extremism, I would like to return once more to the notion of disgust. By now you should be well aware of the relationship between disgust and the intensity of one's moral sentiment. Let us shift to the issue of *self-disgust*. To make this point I would like to call your attention to a very interesting study conducted some eight years ago by Bunmi Olatunji, Bieke David, and Bethany Ciesielski.[17] Using Overton's Self-Disgust Scale (a four-item measure of self-disgust, i.e., "*the way I behave makes me despise myself*"; "*I often do things I find revolting*", etc.), Olatunji and his team sought to test the hypothesis that one's self-perception as "dirty" rendered him unable or unwilling to evaluate moral transgressors negatively.

Participants were exposed to 19 statements across three levels of offense (non-offense: "*C.P. ate an entire gallon of ice cream*", moderate offense: "*R.S. spread harmful rumors about a coworker*", and severe offense: "*G.W. murdered two people in their home*") and then asked them to rate the level of disgust they experienced at the person's action presented in the statement, as well as the level of punishment they felt the person deserved on a scale between 0 (least disgusted/least deserving of punishment) and 7 (most disgusted/most deserving of punishment). Interestingly, Olatunji's team found that self-disgust was significantly *positively* associated with disgust and punishment ratings of non-moral offenses and significantly *negatively* associated with disgust and punishment ratings of severe moral offenses. In controlling for both participant's depressive symptoms and disgust proneness, the researchers found that only self-disgust explained significant variance in disgust/punishment ratings for non-offenses and severe offenses. In summation, the team was able to demonstrate that self-disgust is associated with less punishment of moral transgressions. In their conclusion, the team remarks that,

> The impaired moral perception, in the form of assigning less harsh punishment to severe offenses, may be mediated by affective appraisals that may accompany self-disgust (i.e., shame, guilt), perhaps to broaden the in-group.

17 Olatunji, B. O., David, B., & Ciesielski, B. G. (2012). Who am I to judge? Self-disgust predicts less punishment of severe transgressions. *Emotion, 12*(1), 169–173.

However, it is important to note that self-disgust explained significant unique variance in predicting more disgust and punishment ratings of non-offenses. That is, those high in self-disgust appear to be more prone to finding events where no moral wrong-doing is committed more disgusting and more deserving of punishment. This finding suggests that pervasive feelings of self-disgust may be associated with a bias in moral decision making. Such a bias may emerge as a result of the contamination of information used to appraise the severity of moral transgressions and non-offenses (eating an entire gallon of ice cream).

Furthermore, they state the following,

The present findings suggest that self-disgust, unlike other disgust-based personality traits (i.e., disgust sensitivity), may be marked by an internal moral unbalance that is associated with the tendency to assign more punishment for non-offenses and less punishment for severe moral offenses.

Perhaps these individuals feel a greater sense of repulsion at certain inoffensive actions (such as eating a gallon of ice cream) because the physical feeling which gluttony produces is so unpleasant. Perhaps they are performing some rational calculation and detecting how such actions would negatively impact their market value. Perhaps it signifies an internalized dual moral code. Or perhaps, considering most of the participants were college aged women, we can attribute such outcomes to wholly uncomplicated and non-abstract factors. What is of interest to me is the researchers' emphasis on "*the contamination of information used to appraise the severity of moral transgressions*" and the "*internal moral unbalance*" which their participants demonstrated throughout the experiment.

Whatever genetic precursors we may find that incline an individual to feelings of self-disgust, they will always depend on the larger cultural trends to elicit and expand upon them.[18] I am taking a bit of a leap in saying this, as this is a deeply impoverished area of study and it is presently impossible to know the degree

18   That is to say, the narratives, parables, images, symbols, and myths which culture generates.

of influence feelings of self-disgust have on moral judgments at large—nonetheless—I argue that we should view feelings such as self-disgust as the inevitable result of the dual techniques of responsibilism and mythic appropriation which prey upon man's psyche as effortlessly as a virtuoso plucks the strings of his guitar. In spite of the dearth of empirical proof necessary to justify my arguments, I find that this study lends credibility to many of the claims I've made throughout this book, namely that the propagandistic appropriation of mythic wisdom leads to a moral overcoding which demoralizes the individual and impairs his capacity for decision-making. He begins to hold himself to the punishing moral code of his enemy, thus falling into a state of despair and agony which cripples his moral judgment. In the end, he is psychologically disarmed and seeks to make the entire world his friend and thus becomes ill-equipped to morally correct his peers because 1) he's just as bad if not worse than them, and 2) they are part of his extended family anyway, and in the neoliberal world where morally rebuking someone is quite literally a sin, he should not commit such an atrocity against his kin. (Or more accurately, rebuking them in accordance with a morality antipodal to that of the pathocratic ruling class is sinful.)

The individual must be psychologically liberated if we are to achieve any kind of reform or overthrow of the current pathocratic regime. Self-disgust is tantamount to self-recrimination. And while it can be quite good and healthy to feel revolted by one's own actions, good and honest people all over the North American continent suffer tremendously under this psychologically induced tyranny. Pathocrats wish us to normalize all manner of bestial and uncivilized conduct, for the continual barrage of demoralizing and health-depleting practices weaken us as individuals, but also as political subjects. Alongside the normalization of the antisocial, is the pathologizing of the eusocial (e.g., discrimination, judgment, et cetera). And while the pathocracy may never achieve the absolute limit of psychological reduction, they merely need to strike a minimum limit to cripple the population. We are rapidly approaching that limit. (Individuals more pessimistic than I might say that we have already surpassed that limit.) It is not enough to simply say that America must be more courageous, or more cunning, for Americans first need to be healed. The psychic wound which impairs accurate self-evaluations, which impairs the ability to make sound moral judgments, must be sutured. Much has been made of the victim culture which has overtaken the United States. As I have pointed out, we are in fact a nation of victims. But that is not where the conversation ends; from this point we must be able to identify who our victimizers are, to disassociate from them, and to reject the systems and practices implemented by them against us.

If one wishes to diminish the threat that extremism poses, then one can only do so by rejecting the moral framework of the pathocratic class. This is no small task, as doing so necessitates rejecting the incentives provided by the pathocracy (incentives such as material wealth and social status). One must have the courage to step outside of the life that they know and the fortitude to withstand the turbulence such opposition will undoubtedly generate. By standing in solidarity (even if only passively) with the pathocracy, one makes himself an avatar of its hideousness.

And if one is concerned with the threat that some extremists and radicals pose, then he must also help them to reject the affectively reactionary contrarianism which traps their thinking. Anti-extremist initiatives (which so often function as re-educational programs designed to bring heretics back into the church of neoliberalism) ought to be concerned with introducing a more philosophical mode of thinking to the minds of troubled individuals, whose lives are typically marked by chaotic trauma, stultifying platitudes, and soul-impoverishing propaganda. I do not intend to draw any comparison or equivalency between extremism and radicalism, having sufficiently explicated the differences between them throughout this text, but just as extremism does not necessarily entail violence, neither does radicalism necessarily entail ideological correctness. The truly radical man is invariably political, but as I have hopefully made clear in this work, the extremism of our hegemonic apparatuses increasingly makes radicals of us all (however politically active we may or may not be). Our leaders, in neglecting their duty as shepherds, have abandoned their flock. We must now assume that responsibility for ourselves. The goal is not to convert people to a particular mode of thought, but to return them to a condition where they can simply *think*. And even if, in the end, they elect to let someone they know do the thinking for them, at the least they will have chosen that for themselves (and they will have chosen someone they know and trust rather than deferring to simulacra of intimacy and parasociality provided to them by the media complex).

But truly, the most impactful thing *anyone* who is worried about the state of the world can do is to build for themselves that which has been denied to them: faith, love, family, and honor. Or to say it another way, one should seek a life of virtue. The best strategy for combating extremism may be found in rejecting the modern arrogance of man, his desire to turn all objects (including other people) into materials which he can exploit, his desire to control all outcomes and circumstances, and instead returning to a spiritual minimalism or humility which isn't meek, disengaged, and powerless, but rather is secure in the power which it truly holds. An even simpler (though no less courageous) course of action would be to encourage the most basic form of intimacy which any two humans are capable of: free and uncomplicated speech. I do not speak of free speech in its modern form (the freedom to be callous and cruel, to be transgressive for its own sake, to be frivolous when circumstances demand grave seriousness, to be senselessly vulgar and stupid), but rather the freedom to pursue one's own generous and noble curiosity. The freedom I am describing is one which secures the ability to speak plainly about one's own fears and angst, his dreams and his hopes, his criticisms and his convictions, and all that is dearest to his soul. Perhaps most importantly, the freedom to speak and not be intentionally misunderstood and punished, marginalized and demonized, and ultimately shunned from society itself. Perhaps the first step toward truly combating political extremism may be found in the project of de-pathologizing speech and thought, particularly the kinds which challenge enshrined ideophilic dogma. Without the ability to speak openly about our thoughts and feelings in a non-hostile and non-accusatory way, our only recourse is violence. And as tantalizing and primal as violence may be, it is not a solution which can be neatly rescinded once placed on the table.

These are not particularly glamorous solutions, and neither

are they especially concrete. For that, I can only offer my sincere apology. After all, description is always easier than prescription. If all I have offered is a better, more accurate understanding of the problems we face than perhaps better men may pick up where I left off and work to usher in a future worth living for. One, I hope, that will be worth fighting for.

BIBLIOGRAPHY

ADL. "Murder and Extremism in the United States in 2017", *An ADL Center on Extremism Report,* https://www.adl.org/resources/reports/murder-and-extremism-in-the-united-states-in-2017.

—————. "Murder and Extremism in the United States in 2018", *An ADL Center on Extremism Report,* https://www.adl.org/murder-and-extremism-2018.

—————. "Murder and Extremism in the United States in 2019", *An ADL Center on Extremism Report,* https://www.adl.org/murder-and-extremism-2019.

Adorno, T.W. & E. Frenkel-Brunswik, D.J. Levinson, D.J., R.N. Sanford. *The Authoritarian Personality,* (Harper & Brothers, 1950).

Akiskal, Karen K., Mario Salvino & Hagop S. Akiskal. "Temperament profiles in physicians, lawyers, managers, industrialists, architects, journalists, and artists: a study in psychiatric outpatients", *Journal of Affective Disorders,* Vol. 85, Issues 1-2, March 2005, pp. 201-206.

Alexander, Audrey. "Digital Decay? Tracing Change Over Time Among English-Language Islamic State Sympathizers on Twitter", *The Program on Extremism at George Washington University,* 2017 https://extremism.gwu.edu/sites/g/files/zaxdzs2191/f/DigitalDecayFinal_0.pdf.

Alizadeh, Meysam & Ingmar Weber, Claudio Cioffi-Revilla, Santo Fortunato, Michael Macy. "Psychological and Personality Profiles of Political Extremists", *Computation and Language,* April 1st, 2017.

Almond, Steven. "Our dangerous macho delusions: Brian Williams' fraudulence – and our own", *Salon,* February 9th, 2015 https://www.salon.com/test2/2015/02/09/our_dangerous_macho_delusions_brian_williams_fraudulence_and_our_own/.

Aoki, Yuta & Estelle Malcolm, Sosei Yamaguchi, Graham Thornicroft,

Claire Henderson. "Mental illness among journalists: A systematic review", *International Journal of Social Psychiatry, Vol. 59, Issue: 4, March 8th, 2012, pp. 377-390.*

Bennett, Eric. "Dear Humanities Profs: We Are The Problem", *The Chronicle of Higher Education,* April 13th, 2018, https://www.chronicle.com/article/Dear-Humanities-Profs-We-Are/243100.

Berhulst, Brad & Lindon J. Eaves, Peter K. Hatemi. "Correlation not Causation: The Relationship between Personality Traits and Political Ideologies", *American Journal of Political Science,* Vol. 56, Issue 1, 2012, 34-51.

Berlatsky, Noah. "Let's Put An End To Horseshoe Theory Once And For All", *Pacific Standard,* published on Feburary 9th, 2018, https://psmag.com/social-justice/an-end-to-horseshoe-theory.

—————. "How Anti-Leftism Has Made Jordan Peterson A Mark For Fascist Propaganda", *Pacific Standard,* March 2nd, 2018, https://psmag.com/education/jordan-peterson-sliding-toward-fascism.

Bekiempis, Victoria. "Ghislaine Maxwell trained underage girls as sex slaves, document alleges", *The Guardian,* July 31st 2020, https://www.theguardian.com/us-news/2020/jul/31/ghislaine-maxwell-underage-girls-sex-jeffrey-epstein.

Bilefsky, Dan &Ian Austen. "Toronto Van Attack Suspect Expressed Anger at Women", *The New York Times,* April 14th, 2018, https://www.nytimes.com/2018/04/24/world/canada/toronto-van-rampage.html.

Bond, C.A. *Nemesis,* (Imperium Press, 2019).

Borger, Julian. "Guantanamo: psychologists who designed CIA torture program to testify", *The Guardian,* January 20th, 2020 https://www.theguardian.com/us-news/2020/jan/20/guantanamo-psychologists-cia-torture-program-testify.

Brahmin, Mark. "The Caducean Phenomenon", *The Apollonian Transmission,* May 3, 2019, http://theapolloniantransmission.com/2019/05/03/the-caducean-phenomenon/.

Bratsberg, Bernt & Ole Rogeberg, "Flynn effect and its reversal are both environmentally caused", *Proceedings of the National Academy of Sciences,* Vol. 115, No. 26, June 26th, 2018.

Brenan, Megan. "Americans' Trust in Mass Media Edges Down to 41%",

Gallup, September 26th, 2019, https://news.gallup.com/poll/267047/americans-trust-mass-media-edges-down.aspx.

Broadly Staff. "Gym Bros More Likely to be Right-Wing Assholes, Science Confirms", *Vice,* May 25th, 2017, https://www.vice.com/en_us/article/j5e3z7/gym-bros-more-likely-to-be-right-wing-assholes-science-confirms.

Brooker, Ben. "The 14 rules For Eternal Fascism: Jordan Peterson and the far right", *Overland,* February 14th, 2019, https://overland.org.au/2019/02/the-14-rules-for-eternal-fascism-jordan-peterson-and-the-far-right/.

Bruney, Gabriel. "A Very Abbreviated History of the Destruction of Black Neighborhoods", *Esquire,* May 30, 2020 https://www.esquire.com/news-politics/a32719786/george-floyd-protests-riots-black-comminity-destruction-history/.

Burraston, Bert & Stephen J. Watts, James C. McCutcheon, Karli Province. "Relative Deprivation, Absolute Deprivation, and Homicide: Testing an Interaction Between Income Inequality and Disadvantage", *Homicide Studies,* Vol. 23, Issue 1, February 1st, 2019, 3-19.

Caldwell, Christopher. *The Age of Entitlement: America Since the Sixties,* (Simon & Schuster, 2020).

Cantoni, Davide & David Y. Yang, Noam Yuchtman, Y. Jane Zhang. "The Fundamental Determinants of Anti-Authoritarianism", UC-Berkeley, unpublished, November 16th, 2016.

Capehart, Jonathan. "'Hands up, don't shoot' was built on a lie", *The Washington Post,* March 16th, 2015, https://www.washingtonpost.com/blogs/post-partisan/wp/2015/03/16/lesson-learned-from-the-shooting-of-michael-brown/.

Carmelo M. Vicario, Carmelo M. & Robert D. Rafal, Davide Martino, Alessio Avenanti, "Core, social and moral disgust are bounded: A review on behavioral and neural bases of repugnance in clinical disorders", *Neuroscience & Biobehavioral Reviews,* Vol. 80, September 2017, 185-200.

Chambers, R. Andrews & Marc N. Potenza. "Neurodevelopment, Impulsivity, and Adolescent Gambling", *Journal of Gambling Studies,* Vol. 19, March 2003, 53-84.

Charnigo, Richard & Seth M. Noar, Christopher Garnett, Richard

Crosby, Philip Palmgreen, Rick S. Zimmerman. "Sensation Seeking and Impulsivity: Combined Associations with Risky Sexual Behaviors in a Large Sample of Young Adults", *The Journal of Sex Research,* Vol. 50, Issue 5, March 28th, 2012, 480-488.

Chase, Alston. "Harvard and the Making of the Unabomber", *The Atlantic,* June 2000, https://www.theatlantic.com/magazine/archive/2000/06/harvard-and-the-making-of-the-unabomber/378239/.

Chatterjee, Rhitu. "Americans Are a Lonely Lot, and Young People Bear the Heaviest Burden", *NPR,* May 1st, 2018 https://www.npr.org/sections/health-shots/2018/05/01/606588504/americans-are-a-lonely-lot-and-young-people-bear-the-heaviest-burden.

Choat, Simon. "Horseshoe theory is nonsense – the far right and far left have little in common", *The Conversation*, published on May 12th, 2017, https://www.thedailybeast.com/the-lefts-witch-hunt-against-muslims?ref=scroll.

Cioran, E.M. *Drawn and Quartered,* (Arcade Publishing, 1979).

Cixous, Helene. "The Laugh of the Medusa", *Signs,* Vol. 1, no. 4, (Summer, 1976), 875-893.

Cofnas, Nathan. "Deplatforming Won't Work", *Quillette,* July 8th, 2019, https://quillette.com/2019/07/08/deplatforming-wont-work/.

Conway, Lucian Gideon & Shannon C. Houck, Laura Janelle Gornick, Meredith A. Repke. "Finding the Loch Ness monster: Left-Wing Authoritarianism in the United States", *Political Psychology,* Vol. 39, Issue 5, October 2018, 1049-1067.

Costello, Thomas & Shauna Bowes, Sean Steverns, Irwin Waldman, Scott O. Lilienfeld. "Clarifying the Structure and Nature of Left-Wing Authoritarianism", *PsyArXiv,* 11, May 2020.

Coward, Harold G. *Jung and Eastern Thought* (State University of the New York Press, 1985), 153.

Cratty, Carol. "25-year sentence in Family Research Council shooting", *CNN,* September 19th, 2013, https://www.cnn.com/2013/09/19/justice/dc-family-research-council-shooting/index.html.

Dai, Juntao Doris. "#NotAllWhites: Liberal-leaning Whites Racially Disidentify in Response to Trump-Related Group-Image Threat", *ResearchWorks Archive*, 2020.

Davidson, Richard J. & Paul Ekman, Clifford D. Saron, Joseph A. Senu-lis, Wallace V. Friesen. "Approach-withdrawal and cerebral asymmetry: Emotional expression and brain physiology: I", *Journal of Personaliy and Social Psychology,* Vol. 58, Issue 2, 1990, 330-341.

De Regt, Sabrina & Dimitri Mortelmans, Tim Smits. "Left-wing authoritarianism is not a myth, but a worrisome reality. Evidence from 13 Eastern European countries", *Communist and Post-Communist Studies,* Vol. 44, Issue 4, December 2011, 299-308.

Derrida, Jacques. *Writing and Difference* (Editions du Seuil, 1967).

Debord, Guy. *The Society of the Spectacle* (Paris: Editions Buchet-Chastel, 1967), 117

Derzsy, Noemi. "Strategies for combating online hate", *Nature,* August 21st, 2019 https://www.nature.com/articles/d41586-019-02447-1.

DiAngelo, Robin, *White Fragility* (Massachusetts: Beacon Press, 2018).

Dutton, Edward & Dimitri van der Linden, Richard Lynn, "The negative Flynn Effect: A systematic literature review", *Intelligence,* Vol. 59, November-December 2016, 163-169.

Eddy, Bill. "Are Narcissists and Sociopaths Increasing?", *Psychology Today,* April 30th 2018, https://www.psychologytoday.com/us/blog/5-types-people-who-can-ruin-your-life/201804/are-narcissists-and-sociopaths-increasing.

Chandrasekharan, Eshwar, et al. "You Can't Stay Here: The Efficacy of Reddit's 2015 Ban Examined Through Hate Speech", *Proceedings of the ACM on Human-Computer Interaction*, Vol.1 , No.2, Article 31, November 2017.

Family Research Council. *Southern Poverty Law Center,* https://www.splcenter.org/fighting-hate/extremist-files/group/family-research-council.

Faye, Jean-Pierre. *Le Siecle des ideologies* (Pocket, 2002), 12-22.

Feinreich, Dan. "The ADL Murder and Extremism Report is a fraud", *The Times Of Israel,* January 29th, 2019, https://blogs.timesofisrael.com/the-adl-murder-and-extremism-report-is-a-fraud/.

Ferguson, Mark A. & Nyla R. Branscombe. "The social psychology of collective guilt", *Collective emotions: Perspectives from psychology, phi-*

losophy, and sociology, 251-265, (Oxford, January 2014).

Fisher, Mark. *Capitalist Realism: Is There No Alternative?* (Zero Books, 2009).

Fleischer, Tzvi. "The Political Horseshoe again", *Australia/Israel & Jewish Affairs Council,* posted in November of 2006, http://www.aijac.org.au/review/2006/31-11/scribb31-11.htm.

Fluss, Harrison. "Jordan Peterson's Bullshit", *Jacobin,* February 2018, https://jacobinmag.com/2018/02/jordan-peterson-enlightenment-nietzsche-alt-right.

Fossett, Katelynn. "16 worst predictions of 2016", *Politico,* November 6th, 2016, https://www.politico.com/story/2016/11/2016-election-worst-predictions-230806.

Foucault, Michel. *The Birth of Biopolitics: Lectures at the College de France, 1978-1979,* (Picador, 2010).

Freud, Sigmund. *Beyond the Pleasure Principle* (1920).

—————. *Totem and Taboo* (Beacon Press, 1913), 92.

Feuerherd, Ben. "Court doc details Maxwell's 'constant' orgies with young girls on Epstein's island", *New York Post,* July 31st 2020, https://nypost.com/2020/07/31/ghislaine-maxwell-had-continuous-sex-with-young-girls-on-epstein-island/.

Gass, Nick. "'Hands up, don't shoot' ranked one of biggest 'Pinocchios' of 2015", *Politico,* December 14th, 2015, https://www.politico.com/story/2015/12/hands-up-dont-shoot-false-216736.

Gitlin, Todd. "The Wonderful American World of Informers and Agent Provocateurs." *The Nation,* June 27, 2013, www.thenation.com/article/archive/wonderful-american-world-informers-and-agents-provocateurs/.

Goldberg, Arnold. *The problem of perversion: The view from self psychology* (Yale University Press, 1995).

Graham, Jesse & Jonathan Haidt, Brian A. Nosek. "Liberals and Conservatives Rely on Different Sets of Moral Foundations", *Journal of Personality and Social Psychology,* Vol. 96, No. 5, 2009, 1029-1046.

Greenwald, Glenn & Andrew Fishman. "Latest FBI Claim of Disrupted Terror Plot Deserves Much Scrutiny and Skepticism." *The Intercept*, January 16, 2015, www.theintercept.com/2015/01/16/latest-fbi-boast-disrupting-terror-u-s-plot-deserves-scrutiny-skepticism/.

Goldberg, Zach. "America's White Saviors", *Tablet Magazine*, June 5th, 2019, https://www.tabletmag.com/sections/news/articles/americas-white-saviors.

Hadas Gold. "Survey: 7 percent of reporters identify as Republican", *Politico*, May 6th, 2014, https://www.politico.com/blogs/media/2014/05/survey-7-percent-of-reporters-identify-as-republican-188053.

Hamilton, Brady E. & Joyce A. Martin, Michelle J.K. Osterman, Lauren M. Rossen. "Births: Provisional Data for 2018", *National Center for Health Statistics*, Report no. 007, May 2019.

Hannah-Jones, Nikole. "The 1619 Project", *The New York Times*, August 14th, 2019, https://www.nytimes.com/interactive/2019/08/14/magazine/1619-america-slavery.html.

Harris, Adam. "America is Divided by Education", *The Atlantic*, published on November 7th, 2018, https://www.theatlantic.com/education/archive/2018/11/education-gap-explains-american-politics/575113/.

Hassell, Hans J.G. & John B., Holbein, Matthew R. Miles. "There is no liberal media bias in which news stories political journalists choose to cover", *Science Advances*, Vol. 6, no. 14, April 1st, 2020.

Helliwell, J., & R. Layard, J. Sachs. "World Happiness Report 2019", *New York: Sustainable Development Solutions Network*.

Herman, Edward S. & Noam Chomsky, *Manufacturing Consent: The Political Economy of the Mass Media* (Pantheon Books, 1988).

Hirsh, Jacob B. & Colin G. DeYoung, Xiaowen Xu, Jordan B. Peterson. "Compassionate Liberals and Polite Conservatives: Associations of Agreeableness With Political Ideology and Moral Values", *Personality and Social Psychology Bulletin*, Vol. 36, Issue. 5, April 6th, 2010, pp. 655-664.

Hirschowitz, Rosaline & Victor Neil. "The Relationship between Need for Power and the Life Style of South African Journalists", *The Journal of Social Psychology*, Vol. 121, Issue 2, March 8th, 1983, 297-304.

Hood, Gregory & Jared Taylor, "Media Promote ADL Propaganda on 'Extremist Terrorism'", *American Renaissance*, April 10th, 2019, https://

www.amren.com/commentary/2019/04/media-promote-adl-propaganda-on-extremist-terrorism/.

Human Rights Watch. "US: terrorism Prosecutions Often An Illusion." *Human Rights Watch,* July 21, 2014, www.hrw.org/news/2014/07/21/us-terrorism-prosecutions-often-illusion#

Inbar, Yoel & David Pizarro, Ravi Iyer, Jonathan Haidt. "Disgust Sensitivity, Political Conservatism, and Voting", *Social Psychological and Personality Science*, Vol. 3, Issue 5, December 6th, 2011, 537-544.

Ingraham, Christopher. "The dramatic shift among college professors that's hurting students' education", *The Washington Post,* January 11th, 2016, https://www.washingtonpost.com/news/wonk/wp/2016/01/11/the-dramatic-shift-among-college-professors-thats-hurting-students-education/.

Iqbal, Nosheen. "Donna Zuckerberg: 'Social Media has elevated misogyny to new levels of violence'", *The Guardian,* November 11th, 2018 https://www.theguardian.com/books/2018/nov/11/donna-zuckerberg-social-media-misoyny-violence-classical-antiquity-not-all-dead-white-men.

Institute for Research: Middle Eastern Policy. "FBI files reveal ADL's long history spying on peace, pro-Palestinian and Arab diplomat groups", *Cision PR Newswire,* May 16th, 2013, https://www.prnewswire.com/news-releases/fbi-files-reveal-adls-long-history-spying-on-peace-pro-palestinian-and-arab-diplomat-groups-207706361.html.

Iyengar, S.S. & M.R. Lepper. "When choice is demotivating: Can one desire too much of a good thing?" *Journal of Personality and Social Psychology,* Vol. 79, Issue 6, 2000, pp. 995-1006.

Jaschik, Scott. "Professors and Politics: What the Research Says", *Inside Higher Ed,* February 27, 2017, https://www.chronicle.com/article/Dear-Humanities-Profs-We-Are/243100.

Johnson, N.F., et al, "Hidden resilience and adaptive dynamics of the global online hate ecology", *Nature*, 573, 261-265, 2019.

Joiner, Lottie. "The truth about the party that brought 'Power to the People'." *The Undefeated,* December 20, 2016, www.theundefeated.com/features/the-truth-about-the-party-that-brought-power-to-the-people/.

Jones, Alexi & Wendy Sawyer. "Not just a "few bad apples": U.S. police kill civilians at much higher rates than other countries", *Prison Policy Initiative*, June 5th, 2020 https://www.prisonpolicy.org/blog/2020/06/05/policekillings/.

Jones, E. Michael. *The Slaughter of Cities: Urban Renewal as Ethnic Cleansing*, (St. Augustine's Press, 2002).

Kaplan, Karen. "Americans are having less sex now than 20 years ago", *Los Angeles Times*, June 12, 2020 https://www.latimes.com/science/story/2020-06-12/americans-are-having-less-sex-now-than-they-did-20-years-ago.

Katz, Barry M. "The Criticism of Arms: The Frankfurt School Goes to War", *The Journal of Modern History*, Vol. 59, No. 3, September 1987, pp. 439-478.

Katz, Josh. "Who Will Be President?", *The New York Times*, November 8th, 2016, https://www.nytimes.com/interactive/2016/upshot/presidential-polls-forecast.html.

Kaye, Richard. "Losing His Religion: Saint Sebastian as Contemporary Gay Martyr", *Outlooks: Lesbian and Gay Sexualities and Visual Cultures*, (New York, Routledge, 1996).

Kiehl, K.A. & M.B. Hoffman. "The Criminal Psychopath: History, Neuroscience, Treatment, And Economics", *Jurimetrics*, Vol. 51, June 16th, 2011, 355-397.

Koebler, Jason. "Deplatforming Works", *Vice*, August 10th, 2018, https://www.vice.com/en_us/article/bjbp9d/do-social-media-bans-work.

Kramer, Ronald C. "Poverty, Inequality, and Youth Violence", *The ANNALS of the American Academy of Political and Social Science*, Vol. 567, Issue 1, January 1st, 2000, 123-139.

Kreml, William P. *The Anti-Authoritarian Personality*, (Pergamon, 1977).

Lalkar. "Vygotsky – a pioneering Soviet psychologist who derived his genius from Marxism", Issue July/August 2016 http://www.lalkar.org/article/2455/vygotsky-a-pioneering-soviet-psychologist-who-derived-his-genius-from-marxism.

Langbert, Mitchell. "Homogenous: The Political Affiliations of Elite Liberal Arts College Faculty", *National Association of Scholars*, Summer 2018, https://www.nas.org/academic-questions/31/2/homogenous_the_political_affiliations_of_elite_liberal_arts_college_faculty.

Lasch, Christopher. *The Culture of Narcissism,* (W.W. Norton & Company, 1979).

Le Bon, Gustav. *The Crowd: A Study of the Popular Mind,* (1895).

Lehman, Charles Fain. "The Wages of Woke", *Washington Free Beacon,* July 25th, 2020 https://freebeacon.com/culture/the-wages-of-woke-2/.

Leibler, Isi. "Fight on campuses, don't condemn Israel's prime minister", *The Jerusalem Post,* September 15th, 2016, https://www.jpost.com/Opinion/Fight-on-campuses-dont-condemn-Israels-prime-minister-467845#/.

Levine, Bruce. "Curious "Anti-Authoritarian" Definitions and Divides", *Counterpunch,* September 5th, 2019, https://www.counterpunch.org/2019/09/05/curious-anti-authoritarian-definitions-and-divides/.

Lilienfeld, S.O. & I.D. Waldman, K. Landfield, A.L. Watts, S. Rubenzer, T.R. Faschingbauer. "Fearless dominance and the U.S. presidency: Implications of psychopathic personality traits for successful and unsuccessful political leadership.", *Journal of Personality and Social Psychology,* Vol. 103, Issue 3, 2012, 489-505.

Linker, Damon. "Where are all the conservative university professors?", *The Week,* November, 4th, 2015, https://theweek.com/articles/586794/where-are-all-conservative-university-professors.

Liptak, Adam. "US: Inmate Count in U.S. Dwarfs Other Nations'", *The New York Times,* March 23rd, 2008, http://www.mapinc.org/drugnews/v08/n417/a04.html.

Liu, Yunzhe & Wanjun Lin, Pengfei Xu, Dandan Zhang, Yuejia Luo. "Neural basis of disgust perception in racial prejudice", *Human Brain Mapping,* Vol. 36, Issue 12, December 2015, 5275-5286.

Lobaczewski, Andrzej. *Political Ponerology: A Science on the Nature of Evil Adjusted for Political Purposes,* (Red Pill Press, 2006).

Ludeke, Steven G. & Stig Hebbelstrup Rye Rasmussen. "Personality correlates of sociopolitical attitudes in the Big Five and Eysenckian models", *Personality and Individual Differences,* Vol. 98, August 2016, 30-36.

Maher, Heather. "How the FBI Helps Terrorists Succeed." *The Atlantic,* February 26, 2013, www.theatlantic.com/international/archive/2013/02/how-the-fbi-helps-terrorists-succeed/273537/.

Martinez, Michael. "George Zimmerman sues NBC Universal over edited 911 call", *CNN,* December 7th, 2012, https://www.cnn.com/2012/12/06/us/florida-zimmerman-nbc-lawsuit/index.html.

Mather, Robert D. "U.S. Government Mind Control Experiments", *Psychology Today,* April 26th, 2020 https://www.psychologytoday.com/us/blog/the-conservative-social-psychologist/202004/us-government-mind-control-experiments.

Meshi D. & O. Turel O., D. Henley. "Snapchat vs. Facebook: Differences in problematic use, behavior change attempts, and trait social reward preferences", *Addictive Behaviors Reports* vol. 12, December 2020.

McGrath, Melanie J. & Kathryn Randall-Dzerdz, Melissa A. Wheeler, Sean Murphy, Nick Haslam. "Concept creepers: Individual differences in harm-related concepts and their correlates", *Personality and Individual Differences,* Vol. 147, Issue 1, September 2019, 79-84.

McLaughlin, Dan. "The 1619 Project Wins a Pulitzer Prize for Agitprop", *Yahoo! News,* May 7th, 2020 https://news.yahoo.com/1619-project-wins-pulitzer-prize-103005628.html.

Mendez, Mario F. "A Neurology of the Conservative-Liberal Dimension of Political Ideology", *Journal of Neuropsychiatry and Clinical Neuroscience,* Vol. 29, Issue 2, Spring 2017, 86-94.

Mirowsky, John. "Cognitive Decline and the Default American Lifestyle", *The Journals of Gerontology Series B: Psychological Sciences and Social Sciences,* Vol. 66B, Issue 1, July 2011, 50-58.

Mishra, Pankaj, "Jordan Peterson & Fascist Mysticism", *The New York Review of Books,* March 19th, 2018, https://www.nybooks.com/daily/2018/03/19/jordan-peterson-and-fascist-mysticism/.

Montefiore, H.W. "Jesus the Revelation of God", in *Christ for Us Today: Papers read at the Conference of Modern Churchmen,* Somerville College, Oxford, July 1967 (SCM Press, London: 1968).

Mooney, Chris. "Your Hormones Tell You How to Vote", *Mother Jones,* published on June 14th, 2013, https://www.motherjones.com/politics/2013/06/how-hormones-influence-our-political-opinions/.

Morse, Dan. "Equal Treatment? No Blacks in Center's Leadership", *Montgomery Advertiser,* February 16th, 1994, https://rkeefe57.wordpress.com/montgomery-advertiser-series/.

Moser, Bob. "The Reckoning of Morris Dees And The Southern Poverty Law Center", *The New Yorker,* March 21st, 2019, https://www.newyorker.com/news/news-desk/the-reckoning-of-morris-dees-and-the-southern-poverty-law-center.

Mulhall, Joe. "Deplatforming works: Let's get on with it", *Hope Not Hate,* April 10th, 2019, https://www.hopenothate.org.uk/2019/10/04/deplatforming-works-lets-get-on-with-it/.

Nagourney, Adam & Michael Cieply, Alan Feuer, Ian Lovett. "Before Brief, Deadly Spree, Trouble Since Age 8", *The New York Times,* June 1st, 2014 https://www.nytimes.com/2014/06/02/us/elliot-rodger-killings-in-california-followed-years-of-withdrawal.html.

Navarrete, Carlos David & Daniel M.T. Fessler. "Disease avoidance and ethnocentrism: the effects of disease vulnerability and disgust sensitivity on intergroup attitudes", *Evolution and Human Behavior,* Vol. 27, Issue 4, July 2006, 270-282.

Nawaz, Maajid. "The Left's Witch Hunt Against Muslims", *The Daily Beast,* published on December 14th, 2015, https://www.thedailybeast.com/the-lefts-witch-hunt-against-muslims?ref=scroll.

Nouri, Lella & Nuria Lorenzo-Dus, Amy-Louise Watkin. "Following the Whack-a-Mole: Britain First's Visual Strategy from Facebook to Gab", *Global Research Network on Terrorism and Technology,* Paper no. 4, July 2019.

Olatunji, B. O. & B. David, B.G. Ciesielski. "Who am I to judge? Self-disgust predicts less punishment of severe transgressions." *Emotion,* 2012, *12*(1), 169–173.

Ondercin, Heather Louise, & Mary Kate Lizotte. "You've Lost That Loving Feeling: How Gender Shapes Affective Polarization", *SAGE Journals*, November 18, 2020

Oxley, Douglas R. & Kevin B. Smith, John R. Alford, Matthew V. Hibbing, Jennifer L. Miller, Mario Scalora, Peter K. Hatemi, John R. Hibbing. "Political Attitudes Vary with Physiological Traits", *Political Science,* 321:5897, September 19th, 2008, 1667-1670.

Packer, Martin J. "Is Vygotsky Relevant? Vygotsky's Marxist Psychology", *Mind, Culture, and Activity,* Vol. 15, Issue 1, January 15th 2008.

Patterson, E. Britt. "Poverty, Income, Inequality, And Community Crime Rates", *Criminology*, Vol. 29, Issue 4, November 1991, 755-776.

Pearce, Matt. "Southern Poverty Law Center fires co-founder Morris Dees amid employee uproar", *The Los Angeles Times*, March 14th, 2019, https://www.latimes.com/nation/la-na-splc-morris-dees-20190314-story.html.

Pew Research Center. "Political Polarization in the American Public", *U.S. Politics and Policy*, June 12th, 2014, https://www.people-press.org/2014/06/12/political-polarization-in-the-american-public/.

Plumer, Brad. "How Obama demobilized the antiwar movement", *The Washington Post*, August 29th, 2013, https://www.washingtonpost.com/news/wonk/wp/2013/08/29/where-did-the-antiwar-movement-go/.

Phelan, Nicholas & John E. Edlund. "How Disgust Affects Romantic Attraction: the Influence of Moods on Judgments of Attractiveness", *Evolutionary Psychological Science,* Vol. 2, September 24th, 2015, 16-23.

Post Editorial Board. "The Anti-Defamation League turns anti-Israel, possible hush money from a Clinton ally & other notable comments", *The New York Post,* September 15th, 2016, https://nypost.com/2016/09/15/the-anti-defamation-league-turns-anti-israel-possible-hush-money-from-a-clinton-ally-other-notable-comments/.

Potok, Mark. "The Year in Hate and Extremism", *Southern Poverty Law Center,* 2017 Spring Issue, https://www.splcenter.org/fighting-hate/intelligence-report/2017/year-hate-and-extremism.

Putnam, Robert D. *Bowling Alone: The Collapse and Revival of American Community,* (Touchstone Books, by Simon & Schuster, 2001).

Ray, John J. "Half of All Authoritarians Are Left Wing: A Reply to Eysenck and Stone" *Political Psychology,* Vol. 4, No. 1, March 1983, 139-143.

Remnick, David. "25 Years of Nightmares", *The Washington Post,* July 28th, 1985 https://www.washingtonpost.com/archive/lifestyle/1985/07/28/25-years-of-nightmares/cb836420-9c72-4d3c-ae60-70a8f13c4ceb/.

Robinson, Nathan J. "The Southern Poverty Law Center Is Everything Wrong With Liberalism", *Current Affairs,* March 26th, 2019, https://www.currentaffairs.org/2019/03/the-southern-poverty-law-center-is-everything-thats-wrong-with-liberalism.

Rogers, Richard. "Deplatforming: Following extreme Internet celebrities to Telegram and alternative social media", *European Journal of Communication,* Vol. 35(3), 213-229, 2020.

Rogers, Robert D. & Frederick G. Moeller, Alan C. Swann, Luke Clark. "Recent Research on Impulsivity in Individuals with Drug Use and Mental Health Disorders: Implications for Alcoholism", *Alcoholism: Clinical & Experimental Research*, Vol. 34, Issue 8, August 2010, 1319-1333.

Roccas, Sonia & Yechiel Klar, Ido Liviatan. "The paradox of group-based guilt: Modes of national identification, conflict, vehemence, and reactions to the in-group's moral violations", *Journal of Personality and Social Psychology,* Vol. 91, Issue. 4, 2006, 698-711.

Rohrmann, Sonja & Henrik Hopp, Markus Quirin. "Gender Differences in Psychophysiological Responses to Disgust", *Journal of Psychophysiology,* Vol. 22, 2008, 65-75.

Rozin, Paul & Jonathan Haidt, Clark R. McCauley. "Disgust", *Handbook of emotions*, pp.757-776, (The Guilford Press, 2008).

Saad, Lydia & Jeffrey M. Jones, Megan Brenan. "Understanding Shifts in Democratic Party Ideology", *Gallup,* February 19th, 2019, https://news.gallup.com/poll/246806/understanding-shifts-democratic-party-ideology.aspx.

Sadlier, Allison. "1 in 4 Americans feel they have no one to confide in", *New York Post,* April 30th, 2019 https://nypost.com/2019/04/30/1-in-4-americans-feel-they-have-no-one-to-confide-in/.

Saiidi, Uptin. "Social media makes millennials less social: Study", *CNBC,* October 17th, 2015 https://www.cnbc.com/2015/10/15/social-media-making-millennials-less-social-study.html.

Sailer, Steve. "Scandal-Plagued SPLC's Net Worth Still Grew $52 Million to $545 Million", *The Unz Review: An Alternative Media Selection,* April 30th, 2020, https://www.unz.com/isteve/scandal-plagued-splcs-net-worth-still-grew-52-million-to-545-million/.

—————. "The KKKrazy Glue That Holds the Obama Coalition Together", *Taki's Magazine,* March 13th, 2013 https://www.takimag.com/article/the_kkkrazy_glue_that_holds_the_obama_coalition_together_steve_sailer/.

Savan, Leslie. "Finally, Someone pays for Iraq War Lies – Brian Williams", *The Nation,* February 12th, 2015 https://www.thenation.com/article/archive/finally-someone-pays-iraq-war-lies-brian-williams/.

Schepers, Emile. "Agent provocateurs and the manipulation of the radical left." *People's World,* September 18, 2017, www.peoplesworld.org/article/agents-provocateurs-and-the-manipulation-of-the-radical-left/.

Scher, Isaac. "Rumors are swirling over footage showing a shadowy figure dubbed 'umbrella man' breaking windows during the Minneapolis protests." *Insider,* May 29, 2020, www.insider.com/minneapolis-protesters-social-media-users-suspicious-of-umbrella-man-2020-5.

Schutte, N. & G. Blickle, R. Frieder, F. Schnitzler, J. Heupel. "The role of interpersonal influence in counterbalancing psychopathic personality trait facets at work", *Journal of Management,* Vol. 10, Issue 4, 2016, 1338-1368

Sheftall, Arielle H. & Charles W. Mathias, R. Michael Furr, Donald M. Dougherty. "Adolescent attachment security, family functioning, and suicide attempts", *Attachment and Human Development,* Vol. 15, Issue 4, April 8th 2013, 368-383.

Shihadeh, Edward S. & Graham C. Ousey. "Industrial Restructuring and Violence: The Link between Entry-Level Jobs, Economic Deprivation, and Black and White Homicide", *Social Forces,* Vol. 77, Issue 1, September 1998.

Shipler, David. "Terrorist Plots, Hatched by the F.B.I." *The New York Times,* April 28, 2012, www.nytimes.com/2012/04/29/opinion/sunday/terrorist-plots-helped-along-by-the-fbi.html.

Sinn, Jeffrey S. & Matthew W. Hayes, "Replacing the Moral Foundations: An Evolutionary-Coalitional Theory of Liberal-Conservative Differences", *Political Psychology,* Vol. 38, Issue 6, December 2017, 1043-1064.

Solon, Olivia. "Ex-Facebook president Sean Parker: site made to exploit human 'vulnerability'", *The Guardian,* November 9th, 2017 https://www.theguardian.com/technology/2017/nov/09/facebook-sean-parker-vulnerability-brain-psychology.

Spielrein, Sabina. "Destruction as the Cause of Coming into Being", *Journal for Psychoanalytic and Psychopathological Research,* Vol. 4, 1912, 464-503.

Steffin, John. "Solzhenitsyn and Jordan Peterson: Fascism, white supremacy and patriarchy", *Worker's World,* December 9th, 2018, https://www.workers.org/2018/12/40081/.

Stone, William F. "The Myth of Left-Wing Authoritarianism", *Political Psychology,* Vol. 2, No. 3/4, Autumn-Winter 1980, 3-19.

Stout, Martha. *The Sociopath Next Door* (Harmony, 2006).

Striker, Eric. "The Base: Inside the FBI's Newest Scary Story." *National Justice,* January 18, 2020, www.national-justice.com/base-inside-fbis-newest-scary-story.

—————. "Skinhead Group Members Sentenced To Decades In Prison After FBI Entrapped Them and Then Destroyed Exonerating Evidence", *National Justice,* July 23rd 2020, https://national-justice.com/current-events/skinhead-group-members-sentenced-decades-prison-after-fbi-entrapped-them-and-then.

Sunstein, Cass R. & Adrian Vermule, "Conspiracy Theories", *Harvard Public Law Working Paper,* No.8-03, January 15th, 2018.

Taibbi, Matt. "16 Years Later, How the Press That Sold the Iraq War Got Away With It", *Rolling Stone,* March 22nd, 2019, https://www.rollingstone.com/politics/politics-features/iraq-war-media-fail-matt-taibbi-812230/.

Tasca, Giorgio A. & Leah Szadkowski, Vanessa Illing, Anne Trineer, Renee Grenon, Natasha Demidenko, Valerie Krysanski, Louise Balfou, Hany Bissada. "Adult attachment, depression, and eating disorder symptoms: The mediating role of affect regulation strategies", *Personality and Individual Differences,* Vol. 47, Issue 6, October 2009, 662-667.

Thaler, Richard H. & Cass Sunstein, *Nudge: Improving Decisions About Health, Wealth, and Happiness,* (Penguin Books: 2009).

Thurman, N. & A. Cornia, J. Kunert "Journalists in the UK", *UK: Reuters Institute for the Study of Journalism,* 2016, 12-13.

Tiihonen, Jari & Marja Koskuvi, Markku Lahteenvuo, Pekka L.J. Virtanen, Ilkka Ojansuu, Olli Vaurio, Yanyan Gao, Ida Hyotylainen, Katja A. Puttonen, Eila Repo-Tiihonen, Tiina Paunio, Marja-Riitta Rautiainen, Sasu Tyni, Jari Koistinaho, Sarka Lehtonen. "Neurobiological roots of psychopathy", *Molecular Psychiatry,* February 21st, 2019 https://www.nature.com/articles/s41380-019-0488-z.pdf?origin=ppub.

Tomkins, S.S., *Affect Imagery Consciousness,* Vol.1 (New York: Springer, 1962).

Twenge, Jean M. & A. Bell Cooper, Thomas E. Joiner, Mary E. Duffy, Sarah G. Binau. "Age, period, and cohort trends in mood disorder indicators and suicide-related outcomes in a nationally representative dataset, 2005-2017", *Journal of Abnormal Psychology,* Vol. 128, Issue 3, March 15th, 2019, pp. 185-199.

Van Dijk, T.A. "Politics, Ideology, and Discourse", *Discourse in Society,* 2006, 728-740.

Kennedy, Emmet. ""Ideology" from Destutt De Tracy to Marx", *Journal of the History of Ideas,* Vol. 40, No. 3, July-September 1979, 353-368.

VanNess, Alex. "Jonathan Greeblatt is destroying the Anti-Defamation League", *The New York Post,* December 9th, 2016, https://nypost.com/2016/12/09/jonathan-greenblatt-is-destroying-the-anti-defamation-league/.

Vartanian, Lenny R. & Tara Trewartha, Eric J. Vanman. "Disgust predicts prejudice and discrimination toward individuals with obesity", *Journal of Applied Social Psychology,* Vol. 46, Issue 6, June 2016, 369-375.

Walker, James. "Jacob Wohl Mocked After Claiming Elizabeth Warren Sex Scandal, Says 2020 Candidate Had Affair with 24-Year-Old Marine", *Newsweek,* October 3rd, 2019, https://www.newsweek.com/jacob-wohl-mocked-after-claiming-elizabeth-warren-sex-scandal-says-2020-candidate-had-affair-1462895.

Wan, William & Heather Long, "Coronavirus has caused a huge spike in drug overdoses", *The Washington Post,* July 1st, 2020, https://www.washingtonpost.com/health/2020/07/01/coronavirus-drug-overdose/.

Waytz, Adam & Ravi Iyer, Liane Young, Jesse Graham. "Ideological Differences in the Expanse of Empathy", *Claremont symposium on applied social psychology series. Social psychology of political polarization,* 2016, 61-77.

Webb, Whitney. "YouTube To Censor "Controversial" Content with ADL Assistance", *Mint Press News,* August 7th, 2017, https://www.mintpressnews.com/youtube-censor-controversial-content-adl/230530/.

WebFX Team. "The 6 Companies That Own (Almost) All Media [Infographic]", *WebFX,* January 30th, 2020, https://www.webfx.com/blog/

internet/the-6-companies-that-own-almost-all-media-infographic/.

Weede, Eric. "Some new evidence on correlates of political violence: income inequality, regime repressiveness, and economic development", *European Sociological Review,* Vol. 3, Issue 2, September 1987, 97-108.

Weeks, Linton. "Whatever Happened To The Anti-War Movement?", *NPR,* April 15th, 2011, https://www.npr.org/2011/04/15/135391188/whatever-happened-to-the-anti-war-movement.

Werner, Kimberly B. & Lauren R. Few, Kathleen K. Bucholz. "Epidemiology, Comorbidity, and Behavioral Genetics of Antisocial Personality Disorder and Psychopathy", *Psychiatric annals,* Vol. 45, Issue 4, April 2015, 195-199.

Westfall, Sandra Sobieraj. "George W. Bush Breaks His Silence on the Direction of the Country Under President Trump: 'I Don't Like the Racism and Name-Calling'", *People,* February 27th, 2017 https://people.com/politics/george-w-bush-on-trump-presidency/.

Williams, Zoe. "Do you boast about fitness? Watch out – you'll unavoidably become rightwing", *The Guardian,* September 27th, 2018, https://www.theguardian.com/commentisfree/2018/sep/27/do-you-boast-about-your-fitness-watch-out-youll-unavoidably-become-rightwing.

Winerman, Lea. "By the numbers: An alarming rise in suicide", *The American Psychological Association,* Vol. 50, No. 1, January 2019, p. 80.

Winnicott, Donald. *The Collected Works of D. W. Winnicott: Volume 5, 1955-1959* (Oxford University Press, 2016), 149.

Woolf, Steven H. & Heidi Schoomaker, "Life Expectancy and Mortality Rates in the United States, 1959-2017", *Journal of the American Medical Association,* Vol. 32, Issue 20, December 2019.

World Population Review. "Police Killings By Country 2020", https://worldpopulationreview.com/country-rankings/police-killings-by-country.

Yarvin, Curtis. "A Gentle Introduction To Unqualified Reservations", *Unqualified Reservations,* January 8th, 2009, https://www.unqualified-reservations.org/2009/01/gentle-introduction-to-unqualified/.

Zuckerberg, Donna. *Not All Dead White Men: Classics and Misogyny in the Digital Age*, (Harvard University Press, 2008).

INDEX

Lightning Source UK Ltd.
Milton Keynes UK
UKHW022021080221
378452UK00007B/220